KU-324-557

The Managerial Challenge of New Office Technology

Editors:
Harry J. Otway
Malcolm Peltu

A publication from the INSIS (Inter-institutional Integrated Services Information System) Programme of the Commission of the European Communities

Butterworths
London Boston Durban Singapore Sydney
Toronto Wellington

First published in Great Britain in 1984
by Butterworths & Co (Publishers) Ltd

Publication arrangements by the Commission of the European Communities Directorate-General Information Market and Innovation, Luxembourg

British Library Cataloguing in Publication Data

The Managerial challenge of new office technology.
1. Office practice—Automation 2. Office management
I. Otway, Harry J. II. Peltu, Malcolm
III. INSIS
651 HF5548.2

ISBN 0-408-01533-0

Library of Congress Cataloging in Publication Data

Main entry under title:

The Managerial challenge of new office technology

'A publication from the INSIS (Inter-institutional Integrated Services Information System) Programme of the Commission of the European Communities.'
Includes index.
1.Electronic data processing departments——Management——Addresses, essays, lectures. I. Otway, Harry J., 1935- . II. Peltu, M. (Malcolm)
III. Commission of the European Communities, INSIS Programme.
HF5548,2,m295 1984 658'.054 84—9596
ISBN 0-408-01533-0

Typeset by West Farthing Grange, London SW10 9DS
Printed and bound in Great Britain by Robert Hartnoll Ltd., Bodmin, Cornwall

Foreword

It is now generally accepted that information technologies will be a major source of economic growth and social development into the next century. In order to ensure that the technology can be of maximum benefit, the Council, Member State governments and the Commission of the European Communities (CEC) are committed to a strategy for the 'information age' that blends social, political, economic and industrial goals. An important part of this commitment is the Inter-institutional iNtegrated Services Information Systems, known as INSIS. Its main objectives are to accelerate the implementation of advanced information systems within the EEC and to stimulate the growth of European information technology and information industries. Within this programme, co-ordinated projects are being initiated to introduce advanced office technology and communications services into public institutions and representative bodies from the EEC and its Member States.

When introducing new technology, there is always a temptation to try to gain the potential benefits as quickly as possible. The experience of many users of computer-based systems clearly indicates that the benefits will not materialize unless adequate attention is paid to the broad impact of new systems on all aspects of the user environment. Managers hold the key to success: they must know what the technology can and cannot do, be sensitive to the needs of users when guiding the implementation of new systems and, especially, be prepared to become users themselves if the full potential of the technology is to be realized.

The Commission and the INSIS management see this book as another step in the elaboration of an approach that will allow major changes in the way people work and live to proceed smoothly and effectively. We are pleased that such distinguished contributors agreed to work closely with Dr Otway and Mr Peltu to produce this timely book.

Richard Hay
Deputy Director General for
Personnel Administration, CEC,
and Chairman, INSIS
Supervisory Board

Hans Jørgen Helms
Director of Programmes
Joint Research Centre, CEC,
and Member, INSIS
Supervisory Board

Acknowledgements

We appreciate the collaborative spirit shown by the contributors throughout the preparation of the book. Their wholehearted participation in co-ordination meetings allowed each chapter to benefit from a generous sharing of ideas. They generally met deadlines and patiently accepted our extensive rewriting, making individual sacrifices in the interest of having a uniform style and better continuity of their combined efforts.

We are indebted to the INSIS management for having had the foresight to support the preparation of this book. We are also grateful to many of our colleagues in the Commission who helped in various ways, but especially to Ria Volcan, Edith Steffgen, Joep van der Veer and Edward Phillips.

Harry J. Otway
Besozzo

Malcolm Peltu
London

Contents

The Editors

Harry J. Otway and Malcolm Peltu have also co-edited *New Office Technology: Human and Organizational Aspects*, Frances Pinter, London; Ablex, Norwood, N.J. (1983), as part of the INSIS programme (*see* Foreword).

Harry J. Otway is Principal Scientist in the Informatics, Mathematics and Systems Analysis Department of the Commission of European Communities Joint Research Centre at Ispra, Italy, and is responsible for the INSIS Human and Organizational Aspects functions. He joined the Commission from the International Institute of Applied Systems Analysis (IIASA), near Vienna, and has a long-standing and varied interest in the policy issues arising from the interaction between technical and social systems. He has published extensively and has been a consultant to governments and international agencies and a visiting professor at several major universities.

Malcolm Peltu is an information technology consultant and journalist. He became a computing professional in 1965 and has extensive experience of the technology. In 1972 he started working as a journalist. He has been editor of one of Europe's leading technical newspapers, *Computer Weekly*; computer consultant to *New Scientist*; and is an advisor to the international magazine *Datamation*. He specializes in interpreting computer-based technology to the layman and has written many books, including *The Electronic Office* (BBC Publications, London, 1984), *Successful Management of Office Automation* (National Computing Centre, Manchester, 1984) and *Using Computers – A Manager's Guide* (National Computing Centre, Manchester, 1981).

The Contributors

Niels Bjørn-Andersen (Chapter 5) is an Associate Professor in the multidisciplinary Information Systems Research Group at the Copenhagen School of Economics and Business Administration. He has specialized in the design and impact of information systems on the work of managers and other office staff in their organizational context, and is a consultant to many public and private organizations. He gained his doctorate for the study of Decision Support Systems and has been a visiting professor at the Manchester Business School and the universities of Paris IX Dauphine, Lund and Tampere.

Michel Crozier (Chapter 6) has a worldwide reputation as a sociologist and writer. He is a Senior Research Professor at the Centre National de la Recherche Scientifique (CNRS) and Director of the Centre de Sociologie des Organisations in Paris, a research institute which is part of the CNRS. He has been a consultant to many organizations around the world, including the Rand Corporation, Commission of the European Communities and various centres dedicated to management training. He is also a visiting professsor at Harvard University and the University of California at Irvine in the USA.

Gerhard Fischer (Chapter 3) is a Professor of human–computer communication in the Computer Science Department at the University of Stuttgart. He is a director of the INFORM project which is developing and evaluating knowledge-based (expert) systems to improve the way users interact with computer-based information systems. He has been a visiting researcher in North America for several years, including periods at Carnegie Mellon University, Massachusetts Institute of Technology and Xerox Corporation's Palo Alto Research Centre.

Paula Goosens (Chapter 9) is a consultant in the application of new office technologies for the Dutch PTT, the national post and telecommunications authority. She has worked in industry and for one of the largest Dutch banks, ABN, investigating various aspects of new computerized information systems. She is a founder and former chairman of the Social Aspects of Informatization and Automation of the Dutch Computer Society.

Peter G.W. Keen (Chapter 7) is Chairman of Micro Mainframe Inc in the USA. He has held faculty positions at the Sloan School of Management at the Massachusetts Institute of Technology, and Stanford, Wharton and Harvard universities; he is also a visiting lecturer at the London Business School. He is a consultant to private and public sector organizations in the USA, Europe and Latin America, with particular emphasis on decision support systems, the management of organizational change and telecommunications policy. He has written many articles and publications and is editor of the journal *Office: Technology and People*.

Najah Naffah (Chapter 2) is manager of the Advanced Studies Division in Office Systems at Bull-Transac in France. He has led the Kayak Office Information System project at INRIA, France's foremost centre for research and computer-related activities, and has been in charge of Kayak's development of a complete integrated system of sophisticated computer-based workstations that can run a variety of tasks when interlinked through telecommunications networks. This work resulted in the award to him by the Bull Company of the Prix Européen de la Recherche.

Janine E. Nahapiet (Chapter 8) is a Fellow in Organizational Behaviour at the Oxford Centre for Management Studies, where she teaches middle and senior managers, and students from Oxford University, both undergraduates and postgraduates. In addition, she carries out research and consultancy for private and public organizations into the social and managerial aspects of information systems. She has been a visiting professor at the Copenhagen School of Economics and Business Administration, specializing in information systems and accounting.

Gerdie Nillesen (Chapter 9) is an organizational consultant with the Academic Hospital of the University of Amsterdam, where she is concerned with managerial and organizational developments at a time of great change in the hospital. She was previously a consultant at the Netherlands NMB bank, helping with the introduction of new information systems. She has also lectured at the University of Nijmegen on the social and individual psychology of work and organization.

Francis Pavé (Chapter 6) is a researcher at the Centre de Sociologies des Organisations in Paris, part of the French national centre for scientific research, CNRS. He specializes in investigating practical examples of the way computer-based information systems influence the management and operation of organizations. After conducting research into the consequences of computerization in private companies, he has been studying the impact on public administration in France. He has a doctorate in sociology and has taught at the Paris Institut August Comte.

Larry D. Phillips (Chapter 4) is Director of the Decision Analysis Unit at the London School of Economics and Political Science. His background is in electrical engineering and psychology and he is a member of the American Institute of Decision Sciences, the American Psychological Society and the British Psychological Society. He has been a senior lecturer at Brunel University in the UK and a senior research analyst at Decisions and Design Inc in the USA. He has applied decision technology to problems as varied as the choice of a bridge-collision warning system, strategic planning, analysis for the insurance industry, and new product research and development decisions.

Brian Wynne (Chapter 10) is a lecturer in the multidisciplinary School of Independent Studies, University of Lancaster, and has been a project leader at the International Institute of Applied Systems Analysis (IIASA), near Vienna. He has acted as a consultant on large scale technology policy projects and has published a book on the decision-making process in the energy industry. His professional research has concentrated mainly on the relationship between technological and scientific developments and broader social policy issues.

1

The Challenge of New Managerial Roles

Harry J. Otway and Malcolm Peltu

Introduction

News of an impending reorganization heralds the start of an agonizing period of uncertainty in organizational life. There is a pervasive fear of the unknown: some managers will emerge as winners, others will be losers; power balances will change; long standing work relationships may be disrupted; new communications channels will open, others will close; the context of jobs and work practices will be different. New office technology implicitly brings with it these kinds of far reaching changes, which create a unique challenge to management to participate actively in guiding such potentially revolutionary changes in a constructive way, rather than passively accepting them as occurrences beyond their control.

This chapter explains why the challenges posed by computer-based office systems require that managers must master a number of new and unfamiliar roles. There is a discussion of the nature of management responsibilities for the selection, design, introduction and supervision of new systems, and for their resultant widespread personal and organizational impacts. The subjects and themes developed in the remainder of the book are introduced and the contents of each chapter are summarized.

Management and organizational change

Not only must managers handle the introduction of new office technology, but they must also cope with the fact that the systems affect a different group of people than previous technologies which have automated jobs. This time, managerial staff, including the most senior levels, are being displaced and having to adjust to new ways of working.

In a survey of middle managers in 1200 major companies in the USA, 85 per cent of respondents reported that computer-based information is essential to their work and that computer access was increasing the number and variety of the responsibilities they could handle[1]. At about 500 of these companies, middle management had been reduced. Some of this was due to general economic and market conditions, but 41 per cent believed that 'the continued integration of the computer into managerial operations is likely to lead to further consolidations of departments and functions'. Many organizations cannot operate for long without computers. According to a study at the University of Minnesota, modern banks could survive for no more than two days without their computers, distribution industries for about three days, and insurance companies for less than six days.

The importance of computer-based systems in today's world cannot be denied. There have, however, been many other technological developments in the twentieth century that have also led to radical changes in working methods. Techniques for production automation pioneered by Henry Ford in 1914, for example, revolutionized manufacturing. Computers themselves are not new. They were first used extensively in the 1960s. So, why should new office technology be any different? Are the challenges posed by these new systems really more significant than innovations that have already been assimilated?

The unprecedented challenge

New office technology cannot be regarded as just another step in a long history of technological automation of work. It represents a giant stride, with radical implications for managers, both for their personal development and for the changes it will cause in how organizations function. There is something special about this innovation for the following reasons:

(1) *This is a potential source of exceptional and unaccustomed stress.* In the past, managers have planned and implemented technological developments that have generally changed, or eliminated, *other people's jobs*. With new office technology, managers must still do this but, at the same time, they must cope with impacts on their own jobs which may be threatening to their current status, skills and career development.

(2) *Change is taking place in many activities at the same time.* New office systems are an integral part of other computer-

based technologies which can affect virtually every aspect of an organization's operations., Previous workplace developments in new technologies have tended to have an impact on one prime activity, such as the way factory automation altered production processes, but not on how people communicated with each other. An integrated computer system, however, can be used in factory automation *and* general organizational communications systems, as well as many other activities.

(3) *Organization structures and work procedures are also in a state of flux*. New office technology means a change *of* organizations, not just a change *in* organizations. It leads to new allocations of managerial responsibilities, new departmental structures, new communications methods, new job practices; in short, to new ways of working.

(4) *Improving management productivity is a prime target*. New office technology was first aimed at improving the efficiency of typing and clerical tasks. In most organizations, however, managers and professionals represent the major (60-75 per cent) and fastest growing sector of office personnel costs. Computer-based technology has evolved to the point that it can be applied to management activities that were previously thought to be untouchable by technology, such as policy formulation and decision making. The drive to cut management costs provides impetus to make quick and radical changes to management jobs, further increasing the likelihood of management stress.

(5) *Automation is alien to the traditions of office work*. The traditions in white collar office work are very different to those that have prevailed in manufacturing work. Office staff are accustomed to working in a relatively informal environment, with a great deal of discretion in how and when they work, even for the more routine clerical jobs. Office and management work has rarely been subject to the kinds of detailed prestructuring, monitoring and measurement that have been common on production lines, where the concepts and techniques of automation were developed. If these are applied unthinkingly to office work *as office automation*, rather than *computer-assisted* office work, staff motivation and work effectiveness will deteriorate, even though there may seem to be gains in the short term.

(6) *Computers are being applied directly to everyday life on a massive scale*. Early, large computers were used mainly for

routine information processing on high volumes of data, such as in handling accounts and producing customer bills. They were important to many organizations but were directly used by few people and generally led to slow changes in working procedures. Microelectronics have brought computing capabilities to the fingertips of people in most work functions and walks of life. This has implications throughout society. For example, a bank's customer can obtain cash and make account enquiries directly from a computer-based device outside the bank, reducing the need for many clerical and management staff, providing economic benefits to the bank and increasing the convenience to customers. It is also possible for more work to be carried out from home via computer networks. The technology is therefore crossing boundaries between what had been relatively clear demarcations between working and social activities.

(7) *There is little experience to fall back on*. The broad scope and rapid pace of innovation that characterizes computer-based developments mean that new territory is being pioneered continuously. As yet, there is very little experience over a long period to determine exactly how office work will change. Previous implementations of computer systems provide the most relevant guidelines, but took place in a period of greater stability, in different kinds of activities, and used technologies quite different to current systems.

How to cope successfully

When the INSIS programme (*see* Foreword) first started investigating the human and organizational aspect of new office technology, the first task was to identify the nature and extent of these impacts and what was known about them. This work resulted in a book which summarizes the current state of knowledge in these areas[2]. During its preparation, it became evident that a new issue was emerging which demanded special attention: the challenge to management.

One problem is that the variety of aspects involved have been treated by specialists within the framework of their distinct disciplines. There is a considerable body of analysis and experience of management techniques needed to handle organizational change, staff motivation, effective job design, and so on. There is also much work which described the capabilities of computer-based technologies, how they work and the types of task to which they can be applied. Management specialists, however, have seldom examined the implications of computer-based systems in detail, while computing experts have rarely looked beyond their own technological horizons.

The work summarized in this book was therefore initiated to bring together both management and technical specialists to explore the key challenges facing managers and to suggest how to deal successfully with these important developments.

New management roles

Management must play a number of roles in relation to new office technology. Some of these are extensions to existing responsibilities, others are completely new. Many different roles may have to be played simultaneously. The main ones are:

(1) Developing a strategic plan to set, control and co-ordinate long-term plans.
(2) Making detailed decisions about where, when, how and what new systems are to be installed.
(3) Managing organizational changes induced by new office technology especially where many of the changes may emerge only as experience is gained in using systems and in negotiating necessary accommodations to resolve conflicting requirements.
(4) Using technology in management jobs, leading to new work procedures and job responsibilities.
(5) Guiding the implementation, operation and continuing development of computer-based information resources, which requires careful handling of the frequent human and technical adjustments that must be made.

Power and information technology

To some extent, all management is about the power to define agendas, set organizational goals and, thus, to define implicitly what information is valued. Access to information can be an important element in strengthening and extending control by individuals and groups. This is true not only because the control of information is a form of power, but also in the subtler sense that information which is supportive and meaningful to one viewpoint may not be to another. Computer-based information technology, including new office systems, therefore cannot be regarded as neutral in practical terms, because it is always applied within contexts where it can reinforce or weaken established influences. Thus, the management of new office technology must be viewed in the context of the overall power relationships within an organization.

This book makes no assumptions about any particular organizational structure or management style, recognizing that decision-making processes vary widely. In some organizations, individual managers, other than the most senior, may have relatively little discretion in choosing or shaping new information systems. In a more open, consensus-oriented organization, all levels of management and staff may participate fully in reaching decisions. Whatever the organizational set up, the new management roles discussed in this and subsequent chapters will have to be performed in the manner most suited to individual circumstances.

Choosing the route and the signposts

New office technology provides a myriad of options. The prime management tasks are to choose the main directions in which the technology is to travel, its objectives, and when particular journeys are to start. Then, equally important, the manager must specify what criteria are to be used in judging the success of innovations.

Managers often have to decide new courses of action and judge performance according to a variety of indicators. The particular difficulties posed by computer-based systems are the complex set of reactions they trigger throughout the organization, coupled with the unfamiliarity of many managers with the technology itself. As a reaction to complexity, many managers fall back onto simple statements of quantified objectives, which wrongly forces the process of computerization into narrow and short-term perspectives. This will be more pronounced, causing more difficulties, if technical specialist are left to get on with their own design of a system whose implications fall outside their specialized fields of competence. The net result can be systems designed to satisfy technical ambitions and capabilities, rather than human and organizational needs.

The variety of issues involved, and their dependence on specific local circumstances, means that there can be no foolproof management recipe for success. There are, however, some general principles that managers should use in guiding office technology into what is, for the organization and the individuals in it, uncharted territory. First of all, you must have some idea of where you are going. This seems to be an obvious statement, but many organizations enter into new computer-based systems 'because they are there' and without any real idea of what they want to achieve with them. Once the route is mapped, skill and experience are needed to steer systems in the right direction and to overcome problems that arise, such as the repair and maintenance of systems. Management must therefore take seriously the need to receive adequate education and training in the nature, uses, and consequences of the technology. In order to direct office technology developments effectively, it is crucial that management explicitly considers all relevant performance criteria: organizational, social, personal, economic (long term and short term) and technical. Monitoring a system in terms of only technical and short-term economic factors is like driving a car by looking only at the numbers on devices indicating speed and distance while ignoring fuel indicators, the engine temperature, the state of the roads, and so on.

Planning for new systems

Management must be involved directly in planning the details of new systems, monitoring progress, making adjustments, and generally keeping in charge of developments. This responsibility follows on from the establishment of general objectives in the first phase. It must also encompass a broad range of skills and activities, searching beyond the most immediate and obvious aspects to explore the deeper implications for how the organization really functions. This is a task which can take considerable time and effort.

If management fails to carry out this phase effectively, the system will become unbalanced. It will follow the course determined by particular technological developments, or by the group that has most influence on the design, which may not reflect broader organizational priorities. The very nature of computer technology makes it biased towards particular kinds of tasks which can be measured, thus it can create a spurious aura of rationality and objectivity about its results.

Computer-based systems have a considerable degree of flexibility and adaptability. Once they have been established, however, making fundamental changes can be costly and time consuming. It is therefore important that the main requirements are built into the system from its earliest planning phases.

Management must ensure that these requirements are followed through successfully. If any significant changes of course are necessary, the reasons for them should be brought to the surface. Management should approve them explicitly, instead of finding out, when it is too late to do anything about them, that *de facto* alterations have been made in developing or choosing a system.

Managing organizational change

An intrinsic part of most managers' jobs is to help propose and implement organizational and job changes that occur periodically. New office technology adds a new dimension to this task, making it more difficult than most previous organizational changes. The speed and extent of technological developments are the motor of change. In the past, the initiative for change lay primarily in the hands of management or in prevailing economic and market conditions. Now, the market and economic conditions are encouraging managers to introduce new technology which has much more fundamental implications than originally perceived.

The agenda of organizational change, as induced by new technology, is a familar one, but is considerably different with new office technology. If the introduction of the new system is viewed only as a technical activity, many of these aspects may come as a complete surprise. Management must therefore consider, and take action on, the following:

(1) Establishment of new organizational and management structures.
(2) Definition of new management responsibilities and reporting procedures.
(3) Review of personnel policies making necessary adjustments to job descriptions and recruitment criteria.
(4) Handling of staff and labour relations.
(5) Evaluation of new skills and training needs.
(6) Analysis of implications for relations with customers, clients, suppliers, agents, and other external individuals and groups, followed by necessary actions to ensure that the computer-based system improves these interactions, and that any necessary changes are adequately explained to those affected by them.
(7) Establishment of new ventures which may arise from the implementation of new office systems.

Using technology in new management jobs

Some management jobs will involve specific new responsibilities for aspects of the technology, such as its introduction to the workplace, subsequent operation and development. Changes are also likely to occur in most other management activities: in the way managers communicate within and outside the organization, how information is gathered, work is monitored, assessments are made of performance, documents are produced, insights are gained into future developments, problems are defined, choices are made, and so on. Managers will have to learn new skills and new ways of approaching their jobs.

Many of those changes in management jobs and responsibilities will be caused because managers are becoming direct users of computer-based systems. Some managers in the past have been recipients of results and reports produced by computer, which obviously had some effect on how they worked. Such systems, however, were remote from the daily experience of managers and did not cause substantial changes. Once low cost systems became available to fit on managers' desks, the picture changed.

When using new office technology, most managers go through a common learning pattern. At first, the system seems strange, so managers are tentative. They may feel uneasy working with a keyboard, which has been associated with lower status jobs. Managers also have a natural fear of being seen to make mistakes by colleagues, subordinates or superiors. This learning experience can be stressful but, provided the manager can break through the initial barrier and gain first hand experience of how the system can aid his or her work, the rate of progress in learning how to exploit the system's capabilities rapidly increases.

It is therefore important that systems designed for managers are easy to use and provide some immediate practical benefits. Opportunities for learning and experimenting with new systems should be provided in environments where the manager can make the inevitable mistakes of a learner without feeling under pressure or being embarrassed.

Selecting new systems

Some managers will be influential in selecting systems, although their freedom may be constrained by organizational policies and technical requirements. Choosing a computer-based system is a more difficult task than, say, deciding on a typewriter or a photocopier because there are many different types of computer system which can perform a particular task. They are aggressively marketed by a variety of manufacturers and dealers, each eager to bedazzle their customers with an array of glittering technical catchphrases. Even though the cost of computing has fallen dramatically in recent years, an investment in new office technology is a major step for most organizations, with widespread repercussions for the responsible manager if the system, or its supplier, fails to live up to expectations.

When selecting systems, managers must keep the overall objectives of the venture in mind, both for immediate needs and for longer-term strategies. From a pragmatic viewpoint, those who will use the system should have some say in the selection procedure because they are the ones who know best what the work consists of and thus the characteristics required of the new system. Managers must not allow systems to be bought purely on their technological capability or their face-value price. Managers should seek specialist advice to sort out technical problems, but the manager still has the final responsibility for important questions such as judging the financial stability of the supplier, the quality of support and maintenance, the system's ease of use, and its relevance to a particular applications environment.

The selection of one system cannot be made in isolation from the overall strategy for office innovation. Many organizations have found that individuals or groups have gone their own route in buying relatively cheap systems that met their immediate needs, only to discover at a later stage that they could not be extended or could not be made compatible with other systems in the organization.

Managing information system resources

The implementation, operation and development of information system resources needs careful handling, with great attention to detail. It requires an ability to manage the human specialists involved, as well as being in control of new equipment. This may involve the employment of external consultants or having an internal group specializing in information technologies.

When introducing and implementing systems, managers should pay attention to creating a carefully phased plan. Time should be allowed to evaluate systems in the early stages, so that adjustments can be made as users gain experience. The aim should be to proceed at a pace which enables benefits to be achieved as quickly as possible, without pushing the introduction so quickly that the innovation cannot be adequately assimilated.

Managers will have to attend to many small details, such as the provision of a suitable physical environment, appropriate lighting, heating, and so on. Education and training programmes need to be initiated to prepare all those affected by the system. Consideration must also be given to the security of computing resources and providing back-up facilities in case something goes seriously wrong with the running of the system. This requires foresight in budgetary planning so that the entire resources are not invested in hardware that cannot be properly exploited without added investment in training, adapting the physical working environment and ensuring there is adequate maintenance and support.

Routines should be established to monitor and evaluate the performance of the system on a continuing basis, using the original criteria on which the system was initiated. Computer-based systems are likely to evolve as the needs of the organization and individual users change. At some point, major enhancements may be required or a completely new system may need to be installed. Managers should therefore keep in touch with significant new technical developments of relevance to their applications, as well as checking on how well existing systems are fulfilling their expectations.

Office systems are just one element in an integrated range of computer-based information systems developments that also include traditional data processing functions, telecommunications, automated production processes, and many other previously independent functions. New forms of organization and management are needed to coordinate activities that in the past may have been the responsibility of, say, the office or administration manager, data processing department, telephone manager, and mail room supervisor. A senior manager should have overall responsibility for managing all information systems. In smaller organizations, this could be an additional responsibility for a top executive, in larger enterprises an *information manager* could be appointed.

What this book is about

The challenge to management posed by new office technology is a diverse and complex one. It represents radical innovative forces in an area of work that has changed very slowly. For many, it is an opportunity to achieve personal and organizational advancement, for others, it is a threat to well established patterns of work and the satisfaction, pride and status that come from expertise. This book explores these challenges in a practical manner, avoiding jargon, but without oversimplifying the complexities that managers must face when handling the human, organizational and technical changes.

Chapter structure and content

The book can be viewed as having two main sections. Chapters 2 to 5 are primarily concerned with the manager's role as user of the technology. Chapters 6 to 10 focus on management roles concerned with organizational and job changes, and the evaluation, design and introduction of new systems. There is, however, a coherence which binds together all contributions because there is a close interaction between uses of the technology and broader consequences.

Najah Naffah in Chapter 2 provides a description of the main computer-based systems and services that are of direct interest to managers and professionals. He focuses on the functions that can be performed, rather than examining the technical details of the system, because it is what a system can do that is of most interest to managers. He also provides a brief summary of the main principles of computing and defines the key technical terms that managers are likely to encounter in new office technology.

A prime consideration for managers as users of systems, and also in their role in selecting and designing systems, is the ease and effectiveness with which the user interacts with the system. In Chapter 3, Gerhard Fischer provides guidelines on the types of human–computer communication that should provide the most appropriate solutions.

One of the most important management uses of computer-based systems is to assist in making decisions, known as *decision support systems*. This label has been associated with a wide range of products, some of a relatively trivial nature, but others which have crucial influences on the processes of defining and resolving problems. In Chapter 4, Larry Phillips discusses different types of decision support systems, with particular emphasis on the requirements for senior executives.

Chapter 5, by Niels Bjørn-Andersen, explores how the technology could affect management jobs and the relationships between managers and others in the organization. He indicates how job satisfaction could be enhanced or reduced, depending on choices made in the way systems are applied. Advice is given on how to improve management effectiveness, motivation and work enjoyment.

The broader organizational issues are fully explored from Chapter 6 onwards. Michel Crozier and Francis Pavé set the scene by showing the dangers of allowing computer-based systems to be constructed to meet theoretical, formalized ideas of how the organization operates, which may be quite different from how it functions in practice. They suggest how systems can be designed to support the real needs of the organization.

A more detailed look at how an office technology strategy can be developed is provided by Peter Keen in Chapter 7. He discusses the nature of the strategic plan, why it is so important to the ultimate success of the project, and gives examples of specific techniques that can be used to develop, define and implement these plans.

A crucial process in managing new office technology is assessing the options. In Chapter 8, Janine Nahapiet explains how assessments can be made, and identifies the cost and benefit attributes and the time scales on which assessments should be based. She also describes the implications of different assessment approaches.

The way in which the system is selected and introduced is a critical factor in determining its successful operation. In Chapter 9, Gerdie Nillesen and Paula Goosens examine the issues which managers should take into account when preparing for, and implementing a system. These range from providing adequate education and training programmes to ensuring systems have an appropriate physical environment in which to operate. They stress that the monitoring and evaluation of systems should be a continuing process.

Negotiations and bargaining within the organization are integral aspects of most managers' jobs. The skills to carry out these activities are of special importance to the effective use of computer-based systems. Brian Wynne, in Chapter 10, discusses the reasons for this and explains how some of the most important and valuable aspects of management jobs may be changed by new office technology.

The impact on professionals

The use of new office systems also has profound implications for professionals, such as scientists, engineers, product designers and accountants, because many of the systems designed for managers are also used by professionals. Some professionals, of course, fulfil management responsibilities, as well as performing their specialist tasks. With their management hats on, they are in a similar position to any other manager. The technical orientation of many professionals, however, makes them more skilled in, and often more enthusiastic about, technological capabilities. They may therefore be less able to understand and handle the organizational and human consequences of a decision to install new computer aids to their work.

With previous technologies, investment in equipment to assist in specialized functions could be reasonably regarded as a self-contained event, affecting the professionals but having few broader management implications. Now, the computer-based service used by a professional may be integrated with other information systems, and lead to changes, such as the reorganization of support and clerical staff who assist them.

Realism is the keynote

Under the pressures of modern working life, managers must act quickly to solve immediate problems. While they may agree about the relevance of longer-term strategies, they may feel that 'it is all very well in theory, but what am I to do *now*?' This approach is understandable, but is likely to cause long-term difficulties.

The contributors to this book have given advice based on their practical experiences of how people and organizations behave, and of how computer-based systems actually function. However, it will never be possible, even when there has been more experience of new information systems, to provide hard and fast guidelines that can be applied to all circumstances. This is because the success of each application depends on the context in which it takes place, a context determined by organizational style, national culture, economic conditions, and the general social climate at the time of implementation. The context is so important that the same application, implemented in the same organization at different times, might require a different approach each time, perhaps due only to influences external to the organization.

Nevertheless, the recommendations made in this book provide a framework which can be built on and adapted to particular circumstances. It is possible to go ahead blindly, but ignoring potential problems does not make them vanish. They will cause difficulties later, when it is much harder and more costly to sort them out than if preparations had been made beforehand.

Melding human and organizational objectives with technical and economic imperatives is not a luxury; it is a necessity. Properly conceived and implemented, new office technologies can contribute to increased efficiency as well as a more satisfying working environment. Offices are more than just a collection of buildings and equipment. The way people in offices interact, their commitment and motivation, are crucial ingredients in determining the ultimate success of the organization.

Recommendations

(1) Do not regard innovations in office work using computer-based systems as being only relatively small, self-contained changes.
(2) Take a broad view of the implications of new technology for the way organizations really operate and the way people really work.
(3) Recognise that traditional petterns of management jobs may be radically altered when new office systems are introduced.
(4) Ensure that actions to implement new systems are taken within the framework of a comprehensive, flexible strategic plan that establishes the direction and objectives of the changes.
(5) Do not look for generalized, universally applicable checklists when applying computer-based technologies. Each organisation needs to seek the solutions that best fit its management style and organizational goals. The guidelines and techniques summarized in this book can help to master the management challenge of new office technology.

References

1. Special Report, A new era for management, *Business Week*, 34–58, (25th April 1983)
2. Otway, H.J. and Peltu, M. (eds), *New Office Technology; Human and Organizational Aspects*, Frances Pinter, London; Ablex, Norwood, N.J. (1983)

Bibliography

The following publications are also relevant to topics discussed in this chapter.

Bessant, J.R. and Dickson, K.E., *Computers and Employment: A Selected Bibliography*, Heyden & Son Ltd/British Computer Society, London (1982)

Cooper, C.L. and Mumford, E. (eds). *The Quality of Working Life in Western and Eastern Europe*, Associated Business Press, London (1979)

Dertouzos, M.L. and Moses, J. (eds), *The Computer Age: A Twenty Year View*, The MIT Press, Cambridge, Mass (1979)

Evans, A., *What Next at Work?*, Institute of Personnel Management, London (1979)

Wilson, P.A. and Pritchard, J.A.T., *Office Technology Benefits*, National Computing Centre, Manchester (1983)

2

Information Technology for Managers

Najah Naffah

Introduction

Computing technology first made an impact on the world at large in the early 1960s. Microelectronics also emerged publicly around the same time, in the form, for example, of transistor radios. Telecommunications services like the telephone and telegraph were already widely used in the nineteenth century. These three technologies may have come from different roots and may apparently be concerned with different types of activity, but they have a common thread: the raw material they operate on is *information*. They have now melded together into a unified set of methodologies and techniques known as *information technology*.

This chapter examines how information technology is being applied in office work, particularly to the tasks carried out by managers. It does not describe in detail how the technology works because few managers will have to learn about technical intricacies. Instead, the chapter focuses on describing the main options provided by information technology to managers in terms of the types of services, functions and types of systems available. It also defines the key technical terms which will be referred to in the remainder of the book. *Illustrations for this chapter were produced by the author on the Kayak Buroviseur workstation he has helped develop.*

Computer-based office systems

Computers are at the heart of all important new office technology systems. Physical computer equipment, the *hardware*, can memorize, analyse, manipulate and transmit a vast variety of information forms: text, graphics, pictures, voices, handwriting and more. Hardware operation is controlled by *software*, detailed *programs* of instructions that define each step that needs to be carried out to perform a task. The versatility of computer-based systems comes from the fact that the same hardware can be used to perform a multitude of applications by reprogramming it with new software.

Information is stored and processed by computers in an encoded form comprising only the *binary digits* (bits) 0 and 1. Microelectronics has provided transistors that can act as tiny switches; the *on* or *off* state of such a switch can be regarded as equivalent to a 0 or 1. Many thousands of transistors can be packed into a *microchip*. This is a thumbnail-sized slice of *silicon*, a constituent of sand, which is a *semiconductor* that enables electronic pulses to flow in only one direction. It can be used either as computer *memory* to store information or, arranged in complex circuits, as the *processor* which executes software instructions. Large volumes of digital computer information can also be stored in *backing storage*, such as *magnetic disks* or *tapes*, similar to music disks and tapes; the direction of magnetization of tiny magnets in the coating of these media is used to indicate a 0 or 1.

Digital techniques are also being used increasingly in telecommunications because they are more efficient and reliable than traditional *analogue* methods, which send continuously varying signals that represent, for example, the wave pattern of human voices. The switching exchanges in telecommunications networks are also employing computer systems. The main factor that determines what type of information can be sent on a digital communications link is the *bandwidth*, a measurement of the volume of information, in *bits per second* (bps), that can flow down a channel. *Narrowband* links are suitable for services like telex (about 50 bps), computer data (up to 9 600 bps) or telephone speech (about 64 000 bps). *Broadband* or *wideband* connections are needed either where many different services are to be carried or for providing a service that needs high speed transmission, like colour TV which requires almost 100 million bps.

Data processing and office information systems

The earliest use of computing power was in the form of large *mainframe* computers used for *Data Processing* (DP) applications which had to be housed in specially maintained environments. Such systems were applied mainly to tasks with a clearly defined set of rules and routines that could operate on large volumes of *data* (the term used in computing to refer to 'information') structured into organized files. Typical DP work consists of managing accounts, processing pay-rolls, and maintaining and updating records, such as in customer, sales or supplier files. In early DP systems, work had to be physically transported to and from the computer, where it was processed as batches. Gradually, however, external links were developed through devices called *terminals*, which could be in direct *online* communication with the mainframe.

In the 1970s, smaller, more robust and cheaper *minicomputers* were introduced which were eventually capable of being operated in ordinary offices. The process of decentralizing computing capabilities was given a dramatic boost in the 1970s when microelectronics made *microcomputers* available that are far smaller, cheaper, more powerful and versatile than even the minicomputer. It became economically and technically feasible to have sophisticated, computer-based systems on the office desk of a manager, secretary, clerk or technical professional.

There is a great deal of overlap between DP and office systems, but it is worth noting some crucial distinguishing characteristics that arise more from the nature of office work than the technology; similar hardware and software elements can be packaged in different ways for different application needs.

(1) DP work is highly structured, routine and predictable. Office work tends to be more unstructured, variable and unpredictable.

(2) The users of DP systems have been relatively highly trained and have often been skilled computing professionals. Office users, from clerks to top managers, have less specialist training, and should require less. Office users therefore need systems that are much easier to understand and use than the type of complex systems that have been accepted by DP users.

(3) DP systems perform a lot of work carried out in offices, such as accounting and order processing, but have been generally regarded as support services, somewhat remote from everyday operations. New office technology is visible in the mainstream of working life. Its success or failure is more clearly seen to have an impact on overall organizational and job performance.

(4) Those in charge of DP, typically DP departments, have generally been technical specialists who inhabited a different arena to the rest of the organization. Those in charge of new office technology must be more integrated into the general running of the organization (*see* Chapter 7).

New office technology

Office work that can be assisted by computer based systems can be categorized as follows:

(1) *Document production*. The creation of printed text and graphic material.
(2) *Professional aids*. Tools to help with specific tasks, such as *electronic spreadsheets*, which are simple but effective aids to financial management, and systems honed to assist architects, vehicle designers, doctors, etc.
(3) *Filing/retrieval*. The storage of information that can be subsequently searched to find, analyse and present relevant items.
(4) *Communications aids*. The transmission of information and documents between locations.

The main forces in the office systems industry seeking to fulfil these user needs also fall into four categories.

(1) *Word processors*. Primarily for the production of text documents although some do have basic graphic capabilities.
(2) *Integrated systems*. Provide document production, professional aids, filing/retrieval, and other computing capabilities usually within a communications network.
(3) *Personal computers*. Microcomputers that offer a self-contained, general computing resource suitable for relatively small-scale applications, sometimes without any communications ability.
(4) *Mainframe and minicomputers*. Act as central co-ordinating systems making available computing facilities directly to users via online networks.

A *workstation* is the device from which a user accesses computer-based services. The first type of workstation was a terminal linked to mainframe computers. Initially this was a simple and very slow *teletype*, essentially an advanced form of typewriter that can produce printed material under the control of a computer. The next step was to replace the paper with a screen, in what is known as a *Visual Display Terminal* (VDT), *Visual Display Unit* (VDU) or *video terminal*. A keyboard and screen is now the most common basis for a workstation.

Some workstations rely totally on other systems for their computing power and are called *dumb*. Others, referred to as *intelligent*, have their own inbuilt processor and memory. Many systems can act as *stand alone* devices for some tasks and then be interlinked to share resources and communicate with other workstations. A workstation could be a word processor, a personal computer, a VDT or a device built to provide many services, known as an *integrated* or *multifunction* workstation. Office workstations were originally used mainly for clerical and typing tasks. Systems were also developed for specific professional tasks, such as *Computer Aided Design* (CAD) terminals with high performance graphics capabilities for product designers. *Executive workstations* aimed primarily at management tasks started appearing in the early 1980s. This chapter is mainly concerned with workstations for managers and professionals.

There are many techniques and technologies that contribute to new office technology. This chapter, however, concentrates on describing the functions that new office systems can perform in terms of individual services which are aimed at serving one person at a time, in what is called stand alone mode, or co-operative or corporate services, where users share computing resources.

Individual workstation services

In 1979, Visicorp in the US introduced the Visicalc electronic spreadsheet for the Apple II microcomputer. This system marked a turning point in managers' use of computer-based systems. It gave easy to use evidence that computing can be a practical tool in assisting a manager to perform tasks of importance to him or her. By 1983, over one million spreadsheets were in use in over fifty versions, some more powerful than Visicalc. After sampling the advantages of spreadsheets, many managers started exploring other personal computing services of value to them, such as word processing and personal filing.

Word processing software on personal computers has been satisfactory for the requirements of many of its users, but generally has less sophisticated document production capabilities than *dedicated* word processors designed for use by secretaries and clerks. Word processing software for personal computers has, however, improved considerably, while the scope of specialized word processors has been extended to include other services, such as spreadsheets and personal filing.

Word processing and spreadsheets have been important first steps on the road to more advanced computer-based office services. Word processing originally developed as a means of handling text and has now been extended to documents which also have graphs, charts, tables, illustrations, photographs, mathematical and other special symbols. Spreadsheets are a simplified example of software *modelling*. This defines how a system is likely to behave in terms of rules, equations and relationships governing key factors (*variables*). The user can use the model to find out what would happen if certain variables were altered, so are often referred to as *What if?* systems. Software modelling can become extremely complex, managing far more variables and rules than can be handled in a spreadsheet. Software modelling is an important aid in helping managers to make decisions, but does not necessarily constitute a full decision support system (*see* Chapter 4).

In addition to document production and spreadsheets, this section describes other facilities of personal interest to a manager, such as the filing and retrieval of information, and enhancements to telephone services.

Document production

There are five stages in the production of a document where computer-based systems can be of benefit (*see Figure 2.1*).

(1) *Input* that creates information in computerized form. The keyboard is the most common input device, usually in association with a display screen. When a key is touched, the relevant character is created in computer storage. A pointer on the screen, typically a square character called a *cursor*, indicates the current position of the information being manipulated.

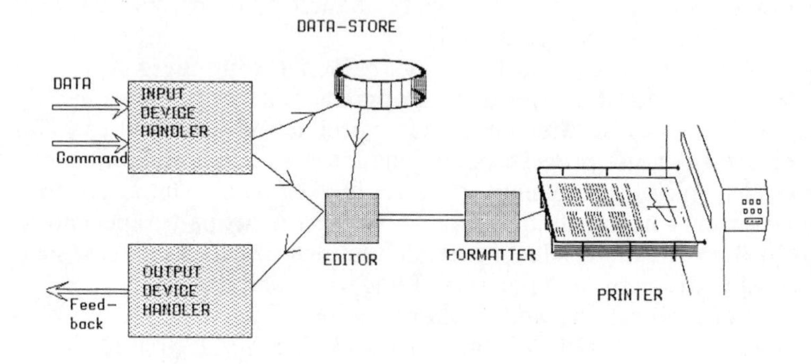

Figure 2.1 Elements in document production

(2) *Data storage* is where information is memorized electronically so that it can be altered during the drafting of a document or stored for subsequent reference. The most popular storage medium is magnetic disks. *Floppy disks* or *diskettes* are like 45 rpm flexible music records and can hold the equivalent of about 100 to 200 pages of A4 text. *Hard disks*, such as compact *Winchester cartridges*, can contain the equivalent of many thousands of pages of A4 text.
(3) *Editing* software that enables the user to manipulate information.
(4) *Formatting* software to allow the user to define how information is presented.
(5) *Output* that presents information. The two most common forms of output are *hardcopy* printout on paper and displays on a screen. The screen can also be regarded as a *window* onto the text information in data storage. This window may be too small to show all stored information, so it may need to be moved (*scrolled*) vertically or horizontally to scan all the information (also known as *browsing*).

The key to computer-aided document production is the software for editing and formatting, which is sometimes known collectively as the *editor*. Products on the market provide this software with varying degrees of quality. When evaluating systems, it is important to determine the ease and effectiveness of its human–computer communication (*see* Chapter 3) and the variety of functions provided which should include the following:

(1) *Editing functions*. The facilities provided by an editor depend on the type of information *objects* being processed, such as:
    (a) Text objects like characters, words, sequences of characters (*strings*), sentences, paragraphs, footnotes and high level entities (chapters, parts, etc.).
    (b) Environmental objects, usually associated with text material, such as authors, table of contents, indexes, annexes and appendixes that are concerned with the beginning and ending the document.
    (c) Graphical information, such as circles, lines, multilines, *splines* (curved lines), freehand drawings, text captions for illustrations, and so on.
    (d) Forms and tables that include areas, such as fields and zones, that need to be manipulated.

    There are some basic actions, such as delete, copy and move, required for all types of objects although their implementa-

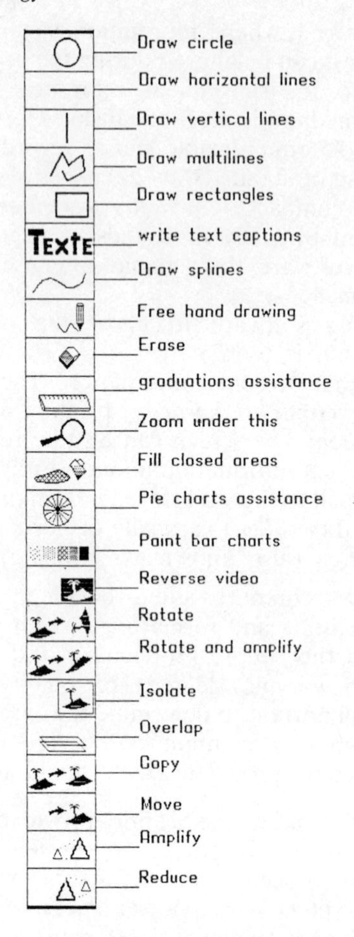

Figure 2.2 Menu of editing commands for graphical information

tion will differ according to the types of data being manipulated. For text editors, there is a minimum set of functions from which fuller editors can be developed (*see Table 2.1*). The types of editing functions needed for graphic systems are illustrated in *Figure 2.2*, which shows a menu from the editor on the Kayak Buroviseur workstation that contains actions to create objects (like 'Draw a Circle') or manipulate them (like 'Rotate').

(2) *Formatting functions*. The formatting process aims to produce a document representing the intentions of the author in terms of meaning and physical appearance (which could be on a screen or paper). The appearance should not detract from the meaning, for example by having a table split over two pages or confusing the reader with too many different type styles. The main functions performed by formatters are summarized in *Table 2.2* and *Figure 2.3*.

Electronic spreadsheets

Spreadsheets consisting of a grid with many rows and columns, produced with paper and pen/pencil, have been used in the past by many accountants and managers using paper and pen/pencil to assist in handling financial information. Electronic spreadsheets provide more efficient, extensive and speedier ways of handling the required data and calculations. The main principles of

Table 2.1 Basic text editing functions

Text editing function	*Action initiated*
Insert	Allows the insertion of a character, word or other text string at the *active position*, the place currently pointed at by the cursor
Delete	Allows the removal of a character or string of characters
Copy	Causes existing text to be copied from the active position to a target position, with the possibility of repeating the copy at other points
Move	Causes text to be moved from the active position to a target position and deletion of the source text from the initial position
Alter	Leads to the replacement of a character or string of characters with a new value. *Global replacement* alters all occurences of a particular string by the new value indicated in the command
Find	Searches for a character or string of characters indicated and positions the cursor at the start of the required string

Table 2.2 Formatting functions

Element acted on	*Functions that can be performed*
Character	Defines how information is to be presented, such as: (1) The style (*fount*), weight (bold or light), size and width (narrow or compressed) (2) The layout of a table vertically (*portrait*) or horizontally (*landscape*) (3) The way information to be presented on a screen is displayed, such as with characters blinking, in *inverse* (character and background colours the reverse of normal) or highlighted in some other way
Block	Constructs words, sentences and paragraphs in appropriate formats, such as having text lined up (*justified*) to the left or right hand margin or having different levels of indention for blocks that form subsections of other text in a structured document
Page	Organizes blocks in pages, with consideration for the height, width, 'white space' margins surrounding text, and other attributes, such as whether it has a landscape or portrait orientation. It also automatically numbers the pages. Care needs to be taken in the way blocks are split over pages, for example, keeping tables and figures on one page
Special commands	Carries out special requirements by embedding codes in the source text which are interpreted by the formatter before organizing the blocks into pages. Such commands relate, for example, to footnotes, forcing a special position (such as the start of a new page) or updating information that needs to be regularly changed (such as the current date)

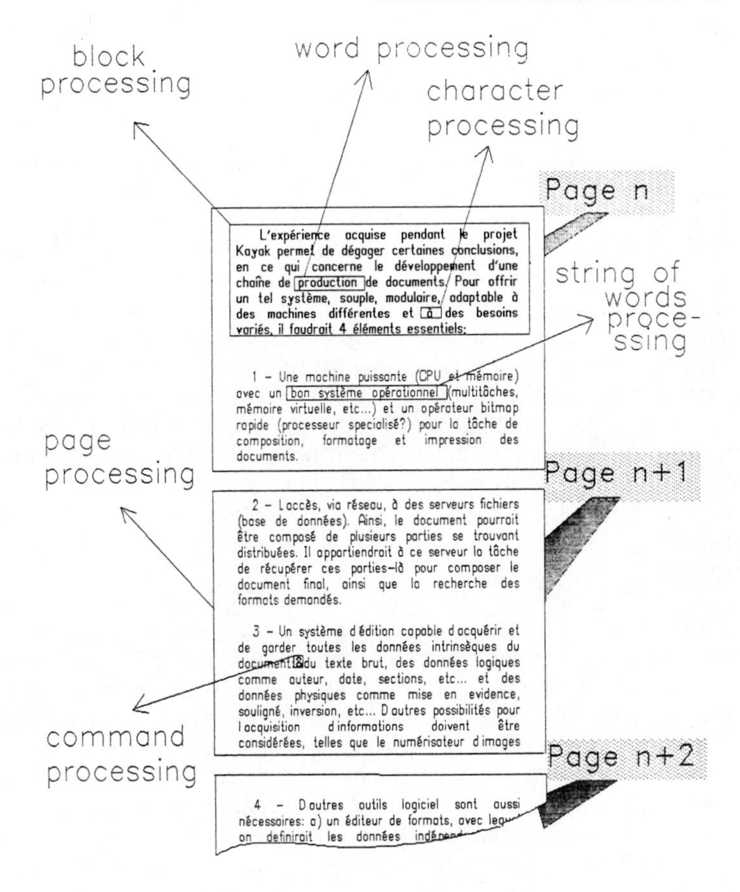

Figure 2.3 Elements acted on by formatting software

spreadsheet techniques are:

(1) Each *cell* can have a *label* (such as price, profit or tax percentage), a *value* and, optionally, *constraints* such as a maximum or minimum value.

(2) The constraints can link one cell to others, say by a formula using arithmetic operations (+,−,×,÷), percentages, averages, logarithmic, trigonometric, logical and other operations. For example, the value of the cell *profit* could be associated with a constraint that is calculated by subtracting the value of cell *costs* from the value of cell *income*.

(3) The fixed information relating to the cell labels, constraints and inter-relations form a model *template*. When new figures are given to particular cells, the model's rules work out the changes to values in all related cells.

An electronic spreadsheet program displays as much of the grid or *table* that can fit in a screen's window (*see Figure 2.4*). Each cell's *address* is its row and column number in the grid. The total number of columns and rows is fixed, typically from 64 to 2000 or more. The user scrolls the window to view the required cells. Some workstations enable the user to look at more than one part of the grid at the same time, as discussed below in the section on multifunction workstations. The most time consuming and tedious part of using an electronic spread sheet is defining relationships between cells, setting constraints, assigning labels to cells, inserting values, and so on. Such setting up, however, is well worth the effort and is likely to be needed only a few times in many years of use. The task is eased if editing functions are available that assist, for example, copying one or more cells, or moving and swapping cells, columns or rows.

Once the spreadsheet model is established, the program automatically performs all the necessary calculations swiftly when the user alters some variables, rules or constraints. In more sophisticated systems, a number of spreadsheets can be interlinked through particular cells; a change in one will trigger the necessary alterations in all others. Electronic spreadsheets are far quicker, more accurate and are able to handle more complex models than traditional paper-based techniques. Spreadsheet programs are used in many different applications, such as sales forecasting, budget planning, currency conversion, and profit-and-loss statements.

Business graphics

Early computer-based systems presented information primarily as text and numbers displayed on green and grey screens or printed, often all in capital letters, on stacks of paper printout. This made many managers shy away from computers because they needed to get on with doing a job rather than spending a lot of time ploughing through difficult to read material.

There are now many *business graphics* software packages that can generate a variety of graphical forms, such as bar charts, line graphs, pie charts (a circle divided into slices) and so on. Such presentations are obviously improved if colour is also available.

Business graphics software is often linked to spreadsheet facilities so that results can be translated automatically into suitable graphs. Some systems also have a graphics editor that can be used to modify the figures generated by the software. A suitable printer is needed to produce hardcopy and, preferably, facilities to create slides that can be used directly at a meeting or conference.

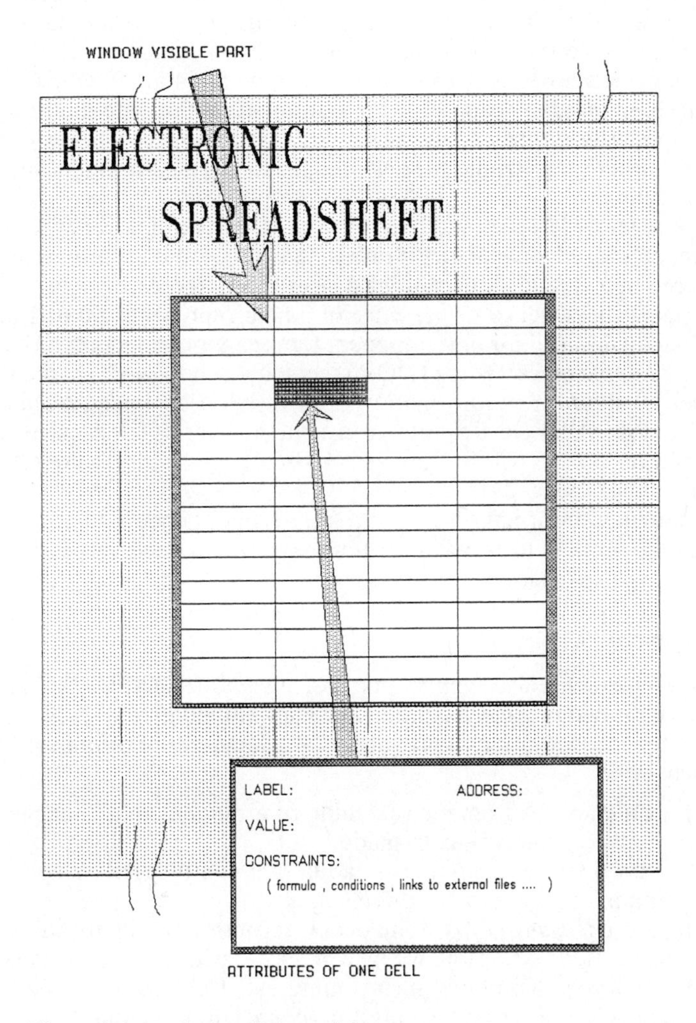

Figure 2.4 An electronic spreadsheet

Personal information management systems

Some information is private to an individual or a group, and is maintained independently from corporate procedures and rules. There are various systems to assist handling such personal information, for example, some microcomputer software helps to create and manage small files of data in the form of the electronic equivalent of a box of reference cards. Systems can also be programmed with *tickler* files which are told by the user to remember certain events and then to give a reminder when the date comes close. *Electronic diaries* can be maintained either as a purely stand alone capability for an individual's private use or in a shared system that allows meetings to be arranged by examining each other's electronic diaries and fixing the appointment automatically.

Images of pictures and pages from a document for personal use can be stored on *video* or *optical disks*. Digital information is stored in a videodisk by shining a laser beam to create holes in the surface; the absence or presence of a hole represents a 0 or 1 bit. Video disks used for entertainment films cannot be recorded over. *Digital Optical Recording* (DOR) techniques, however, enable the user to create new information on a disk via an image scanner. One disk of 30 cm diameter can contain over 500 000 pages of typed text or 25 000 images of A4 sized pages with photographs and illustrations.

Personal information files are stored, maintained and accessed in ways similar to those used for the larger databases described later in this chapter.

Enhanced telephony

Computers can also help to improve telephone services available to an individual, for example, through computerized exchanges and the incorporation of microchips in telephones to offer facilities such as:

(1) *Callback*. Automatic redialling of a number that is engaged until a connection is made.
(2) *Abbreviated dialling*. Initiating frequently used telephone numbers by two or three digits.
(3) *Absent transfer*. Automatically rerouting a call to another specified extension when a person visits another office.
(4) *Hunting*. Routeing an incoming call through a number of possible alternatives until a connection is made, if the

originally dialled number is engaged.

In more sophisticated systems, enhanced telephone services can be offered directly from a workstation. For example, a personal information file containing names and phone numbers can be displayed on the screen, and the person being called indicated by reference to a pointer. Computer-based systems can also record voices in digital form. This can be used to record messages for incoming calls, as in an answering machine. The computer can record the incoming message for subsequent replay when the recipient is free to listen. Systems are also being developed that produce synthesized voices from messages typed at a keyboard.

Managers' programming aids

Software is written in special *programming languages* which have rigid, precisely defined structures and grammars with a limited range of commands and vocabulary that can be used with them. Different programming languages are suitable for different types of task. For example, Cobol is appropriate for commercial data processing and Fortran for scientific work. On microcomputers, the most popular language is Basic because it is extremely easy to learn, although it has limitations for producing complex programs. *Most managers should never have to use a programming language unless they have a special personal interest.* Some professionals may need to learn specialized programming techniques to enable them to develop software tailored to their particular discipline.

There are now many systems available that enable managers to generate software code without having to learn a special programming language. These techniques, known as *end-user, fourth generation* or *applications* languages, or *program generators*, allow the user to provide information to the system in a natural manner. The system then produces the necessary code without requiring the user to become a programming specialist.

Expert systems

A significant computing development which began to make an impact outside research laboratories in the 1980s is that of the *expert system* which contains the distilled knowledge of one or more specialists in a particular subject or *domain*. Initially, expert systems were applied to narrow scientific fields but are now being extended to broader business applications. They are easier to produce when there are sets of rules to be followed rather than when more qualitative decisions need to be made. Some expert system developments are oriented towards replacing human specialists by computers, but other work aims to apply increased computing knowledge and 'intelligence' in a way which is used co-operatively with human expertise (*see* Chapter 3).

Integrated systems

Managers whose main experience of computer-based services has been with personal computers realize that separate software systems are often needed to set up and perform distinct functions, such as word processing, spreadsheets, and communications. One of the most significant trends in new office technology is towards integrating many services into a single system or workstation, as explained later in this chapter.

Co-operative workstation services

People need to share computer-based services to communicate with each other and to gain access to large information libraries or files. The sharing of services can be contained within various levels, such as within a department, a project team that involves individuals from many departments, a building, between organizations, or in a particular discipline (chemical engineers, architects, psychologists, etc.) or market specialization (stockbroking, banking, retailing, etc.).

Electronic mail

Post, Telegraphs and Telecommunications (PTT) were the methods first used to communicate information across long distances. Throughout the world, PTT authorities have been established to provide such services, although it has now become clear that physical postal services are of a different nature to electronic transmission.

Electronic mail, also known as *Computer-Based Message Systems* (CBMS), provides a variety of facilities to assist human communication between locations. These should offer the following basic services (*see Figure 2.5*):

(1) *Message creation by the originator*. The range of information types (text, graphics, etc.) used in messages will depend on the workstation available and the capability of the com-

munications network. A secret password should be given as a security check before the system allows a user access to the network.

(2) *Routeing of messages to the recipient(s)*. The network control software uses information about where the recipient is located and the transmission channels available to deliver the communication to the appropriate workstation(s) in the most efficient and reliable manner.

(3) *Storing incoming mail until the recipient is ready to receive it*. After transmission, the message is filed in computer storage accessible to the recipient, known as an *electronic mailbox*, from where it is extracted at the recipient's convenience. This is called a *store and forward* system.

(4) *Delivery of the message*. The recipient can regularly scan an index to what is in the mailbox which indicates who sent it, a

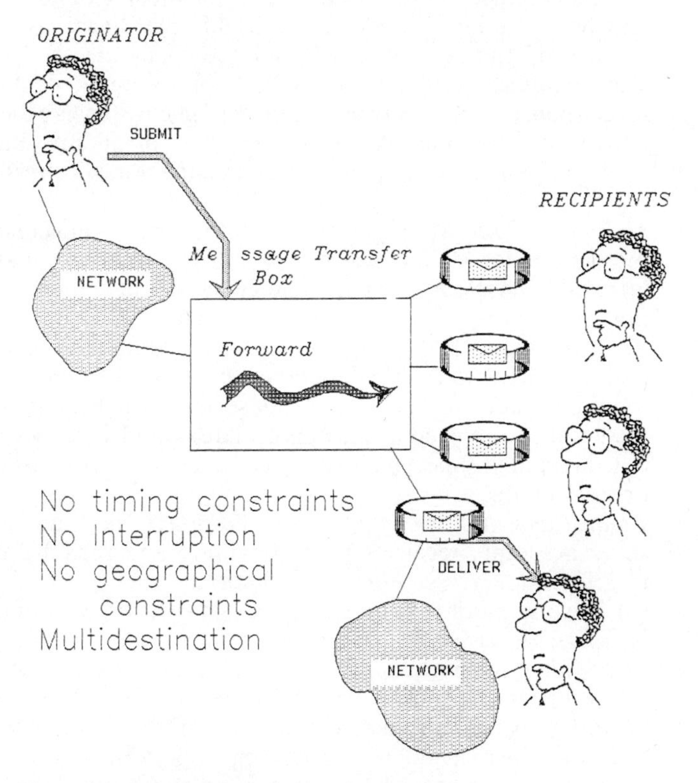

Figure 2.5 Electronic mail: functions and advantages

headline summary of the content, and the degree of priority or urgency. Specific messages can be selected to be displayed on the screen.

Electronic mail services can be of great benefit in assisting communications within and between organizations by providing facilities such as:

(1) *No time constraints*. The originator can compose and send the message at the time and speed she or he wishes without requiring the recipient to be at the other end of the line at the same moment. This is obviously valuable when communicating across different time zones.
(2) *No interruptions*. The store and forward feature means that the recipient is not interrupted every time there is an incoming message.
(3) *No geographical constraints*. Electronic mail extends the telephone's ability to link people in different locations and can lead to the development of a close community feeling. The *computer conferencing* facility, for example, enables subscribers to share in a continuing dialogue by placing ideas into a common file. A participant joins in at any time, reading the latest comments before making a new contribution.
(4) *Multidestination*. Messages can be sent to many recipients at the same time. Mailing lists can be stored in the system and invoked as necessary for particular categories of communication.
(5) *Voice messages*. If the recipient wishes to add a note before sending it back to the sender and/or someone else, she or he should be able to speak a response that will be digitally recorded and relayed at the appropriate point by the person it is directed at. Speech messages are known as *voice memos* or *voicegrams*.
(6) *Control and monitoring of communications*. The time messages are sent, received in the mailbox and read by the recipient can be recorded. In addition:
   (a) The originator can, for example, signal the urgency of the message, causing a light to flash on the recipient's terminal for particularly important ones; request that he or she is informed when the message is delivered and read; specify alternative recipients if the primary one cannot be reached; and allow recipients to know who else received copies or have some *blind* copies that are not

reported to other recipients.

(b) The recipient can, for example, reroute all incoming mail to another workstation if he or she is away for a period, or redirect mail from certain subscribers to other workstations to avoid getting too many unnecessary messages.

(7) *Management of the system*. The system must be administered systematically and effectively. Procedures need to be established to allocate each subscriber an identifying code, password, and appropriate workstation and network facilities. The usage of the system should be monitored to assist in

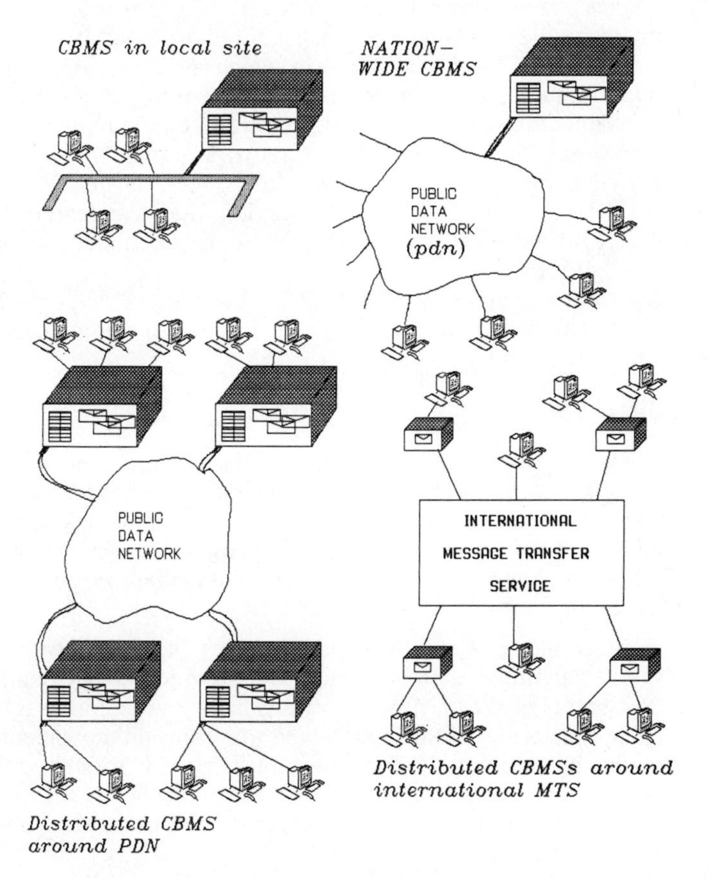

Figure 2.6 Types of electronic mail networks

costing and accounting tasks. Distribution lists and other files must be maintained, such as a *directory file* containing names and attributes of subscribers that could help users, for example, to find all subscribers living on the Champs Elysées.

The workstations, computer storage, printers, computers and other elements that comprise a network can be linked together in a number of different ways, such as in the following list, which refers to the four networks in *Figure 2.6*, moving clockwise from the left hand top corner.

(1) *A local site* with workstations serviced by a nearby micro or minicomputer holding mailboxes, directories, and so on.
(2) *Nationwide centralized service* in which minicomputers and mainframes provide co-ordination and control of workstations linked through a network, often run by the public PTT administration or by a private network supplier.
(3) *Distributed round an international Message Transfer Service* (MTS), the newest type of service that can interlink decentralized local networks or allow direct connection by workstations.
(4) *Distributed around a Public Data Network* (PDN) which allows subscribers to various local networks to communicate with each other.

Teleconferencing

Teleconferencing offers an alternative to face to face meetings. The computer conferencing facility provided by computer based message systems described above can be regarded as a form of teleconferencing, but this term is usually used for services that enable people to interact with each other immediately. The two main types of such teleconferencing are:

(1) *Audioconferences* in which people can talk to, but cannot see, each other. Facilities may be provided to exchange documents electronically or to transmit *telewriting* messages using special electronic input *tablets* that transmit movements made by a pen. Participants must be in rooms with equipment that enables them to talk to and hear others in different locations without the necessity of a handset held to mouth and ear.
(2) *Videoconferences* in which people can see as well as hear each other. The main technical limitation is the need to have

high bandwidth transmission links – moving pictures can require a minimum of 1.5 to 2 million bits per second. Instead of *full motion* conferencing, *freeze frame* services can be provided at less cost, operating at only about 50 000 bits per second. With freeze frame, a still picture is sent about every thirty seconds; this is clearly not as effective as full motion. Special cameras, studios, TV monitors and other equipment are needed for videoconferencing.

Teleconferencing offers potentially attractive services but its use has grown relatively slowly. This is partly because the costs have been high compared to the benefits. As with other computer-based services, microelectronics is reducing costs, which has made motion videoconferencing a cost effective option in many circumstances. Another brake on teleconferencing growth has been the resistance by managers who have found remote communications awkward, particularly when facing cameras. Increasing experience with live systems is helping to give managers more skill in being able to exploit teleconferencing functions.

The teletex service

The Consultative Committee on International Telephones and Telegraphs (CCITT), which represents telecommunications authorities around the world, has defined standards for *teletex*, a 'supertelex' service for exchanging text messages. Teletex enables messages to be created, edited, transmitted across the network and received. Traditional telex devices had built-in printers with only capital letters, but teletex terminals can have a range of facilities, from being an adapted *electronic typewriter* (a word processor with limited memory, software and display capabilities) to specially developed, sophisticated workstations. This gives a vast improvement in quality and speed compared with telex.

Being based on an internationally agreed standard is of great importance for teletex because incompatibilities between computer-based equipment and services is a major barrier to further growth of new office technology. The CCITT teletex standards cover transmission rates (2400 bits per second), the character repertoire that should be available, the basic range of services to be provided, and the communications *protocols*. Rules and procedures that need to be followed when making connections between terminals, checking that transmission has been error free, and so on, are also given. Teletex systems should also be able to link into the telex network.

Viewdata and teletext

Videotex allows the transmission and presentation of information containing graphics as well as text. Interactive videotex (*viewdata*) allows the user to send messages and commands to search through 'pages' of data or, say, to order goods displayed in the sales catalogue held in the system's information store. Viewdata can also be used to exchange electronic mail between subscribers. It provides a relatively simple and low cost way of distributing up to date information to many subscribers: for example, from a company to its dealers or between travel agents. Many public viewdata services have been established, such as Prestel in the UK, Teletel in France, Telidon in Canada and Captains in Japan.

Broadcast videotex (*teletext*) provides one-way transmission of pages of information to many receivers, such as from a TV transmitter to adapted TV sets, using a spare transmission channel not used for sending moving pictures.

Facsimile document transmission

Telefax or *facsimile* (fax) scans a document, transmits its image and reproduces a copy on the receiving device. Early machines were originally rather slow and generated blurred and indistinct copies. Computer-based digital techniques have improved speed and quality and reduced costs. The CCITT has classified telefax machines into four categories. Groups 3 and 4 are the most interesting for the office of the future. Group 3 systems send the copy of a page in less than a minute, perhaps as quickly as 20 seconds. Group 4 must be equally fast and must also be error free. The other two groups are mainly older machines that transmit an A4 page in up to six minutes (Group 1) or three minutes (Group 2).

Corporate databases

Filing, storing and retrieving information are common office activities. Filing cabinets with folders and papers have been an integral part of office work. Computerized *databases* provide new means of managing such information to reduce the amount of paper and space needed, speed up the search to extract relevant information, and enable people at many locations to access the same information source.

One of the problems with any database is getting information into it. Data input via a keyboard can be stored directly in computerized form. Techniques to recognize handwriting and human speech have taken longer to develop. Systems have been available for a long time that can read some printed characters (*Optical Character Recognition*, OCR), but it has been harder to get computers to read letters typed unevenly, mixed print and handwriting, drawings and pictures. Storage media that can adequately cope with images, such as optical disks, only started to come on the market in the 1980s.

The most widely used databases have therefore been composed of text and numbers gathered through keyboard entry known as *DataBase Management Systems* (DBMS). These were developed on data processing systems with highly structured data, such as accounting, orders, delivery, customer, client, inventory, supplier and personnel records. Initially, information was handled in computers as separate *filing systems*, similar to manual systems, with each file containing all its own records and fields, although some information could be common between files, such as a part number in order, delivery and inventory files. Such techniques proved inefficient for large scale information handling although they can be satisfactory for the small-scale personal information needs of many users. Full scale DBMS software was needed to store and manage data items in a way that avoided unnecessary duplication in data storage but allowed the user flexibility to make an interconnection between items. Three main types of DBMS have been widely used:

(1) *Hierarchical* models structured similarly to an hierarchical organization. A file can be the 'superior' to one or more files beneath it, linked from top to bottom down branches of the hierarchy. This technique is relatively easy to establish and maintain, but can prove to be too rigid and inefficient because it does not allow files or data records to be linked across branches.

(2) *Network* structures that allow data elements to be interlinked in many ways without being confined only to linkages within vertical branches. Like hierarchical files, the structure of the database and the way elements are linked must be defined when the database is set up. As the network approach allows more options for creating links, it is more complex to set up than hierarchical systems but offers the user greater flexibility.

(3) *Relational* databases represent the newest approach, provid-

ing great ease of use but requiring extremely complex software controls. The database is regarded as a collection of data items whose structure is not defined when the database is set up, as with network and hierarchical structures. Instead, the relationships are formed dynamically according to the tasks being performed. The difficulty of handling many intricate relations can make this software very slow. Techniques have been developed to give hardware boosts to the speed of relational systems, such as implementing some routines in *firmware*, specially constructed microelectronic circuits, or using microprocessors to aid the search for information on disks.

Information retrieval and query languages

The *query language* or other method available to the user to search through databases, make enquiries and retrieve relevant information is of importance to the effectiveness of the whole system. The following are some of the main query techniques.

(1) *Indexed keyword searches* in which items in the files are associated with explicit search keys. *Full text* systems create lists which identify the occurrence of each term and enable the whole text to be searched. *Partially indexed* systems, typified by computerized libraries, are based on searching for attributes, such as author, title, and subject selected by a professional indexer.

(2) *Query by Example* (QBE), developed for relational databases, presents the user with a list of attributes; the user fills in the values of those items being looked for.

(3) *Menus* present the user with a number of options from which to select either the required information or another menu taking the user along a trail to the information.

(4) *Natural language* allows the user to express requirements using phrases similar to the way the query would be normally expressed, such as 'Find me all the customers with orders that have been outstanding for more than two weeks'. Such systems usually 'understand' natural languages only within a predetermined context and recognize only a limited vocabulary.

(5) *Question and answer* in which the system finds out what is wanted by asking the user a number of questions.

(6) *Free text* which enables every part of a document to be explored, even if the specification of what is wanted may be

incorrect (say through a misspelling) or incomplete.

Image banks

Optical disks, discussed earlier in terms of personal information systems, can be combined into *juke boxes* to provide a source of information, held as images, which may be shared by many users. An image scanner is used to transfer documents to the disks. Information about each page is keyed in from a control workstation by providing details of various attributes that will help an associated database management system to retrieve the relevant image and display it on a workstation screen. It is important to remember that information on such disks is stored as images of whole pages. It therefore cannot be searched in detail, as a text database could.

Office workstations

The most common office workstations have been VDTs for clerical staff, word processors for secretaries and typists, and personal computers for managers. The most important workstation developments for managers have been towards high perform-

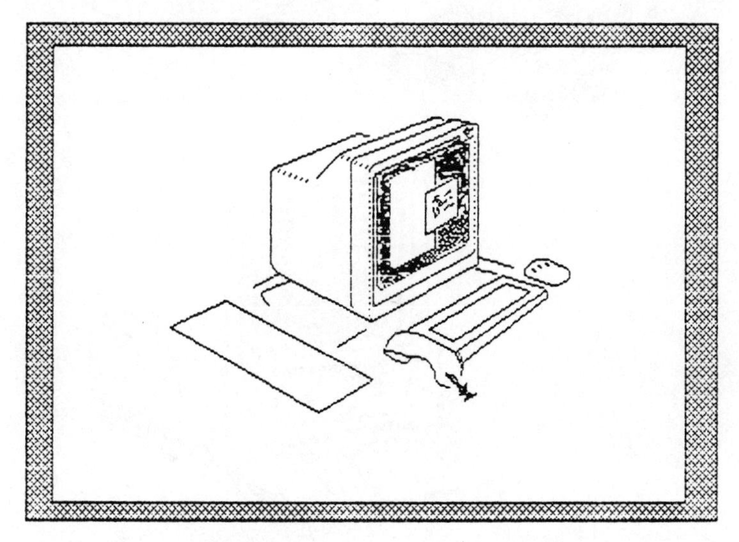

Figure 2.7 A multifunction workstation with a multiwindow display and a mouse to the right of the keyboard

ance, multifunction workstations which integrate a variety of functions (*see Figure 2.7*). In addition, there is a growing variety of other executive workstations and terminals (*see Figure 2.8*).

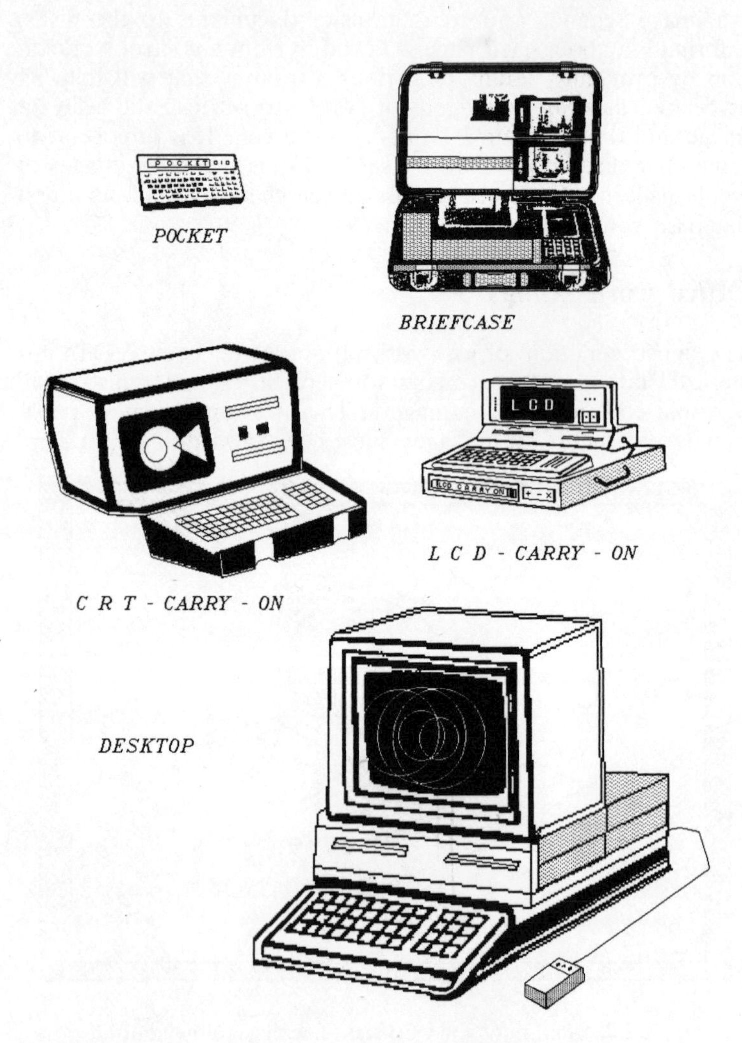

Figure 2.8 Personal workstations for managers

High performance multifunction workstations

The most advanced workstations are systems that are effectively small computers which can operate as a stand alone device or as part of a network. They were pioneered in the 1970s at Xerox Corporation's Palo Alto Research Center (PARC) in California as a way of integrating different tasks and information types (text, graphics, pictures, voice, etc). They first became commercially available in the early 1980s through systems like the Xerox Star and Apple Lisa and Macintosh. Their main attributes include the following facilities:

(1) *Multiwindow displays* that can show different applications being run on the machine at the same time or different parts of the same document or spreadsheet. For example, one window could be used for editing, another for displaying the contents of an electronic mailbox and a third to show an

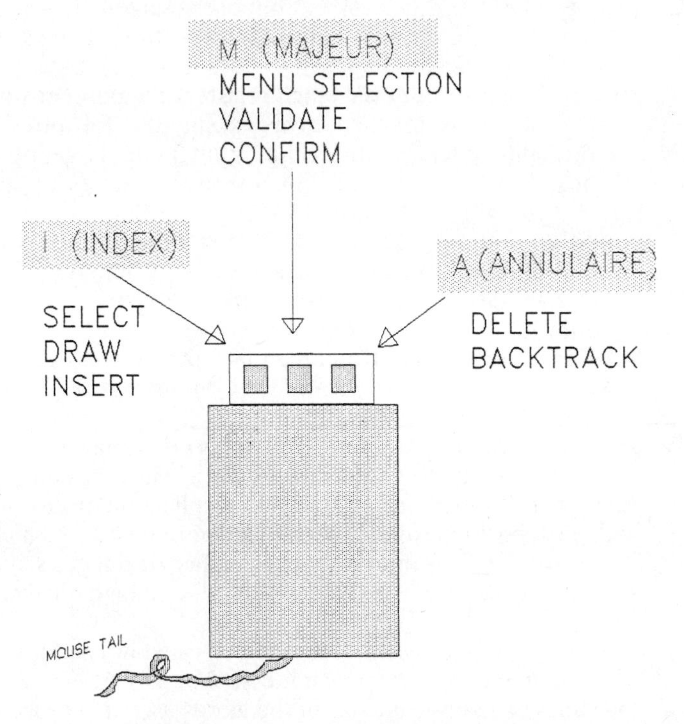

Figure 2.9 Facilities provided by the mouse in the Kayak Buroviseur workstation

electronic telephone directory. In addition, windows can come and go (*pop up*) displaying, for example, editing menus (*see Figure 2.2*) that can switch automatically from, say, text to graphic tasks. Multiwindows are of great importance to managers whose work is likely to consist of having to keep many tasks active at the same time. It also contributes to good human–computer communication (*see* Chapter 3).

(2) *Pointing aids* needed to complement multiwindow systems. They are used, for example, to move windows or other objects on the screen (such as placing a chart in an appropriate place in a document), or to point to a small symbol (*icon*) that represents a function to be performed (*see Figure 2.2*). The main pointing devices include the following:
   (a) *Mouse*, a small object, with a rolling ball in the base, that can be held in the palm of the hand. The cursor on the screen is moved in the direction followed by the mouse as it is rolled over the desk in front of the screen. The mouse can have one or more control buttons to initiate various tasks (*see Figure 2.9*).
   (b) *Touch sensitive screen* which registers the point at which the screen is touched. This is suitable for browsing through systems with menus containing large option boxes, but is unsuitable for use as a pointer to small objects with high accuracy.
   (c) *Tablet*, a flat pad sensitized to register the position where it is touched and used particularly in Computer Aided Design tasks where it is necessary to create detailed drawings.
   (d) *Light pen*, an electronic pen-like device used to input graphic images, particularly for Computer Aided Design tasks.

(3) *High resolution displays* that can display crisp images, usually with black characters and images on a white background. Images are formed on the screen as a collection of tiny dots, with each position called a *pixel*. The more pixels, the higher the resolution and the better the quality of image; screens with about 1024 x 768 pixels can reproduce a high quality A4 page.

(4) *Powerful microprocessors* of similar capabilities to those used in micro and minicomputers, typically 16- or 32-bit machines. The basic bit-size of the words used in a processor are a measure of the power and capability of a system, with 4- and 8-bit systems having relatively limited capabilities.

(5) *Large memory and disk storage* containing up to about 512K or more bytes of *Random Access Memory* (RAM) and from 10M to 100M bytes of hard disk store. (A *byte* is a group of eight bits, equivalent to a character; *RAM* is main memory held in microchips which is immediately accessible to software and which a user can write to or read from; K is an abbreviation for 1024 and M stands for 1 048 576.)

(6) *Full page screen* which displays the equivalent of a full page of A4 text, whereas other screens typically have half a page.

Autonomous personal workstations

It was in the mid 1970s that personal computers, like the Apple II, first helped managers lift the grey curtain of jargon and mystique that shrouded computing during the heyday of mainframe data processing. Personal computers could use ordinary domestic colour TV sets and were originally developed for use in the home to entertain and educate. Many managers found that once they got hands-on experience of a personal computer, they began to appreciate what it could do for them at work, particularly when running software, such as electronic spreadsheets, that provide immediate and obvious benefits.

Personal computers have evolved in two main directions since then. On one hand, they have become smaller and more lightweight so that they can be easily carried around. Moving in the other direction, some personal computers have become increasingly sophisticated. A continuous spectrum of personal computing is available to managers, from pocket computers to powerful multifunction workstations. The choice of which system is most appropriate depends on the nature of the tasks involved, the volume of information being handled, and the money available to invest in a system. Many managers may eventually come to have more than one workstation, say one to work with on a plane or train, one at home and one in the office. Each is likely to be capable of being used on its own or connected to a network. The following are the main categories of personal computers (*see Figure 2.8*), in addition to the multifunction workstations described above.

(1) *Desk-top personal computers* generally have a half page screen (24 lines of 80 characters), possibly with full colour, keyboard, floppy and hard disks, a minimum of 256K bytes of RAM and options for telecommunications links. The *operating system* software available is of crucial importance.

These are collections of routines that organize the hardware resources and determine which software applications packages can run on the machine. Widely used operating systems, like PC-DOS, MS-DOS, CP/M and Unix, are likely to have a broader range of applications software available to users than an operating system used on fewer machines. Many programming languages are likely to be available, some provided in *Read Only Memory* (ROM), microchip main memory that the user cannot overwrite. They generally weigh between 10 and 20 kgs (25 and 50lbs).

(2) *Transportable or carry-on computers* provide similar capabilities to desk top systems but are lighter, from about 4 to 10 kgs (10 to 25 lbs), and come with a case that can be used to carry them around. They may contain a small built-in screen, but can also usually work with a standard display or TV screen. The built-in screen may use a *Cathode Ray Tube* (CRT), which is the basis of TV and VDT displays, or a *Liquid Crystal Display* (LCD), a flat screen also used for calculators and watches.

(3) *Portable or briefcase computers*, generally the size of a book, can be slipped into an ordinary briefcase and are capable of being run off batteries. They usually weigh only a few kilograms, have about two to eight lines of built-in flat screen display, and up to about 32K or 64K of RAM. Cassette tapes or small *microfloppy* disks (5.25 or 3.5 inches in diameter) may be offered for additional storage. These systems are ideal for note taking, electronic mail and preparing shortish letters and reports.

(4) *Pocket computers*, the size of largish pocket calculators usually with one line display, have a small keyboard, up to about 10K bytes of RAM, and the ability to connect to a small printer.

Connected office terminals

There are many devices in the office which are developments from traditional data processing, such as the intelligent VDT, or from telecommunications-oriented information processing (known as *telematics* or *telematique*), such as the telephone, teletex and videotex (*see Figure 2.10*). There are a number of developments to try and combine two or more such terminals into a single workstation, as indicated by the arrows connecting items in *Figure 2.10*. For example, some PTTs are working on terminals that combine teletex and telefax. Videotex and telephone services can be combined in a single unit (public viewdata services already use ordinary telephone lines for communication). The following is a summary of the main types of terminals.

(1) *Intelligent terminal* is typically a VDT including its own microprocessor and main memory.
(2) *Teletypewriter*, usually abbreviated to TTY, is the old fashioned terminal consisting of a keyboard and built-in printer.
(3) *Videotex* terminals are used mainly for viewdata database queries and some electronic mail.
(4) *Telex* is the worldwide text communication system.
(5) *Telephone* network is for voice communications to which computers can add enhanced telephony capabilities.
(6) *Teletex* is text communications as defined by the CCITT.
(7) *Telefax* is document facsimile transmission.

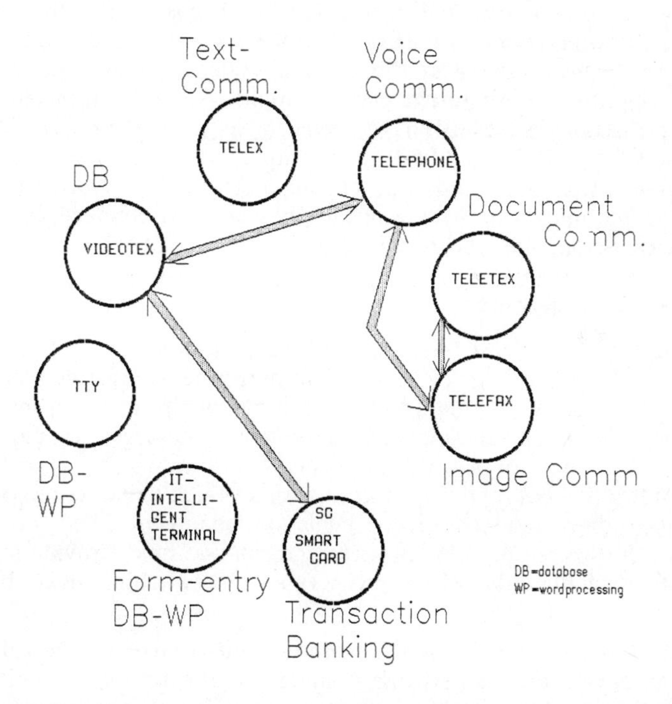

Figure 2.10 Types of telecommunications terminals (arrows indicate services being integrated into combined workstations)

(8) *Smart Card* (SC) is a recent development that puts a microchip on a small plastic card, containing up to 16 000 or more characters, which could be used, for example, to assist security checks or to make payments directly.

Networking capabilities

Networks for office work cover either a particular building or set of offices (*local* distribution) or a broad geographical range (*wide* distribution). For managers, the establishment of the telecommunications infrastructure is a key strategic and tactical issue. The network effectively lays down the standards that determine the types of workstations that can be linked to it and the services offered.

The ultimate aim is to have *open systems*, where any kind of device can be interlinked with any other. To this end, the *International Standards Organization* (ISO) has defined the *Open Systems Interconnection* (OSI) framework. This is divided into seven levels, starting at the basic physical interconnection and moving up to the interchange of complete software applications. Some detailed standards have been established at the lower levels. The CCITT X.21 standard, for example, covers the lowest level, physical transport, and X.25 encompasses the lower three levels for some networks, including the physical X.21 connection, data transmission, and the routeing of messages through a network.

Wide area networks

The telephone and telex networks are traditional examples of *Wide Area Networks* (WANs). The performance of a network is determined by two main factors, the bandwidth of the transmission medium and the method used to route messages through the system. The copper wire of telephone networks is of low bandwidth, but *coaxial cables*, with a thick conducting core, *optical fibres*, which send signals on beams of light through hair-thin glass fibres, microwave and satellite links provide much higher bandwidths. Two main types of switching have been common.

(1) *Circuit switching* is where the circuit connecting the calling device to the network is linked to the receiver circuit by making interconnections through a series of exchanges in the network. This has been the technique used in traditional

telephone exchanges.

(2) *Packet switching* is widely used for digital networks. Data is divided into small packets wrapped around with control information, including a header at the front that contains the address to which it is going. Switches in the network send each packet through the most efficient route to the receiver. Checks are made to ensure the packets arrive intact and in the right order. The X.25 standard applies to packet switched networks.

Private automatic branch exchanges

Many organizations have had locally distributed telecommunications networks for many years in the form of intra-company telephone communications controlled by a private exchange, typically a switchboard operated manually. These are being replaced by computer-based Private Automatic Branch eXchanges, known as *PABX*s or *PBX*s, which can offer a variety of office information services, such as enhanced telephony, electronic mail and audioconferencing. One of the long term limitations on a PABX may be that the existing wiring does not have sufficient bandwidth to carry high volumes of traffic. An important advantage, however, is that a reasonably powerful network can be established without requiring any major rewiring.

Local area networks

PABXs give a local distribution of telecommunications that provides many additional services in addition to the basic transmission of data. Systems that offer high speed local transmission but with few, if any, additional capabilities are known as *Local Area Networks* (LANs). There are two main LAN families:

(1) *Broadband* can transmit many channels on differing frequencies, so that a mix of information can be carried at the same time.
(2) *Baseband* consists of a single channel that allows the transmission of one stream of data at a time.

Broadband networks can be used for a variety of purposes, such as TV broadcasting, multi-channel audio transmission, environmental control, and for local cable TV networks. They generally cover a greater geographic spread than baseband systems, which are usually restricted to cables of no more than about one to three kilometres in length, although independent LANs can be interconnected. The speed required for a baseband service is typically at least one million bits per second. The following are the main types of baseband LAN techniques:

(1) *Broadcast Carrier Sense Multiple Access* (CSMA) is typified by Ethernet, developed at Xerox's PARC centre, which also pioneered research into multifunction office workstations. In these systems each network *station* (representing a connection to one or more devices, workstations of computer systems) can broadcast messages to other stations, which remain constantly on the alert to detect messages addressed to them.
(2) *Ring empty slot systems*, originally developed at Cambridge University in the UK, are where fixed length data slots continually circulate around the link. Stations dump information into vacant slots or detect and pick out data addressed to them.
(3) *Ring or bus token systems* are where stations can transmit only when they are in possession of a token, a special code that circulates with other data. A bus layout has stations connected on a linear link, like stops on a bus route.
(4) *Polling systems* have a central controller that distributes to stations the right to access the network on the basis of a controlled polling sequence.

Standards for various aspects of LANs have been established by internationally recognized authorities, such as the American Institute of Electrical and Electronics Engineers (AIEEE) and the European Computer Manufacturers Association (ECMA). Such standardizations are important steps towards enabling organizations to have greater flexibility in choosing devices to link to the network and in joining up networks.

Choosing and mixing networks

Each type of LAN, or the PBX option for local communications, has particular advantages and disadvantages. The choice of the most appropriate technique for any particular circumstance will depend on existing systems, the types of information being communicated, the costs of linking (*interfacing*) units to the network and of installing the network, overall performance, and so on. For many organizations, a mix of network types may be the solution. For example, it is becoming popular to have baseband systems for local groups, say all offices on one floor of a building, then to link these by a broadband system covering many buildings. It is also possible to have an integrated system (*see Figure 2.11*) consisting of:

(1) One or more local area networks.
(2) Individual computer systems, workstations, databases and input or output devices (known as *servers* in terms of networking).
(3) *Gateways* linking up private and public networks.

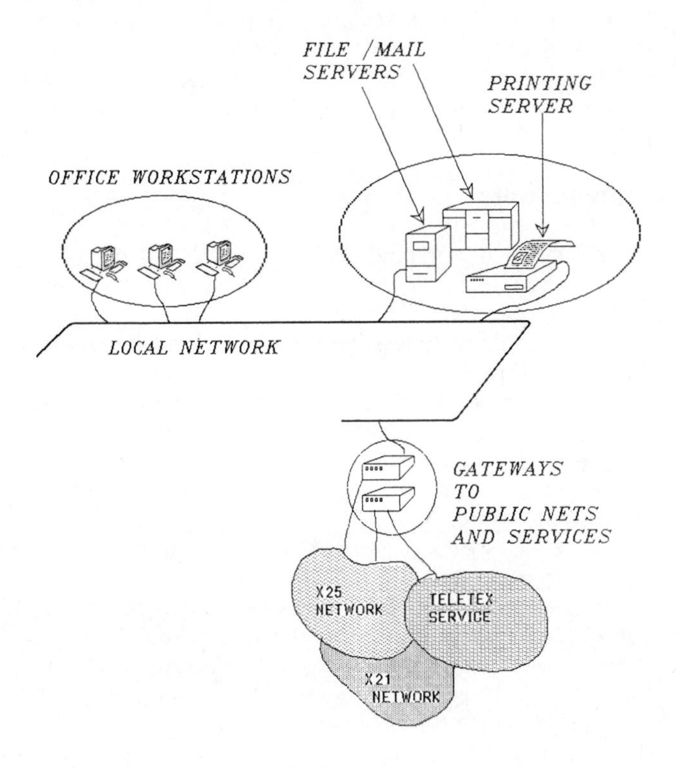

Figure 2.11 Interlinking networks and devices to provide an integrated service

Future trends in new office technology

This chapter has focused on systems and services that have already proven themselves in live business operations. Innovations in computer-based technologies are progressing at a rapid rate and new options are continuously coming onto the market. The main trends are as follows:

(1) Further use of microelectronics to reduce the cost and size of computing, making available increased computing. More software will be turned into firmware as part of this process.
(2) Improved human–computer communication through new input and output aids, such as systems that understand human speech and handwriting, and increased implementation of criteria discussed in Chapter 3.
(3) Greater use of knowledge-based systems and more intelligent software, such as expert systems.

Recommendations

(1) Take time to understand the basic principles of computer-based office technology and the most important services offered. Do not worry about learning technical details, such as programming, unless you have a special personal or business interest.
(2) Avoid jumping at the cheapest product, unless it is to be used purely as an educational aid to get the feel of the technology. Only choose the cheapest if you are sure, after careful evaluation of alternatives, that it is the most effective and appropriate system.
(3) Consider all aspects of possible systems and their relevance to the environment in which the chosen one will operate. Many systems are sold on the basis of long lists of functions, but only a few of these may have any real impact.
(4) When selecting a system consider questions such as:
    (a) How well is it documented and supported by the manufacturer or distributing agent?
    (b) Are there other users of the system? If so, how many, where are they located, what activities are they being applied to, and can some be contacted? Checking with other users is an important way of finding out how systems and their suppliers really perform.

   (c) Is the system a 'paper' machine? Many manufacturers announce systems while they are still in research and development in order to create a pre-production demand.
   (d) Is the system compatible with machines already installed in the company? If not, what is the cost and time involved in converting to the new system?
   (e) Is the system compatible with accepted international and industry standards, where they exist?
   (f) How does the system match the ergonomic and human–computer communication criteria defined in Chapter 3?
   (g) What commitment will the supplier offer regarding performance and reliability?

(5) When evaluating suppliers of systems, consider questions such as:
   (a) How long has the supplier been in business and what experience does it have with the system and application being considered?
   (b) What is the number, location and quality of staff who can support the system and what support and maintenance response can be guaranteed?
   (c) Is the company financially secure?
   (d) If the company or product is new, are any guarantees or special offers provided, such as discounted costs and extra support, to minimize the risks of relying on an innovative venture?

Bibliography

The following publications are relevant to topics discussed in this chapter.

Date, C.J., *An Introduction to Database Systems*, Addison Wesley, Reading, Mass (1981)
Ellis, C.A. and Nutt, G.J., Computer science and office information systems, *ACM Computing Surveys*, **12** (1), 27–60 (1980)
Landau, R., Bair, J.H. and Siegman, J.H., *Emerging Office Systems*, Ablex, Norwood, N.J. (1982)
Naffah, N. (ed), *Office Information Systems: Proceedings of the Second International Workshop on Office Information Systems*, North-Holland, Amsterdam (1982)
Nievergelt, J. (ed), *Document Preparation Systems*, North-Holland, Amsterdam (1983)

3

Human–Computer Communication and Knowledge-based Systems

Gerhard Fischer

Introduction

The microelectronics revolution of the 1970s made computer systems cheaper and more compact, with a greatly increased range of capabilities. Computing moved directly into the workplace to the fingertips of everyone doing office work. Chapter 2 described the rich variety of office tasks that can be assisted by computer-based computing power. Much of this power is wasted, however, if users have difficulty in understanding and using the full potential of their new systems. Too much attention in the past has been given to technical aspects which have provided inadequate solutions to real world problems, imposed unnecessary constraints on users and been too rigid to respond to changing needs.

This chapter examines how to improve the interaction between the user and the system in order to increase effectiveness. It explains why human–computer communication is a crucial determinant of the usefulness of systems and offers guidelines on the ergonomic criteria that should be used when developing and evaluating systems. It emphasizes the importance of software in managing the dialogue between users and computers, particularly in relation to workstations used by managers and professionals. The chapter also explains why, in order to develop systems which fit naturally into office work environments, more 'intelligent' software is needed which has knowledge about the user, the tasks being carried out and the nature of the communications process.

The importance of human–computer communication

The management challenge of introducing computer-based systems is not primarily a technical one. It involves handling a variety of complex human and organizational changes, as well as technical innovations. This means that the design, development and evaluation of new information systems should start with an understanding of the overall social and technical *(socio-technical)* environment in which any particular new technology is embedded. *Ergonomics* and *human factors engineering* are disciplines which pursue this aim of having people and technology working in harmony to meet the desired performance. This *user-centred* approach starts on the 'outside', examining human psychological and behavioural needs, then moves, inwards, through the work tasks carried out to the specific technical details.

A crucial determinant of the effectiveness with which computers are applied to assist people at work is the nature of the *human–computer communication*; that is, the interaction between the user and the system, also known as *Man Machine Interaction (MMI)* or the *user interface*. Managers should understand the key issues in human–computer communication. This will help them to steer the design and implementation of new systems in order to create the appropriate socio-technical environment for the groups under their responsibility. It will also enable them to differentiate between spurious advertising slogans and really important features when evaluating systems. In the past, methodologies for creating and assessing computers were *computer centred*, which is why so many failed to match their actual operating environments (*see* Chapter 6). They started by considering what the hardware and software could do, then built the final system around these computing capabilities. Managers have a responsibility to avoid this attitude in the future.

A systematic approach to human–computer communication should be an important mechanism in implementing strategic plans in order to match successfully the capabilities of new office technology with organizational and personal goals. Detailed prescriptions or check-lists cannot be provided to cover all aspects of human–computer communication because so much is dependent on human *cognitive* abilities – how people behave, think and perceive the world. Such subjective factors are not amenable to be being measured and predicted with the same precision that is possible with elements in the physical environment. This chapter does provide, however, principles of good human–computer communication which can be used as the basis for judging the inevitable trade offs that have to be made when weighing up the advantages and disadvantages of different systems.

Costs of ignoring ergonomics

Concern about the ergonomics of computer-based systems first came to prominence in relation to the possible health hazards for operators using VDTs for clerical and typing tasks. Managers became aware that failure to examine ergonomics could lead to staff anxieties and resistance to technology. Research into hardware ergonomics and the physical work environments (chairs, desks, lighting, ventilation, etc.) clearly showed that poor ergonomics could lead to inefficiencies at work as well as to some physical discomfort and mental stress for users.

If the human–computer communication is too complex, the user will be unable to understand and exploit many of the facilities available. It has been found that *less than 40 per cent* of the potential range of functions is ever used on many systems. If the user interface is difficult to grasp and remember, unforgiving to even the smallest error and generally unfriendly, users will require a great deal of training and the system will be error prone and inefficient in action.

Ergonomics views all elements of a system as a whole. It requires that hardware, software, an individual's psychological needs, group behaviour and dynamic social interactions are considered in a systematic and integrated fashion. By putting the user at the centre of the design, ergonomic and socio-technical methods identify what is needed before looking at how it is done. This leads to important strategic guidelines, independent of any particular technology. For example, it recognizes that individuals and organizations evolve over a period of time. The system should therefore be capable of adapting to meet different requirements, such as allowing a person to move from being a novice to an experienced user within a smooth, consistent framework of human–computer communication.

An ergonomically designed system should enrich jobs and reduce stress (*see* Chapter 5). If the system is forgiving towards user mistakes, say allowing erroneous actions to be corrected through an 'undo' command, users will feel more relaxed and willing to investigate a wider range of applications of the technology. On the other hand, a technology centred design can lead to computers becoming a straight jacket, determining what can and cannot be done. For example, if a workstation handles only text, there is a tendency for the user to ignore other forms of information presentation. This has led to a diminishing use of graphics in papers and reports prepared on word processors. The word processors may have been more productive in terms of the time taken to produce a document. The end-result, however, may be less useful because of the omission of graphics, which can be such an effective means of presenting information.

In order to avoid the costs and problems that can occur when socio-technical and ergonomic needs are ignored, it is important to incorporate the necessary evaluation criteria from the start of a project. Ergonomics research should indicate wrong developments at an early stage. After installation, continuous evaluations should assist the system to evolve in tune with social, human and organizational needs.

The nature of human–computer communication

A user-centred approach to computer systems requires an understanding of:

(1) The skills and knowledge of different types of user.
(2) The structure of tasks to be performed, for example, whether a task can be defined by a clear, predictable specification or is ill structured, with many ambiguities and unexpected occurrences.
(3) The technology involved, say whether the workstation has a basic keyboard and single frame screen or a mouse and keyboard with a multiwindow screen and icons (*see* Chapter 2).

Until the 1970s, the relationship between the user and the computer was so remote that it could be compared more to correspondence by letter than to a conversation. Today, users and computers usually interact directly, in a similar fashion to a conversation. The styles of some interactions are restricted and allow tasks to be accomplished using only a narrow range of techniques. The users in such systems are regarded essentially as operators, be they typists operating a word processor or children manipulating the control stick of a video game. A new era of human–computer communication began when microelectronics decreased the cost and increased the availability and capabilities of hardware. This made it feasible to use computational resources not only to provide particular functions, but also to assist in making those functions usable.

There is a growing understanding that the cognitive limitations of the user are as important to communication with machines as the technology of the machine itself. The increasing richness and complexities of possible communication means that systems designers are often faced with having to resolve conflicting requirements, such as:

(1) Balancing what is best in terms of a person's cognitive thought against what is most efficient for the computer.
(2) Providing systems that must be easy for most people to use, but also must have sufficient power to allow the skilled user to exploit the system for a variety of different and more complex purposes.
(3) The necessity to remain compatible with existing systems while also exploiting the power of new systems and techniques.
(4) Being easy for beginners to use as opposed to the needs of experienced users who require less hand-holding.
(5) Having tight integration between different subsystems but still allowing systems to be composed of independent modules that can be flexibly interlinked and rearranged.

Human–computer communication can become a bottleneck that restricts the growth of successful uses of new office technology and limits the extent to which new information processing and communications technologies can be integrated into our working and living environments. Many techniques are being developed to assist communication.

Advantages of knowledge-based systems

Computer techniques have traditionally been constructed from the logical information handling capabilities of hardware, which are most suited to dealing with factual data and other information and calculations amenable to digital encoding. *Artificial intelligence* (AI) methods, on the other hand, start by using human behaviour as the model of how computers should act. People acquire knowledge through experience and learning and then apply that knowledge to solving problems, communicating, making decisions and acting. *Knowledge-based systems*, also known as *intelligent knowledge-based systems* (IKBS), aim to emulate these human characteristics. Knowledge-based systems have two main ingredients: the store of knowledge and a means of processing that knowledge using programs and rules based on how people reason, deduce and infer. This requires techniques for:

(1) *Knowledge acquisition*. How knowledge can be acquired

most effectively from human experts and data gathered by instruments. This may involve a *knowledge engineer* to interpret the expert's knowledge to the computer. The expert could, however, create and manipulate the knowledge base directly.

(2) *Knowledge representation*. How to represent knowledge in a form that can drive the computer but which is still understandable by users. Traditional software code is generally comprehensible only to specialists who understand programming rather than those who know about the subject (*domain*) to which the programs are being applied.

(3) *Knowledge utilization*. How the knowledge base can be 'browsed through' and relevant knowledge found. The extent to which the system uses its knowledge to assist the user in finding what is needed must also be determined.

One particular IKBS development is the expert system which attempts to match the performance of human experts in a specialized domain. Like a human specialist, it should also be able to communicate, to explain and to give assistance, and so on. A knowledge-based system without good human–computer communication is like a human who knows everything but cannot talk about it. Good human–computer communication without knowledge behind it, however, is like a person who talks all the time but does not know anything.

Knowledge-based systems offer the most promising approach to improving human–computer communication to the level of effectiveness expected when people communicate with each other. They recognize that people and computers have different attributes and so form a cooperative partnership.

Towards better human–computer communication

The following are the key areas where human–computer communication has failed to match the effectiveness of human interaction:

(1) People are able to understand each other and make reasoned judgements although all the elements in the communication have not been made explicit. In all but the simplest exchange, it is likely that a substantial portion of the communicated message is not made explicit and that the information given is incomplete. Nevertheless, people are able to deduce or supply additional information and correct mistakes through their knowledge of the context of the

communication, past experience and so on.

(2) When faced with a problem presented in broad general terms with many details missing, people are still able to apply their reasoning and problem-solving power. People can make sense out of unexpected situations whereas computers have to be preprogrammed to anticipate all eventualities.

(3) If there is a misunderstanding, people are able to articulate the reasons for it and realize the limitations of their own and their partner's knowledge.

(4) People can provide explanations to others of how they reached a conclusion or why they behaved in a particular way.

(5) People can solve problems by taking imaginative leaps, for example by conceiving of an analogous situation of similar characteristics with which they are more fmiliar.

What makes human communication so successful is that it takes place between individuals who have their own knowledge bases to draw on. A manager expects that the people around him or her know what they are doing in their jobs. A secretary, for example, should know whether or not to put a call through to the manager depending on what the manager is doing, who is calling and the importance of the topic the caller wants to discuss. An office worker who has no understanding of the business being carried out is of little support to a manager because of the effort required by

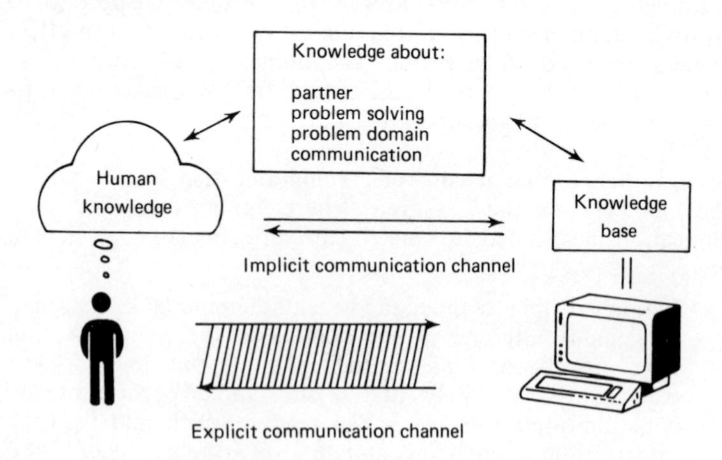

Figure 3.1 Use of a knowledge-based system to assist human–computer communication

the manager when delegating a task. In a similar way, computer aids for managers should also have some knowledge and understanding of what they are doing.

Figure 3.1 summarizes the most promising approach to meet fully the design criteria provided in the remainder of this chapter, although some goals can be met with other techniques. Compared to previous computing methods, the advantages illustrated in this diagram are:

(1) *The explicit communication channel is widened.* This covers the direct interactions with a workstation. Through the use of colour, graphics, icons, multiwindow displays and so on, the workstation has a much wider range of options which can be used to manipulate, explore and analyse information and knowledge held in the computer.
(2) *An implicit communication channel* is opened. This allows for the crucial ability of partners in a communication to understand each other without having to have every last detail spelt out explicitly.

Human–computer communication can therefore become an exchange between two knowledgeable entities, one human and one computerized, rather than between an intelligent person and a dumb machine.

Guidelines on user requirements

A computer-based system cannot be evaluated in isolation from the person using it or from the tasks that it is expected to support. A system that performs well when being used to carry out a narrow range of relatively well-structured tasks is unlikely to be suitable for managers whose workload is varied, unpredictable and unstructured.

Ergonomics research therefore examines the following, in addition to particular technologies.

(1) *The behaviour and perceptions of the user.* In comparison to computer information processing systems, people have both strengths and weaknesses when they deal with information. For example, people have limited short-term memories and a tendency to make errors for a variety of reasons. On the other hand, people have powerful visual systems which give great scope for improving the way information is displayed on workstation screens and for human–computer com-

munication. Some people suffer from fears and anxieties about the technology, which must also be taken into account.

(2) *The nature of the tasks being performed*. The job roles carried out by people in offices consist of a number of tasks. Clerical and secretarial work tend to have a narrow range of tasks which occur in a more predictable and structured way than those of managerial and supervisory work. Systems for office work must be flexible enough to be tailored to meet unexpected situations. They must also be responsive to changing patterns of work and the evolving needs of each user.

Managers are sometimes referred to as *casual* or *discretionary* users because they do not have to operate the system continuously and they have a degree of freedom in choosing when to use computing aids. The work of managers and professionals, which form the main focus of this book, can be differentiated from other office roles by the following characteristics:

(1) *Problems dealt with are often 'fuzzy'*. The precise specification of the problems and challenges to be resolved can be difficult to define in advance. Solutions may be found by moving from a partial solution via a learning from experience to an evolving understanding of the problem.
(2) *Formal analyses are insufficient*. Problems to be faced usually cannot be adequately understood in advance. Techniques of formal analyses of work tasks, such as those favoured in operations research, are inadequate to define job routines and communications channels in sufficient detail to be translated into software.
(3) *Importance of innovation*. The unpredictable and varied nature of the work means that innovative new solutions often have to be generated which depart from systems based on analyses of past behaviour.
(4) *Complex decision making*. Responsibilities for making decision are often difficult to delegate because they cannot be described well enough for an assistant to do them.

How to evaluate the usability of office technology

The human–computer communication ability of a system cannot be defined by a simple measure of 'goodness' or 'badness'. The aspects discussed above indicate the many factors and interactions involved. The following dimensions should be considered when assessing systems.

(1) *Usefulness*. The system should be as supportive as possible in aiding the user to meet her or his goals; knowledge is therefore needed about these goals.

(2) *Functionality*. The range of tasks or functions that a system can perform is known as its functionality. All required functions should be smoothly integrated within a consistent framework.

(3) *Uniformity of interaction*. The style and format of human–computer communication should be consistent and uniform between different tasks and subsystems. This is particularly important for a casual user who does not have the time to learn and understand new techniques.

(4) *Flexibility and adaptability*. The system must not only be able to meet immediate short-term objectives but should be capable of being enhanced, adapted and extended in the future in an evolutionary way, building on skills learnt and systems used in the shorter term.

(5) *Learning and training*. The time needed to learn how to use functions should be short, particularly for busy users who have little time to spare. The aim should be 'no threshold and no ceiling': there should not be a threshold step too high and too complex for a novice but there should also be no ceiling on the degree of complexity to which the system rises. This can be achieved by constructing systems that grow with the experience of the user.

(6) *Error handling*. When an error occurs, the system should generate a meaningful response relating to the task, not to the internal state of the machine. Advice should be provided, clearly and unambiguously, so that the user is able to take corrective action to overcome the problem.

(7) *Robustness*. Errors should not lead to a total breakdown of the system. Users should also be offered the chance to retract (*undo*) previous actions without losing all the relevant information or causing a major disruption in processing. This reduces stress on the user and enhances her or his willingness to innovate and explore new aspects of the system.

(8) *Speed of response*. The computer should respond to the user with sufficient speed so that the user does not get anxious wondering what has happened, but not so quickly that the user is put under unnecessary pressure. If there is likely to be a delay in response because the computer needs time to perform a complex calculation or search through a large

database, the user should be given an indication that the system is still active and, if possible, an idea of when the response will be provided.

(9) *Helpfulness*. The system should provide guidance and advice if the user is unsure what to do next. Such help should be provided in a language that is understandable by the user, and it should be unambiguous and relevant to the situation the user is in at the time.

(10) *Time to implement*. A system should not only provide the appropriate functions and quality but should minimize the amount of time and personnel resources needed to apply the technology efficiently and effectively.

(11) *Quality of service*. The quality of the final service or product, such as a customer enquiry service or printed document, should be at least as good as anything that could be provided by non-computer means.

(12) *Acceptability*. All users should feel the system genuinely enhances their jobs and work environments.

(13) *Group support*. Systems should provide adequate assistance to the sharing of information amongst members of a group, in addition to helping individuals.

(14) *Self-explanatory power*. A knowledge-based system should have the ability to understand what it is doing and to explain to the user how it made inferences which lead it to recommend a particular conclusion.

(15) *Conviviality*. The user must be in control of the system and be able to modify it as required to meet activities and situations not anticipated in the programs.

(16) *Symbiosis*. People and computers should be able to unite in a harmonious, symbiotic relationship where the computer augments human activities rather than replaces people.

Eight pillars of ergonomic wisdom

The following summarize the major principles that have emerged from ergonomic research into the behaviour of users and the tasks they perform. They provide a basis for developing and assessing adequate human–computer communication.

(1) *The limiting resource in human processing of information is human attention and comprehension, not the quantity of information available*. Modern information and communication technologies have dramatically increased the amount of information available to individuals. An important function

in human–computer communication is to allow for the selection of the information you actually want and presentation of it in the most appropriate way.

(2) *In complex situations, the search for an optimal 'rational' solution is a waste of time.* There are limits to the extent to which people can apply rational analyses and judgements to solving complex, unpredictable problems. It is insufficient to ask people to 'Think more clearly' without providing new tools, such as knowledge-based systems, which help extend the boundaries of human rationality. The aim is to achieve the most satisfactory solutions given current knowledge, accepting that 'better' solutions will emerge as the result of experience and enhanced knowledge and understanding.

(3) *The nature of human memory mechanisms are important design considerations.* The limitations and structure of human memory must be taken into account in designing human–computer communication. People have relatively limited short-term memories. Dialogues should, therefore, be constructed which do not expect the user to remember everything and which reinforce, prompt and remind the user of necessary information in a supportive but unobtrusive manner. The way people *recognize* information visually is different to how they *recall* other information. The different recognition and recall memory structures are relevant to judging the advantages and limitations of different user interactions, such as comparing the use of a function key to initiate an operation compared to a menu-based interface (menus are examined later in this chapter).

(4) *The efficient visual processing capabilities of people must be utilized fully.* Traditional displays used with screen-based workstations have been one dimensional, with a single frame on the screen usually filled with lines of text. New technologies have opened ways to exploiting human visual perception more fully, say through the use of multiwindow displays, colour, graphics, icons and mice (*see* Chapter 2).

(5) *The structure of the computer system must be understandable by people using it rather than requiring the user to learn by rote the functions that can be performed.* An adequate understanding of how a system works gives users the knowledge and confidence to explore the full potential of a system, which can have a vast range of possible options. Learning by rote may train the user to operate a limited number of functions but makes it difficult for the user to cope

with unexpected occurrences and inhibits their exploitation of the full potential of the system.

(6) *There is no such thing as 'the' user of a system: there are many different kinds of user and the requirements of an individual user grows with experience.* Computer systems built to a static model of the nature of *the* user of the system are too rigid and limited to meet the demands of a rapidly growing and diverse user community or the evolving needs of each user.

(7) *The 'intelligence' of a complex computer aid must contribute to its ease of use*. Truly intelligent and knowledgeable human communicators, such as good teachers, use a substantial part of their knowledge to explain their expertise to others. In the same way, the 'intelligence' of a computer should be applied to provide effective communication.

(8) *The user interface in a computer system is more than just an additional component: it is an integral and important part of the whole system*. Human–computer communication must be considered at the very earliest stage of the design process so it can be adequately integrated with all other elements.

Ergonomic criteria for human–computer communication

The crucial unresolved issue for human–computer communication in the office of the future is software ergonomics. Hardware and software are closely related and there are important questions in hardware ergonomics still to be investigated. Hardware, however, is no longer the main limiting factor in computing developments, as it once was. Progress in microelectronics and other 'hard' technologies have opened huge spaces within which software can manouevre and which are still under-exploited.

Rapid hardware developments have frequently overtaken ergonomic research. The technology being examined may become obsolescent before the research reaches a conclusion or capabilities previously available only on a few costly systems suddenly become common at a price within the reach of all users. For example, detailed research into the optimal design for keypunches used with punched card equipment is of little value today because keypunches are dying out. At one time, much effort was spent investigating the importance of having terminals and printers which provide both upper- and lower-case characters. Now, most devices offer small and capital letters at a reasonable cost.

Computers now have enough computational power in a compact and low cost form to overcome previous major hardware restrictions such as the lack of graphics, colour and multiwindow displays. The prime question is how to develop software which makes use of this extra power to meet actual user requirements.

Workstation hardware requirements

Research and development in hardware ergonomics and the physical work environment have made substantial progress and is backed by checklists which can be used with a reasonable degree of confidence[1]. This is possible because the human physiological and perceptual systems involved in operating equipment are fairly well understood and more readily amenable to measurement than the subjective factors involved in software ergonomics. These guidelines generally focus on VDT designs for secretarial and clerical tasks and emphasize characteristics such as:

(1) Keyboard detached from screen for optimal positioning, with the display capable of being rotated and tilted.
(2) Avoidance of glare and reflection from the screen.
(3) A flat keyboard (no more than a 15 degree slope) to avoid excessive loads on the hand and arm, with properly shaped keytops labelled with legends that are readable and understandable.
(4) Presentation of stable, legible characters on the screen. The most common (and preferable) method of creating images on a screen, also used for domestic televisions, is *raster scan* generation. The cathode ray tube sweeps an electron beam over the phosphor coated inner surface of the screen, illuminating tiny dots on the screen to form the required characters or other shapes. The image, however, quickly fades and has to be continually refreshed. If the *refresh rate is too low, characters are likely to flicker; a minimum of 50 Hertz (preferably 60 Hertz) is needed for negative presentation* (light characters on a dark background) or 80 Hertz for *positive presentation* (black on white) of flicker-free character displays.

These basic requirements also apply to the personal workstations for use by managers and professionals which will be the dominant feature of office systems in the future, providing considerable local computing power as well as being linked to local area networks and external communication links. It is therefore of great importance that workstations adequately integrate the broad range of tasks required. The following characteristics for workstation ergonomics should therefore be considered, in addition to the general VDT guidelines already mentioned.

(1) *Screens and output*
   (a) The display should be large enough to show a full page of A4 text and make effective use of a multiwindow capability (*see* Chapter 2).
   (b) A graphical capability is vital for many applications and a desirable option for most tasks. Raster display techniques are preferable to *character* or *vector generation*, which produces images as sets of lines rather than groups of dots.
   (c) Colour is also a desirable option for many tasks and a key requirement for specialized activities where it is necessary to differentiate between many objects or types of information.
   (d) It should be possible to identify and select objects on the screen through a pointing device, such as a mouse, a light pen or touch-sensitive screen (*see* Chapter 2).
   (e) Screens and keyboards should have similar functional capabilities so that What you See Is What You Get (WYSIWYG, pronounced 'whizzy-wig'). For example, the screen should have *proportional spacing* where each character has a different width (such as 'm' being wider than an 'i') as is common on many printers. If the screen has a graphics capability, then the printer should also be able to produce similar images; laser printers, for instance, can satisfy this need.

(2) *Input devices*
   (a) Facilities should be provided to handle text (most commonly a keyboard); pointing devices; and choice devices (for example, special buttons or keys which initiate complete functions). Voice and handwriting input will enter commercial applications when they achieve appropriate performance levels; initially they are being used in specialized tasks, for example where a limited speech vocabulary is sufficient or where hand-printed, block characters are written on special forms.
   (b) The way a variety of input methods are used together must be carefully planned and integrated; for example,

there should be a smooth transition when switching between a mouse and keyboard.

(3) *Growth potential.* New technological developments are continuously offering new functions and capabilities. The workstation design must therefore be sufficiently flexible to incorporate enhancements as they become available and are required by the user. The design strategy must also provide a sufficiently coherent and consistent framework so that new facilities can be integrated smoothly with existing capabilities. This can be achieved by following the design criteria for human–computer communication recommended in this chapter.

Software: the key to effective computing

Software mediates between the sophistication of computer-assisted office systems and the human ability to interact with them in a natural, productive manner. It is the bridge between what the technology can do and how the user expects the system to behave. It is, therefore, partly concerned with human behaviour and partly with the technicalities of the system. The sturdiness and usefulness of this bridge is the concern of *software ergonomics*, although this also encompasses psychological and other factors[2]. The subject became recognized as a crucial aspect of computing when word and text processing systems began to be used widely in offices by people who had no previous computing experience. Before that, computer users generally had specialist knowledge and an interest in computers which made them willing to overcome awkward and inefficient interfaces.

Software can be regarded as the implementation of a model of how a system is expected to behave (*see* Chapter 6). In terms of software ergonomics, the challenge is to bring together three models which play a major role in human–computer communication each providing a different perspective on the interface.

(1) *The model of the systems designer.* The person or group designing a system has a concept of the purpose of the system, the kinds of users who will work with it, the tasks and performance to be achieved, and the most appropriate forms of interaction. This, perhaps imperfect, model has a crucial influence on the nature of the systems and in the past has been dominated by the views of technical specialists who often failed to consider the users' needs in full. There is still, however, much that is unknown or unpredictable in relation

to human behaviour, of how an office operates in information processing terms, and of the underlying structures of tasks being carried out. Steps towards better understanding are emerging and it is important that designers are kept on the right track through the involvement of users in the design and assessment of systems, even if most users still have difficulty in articulating the details of their own working methods, let along specifying the future system they would like to have.

(2) *The user's view of the system.* Users often find systems designed by the technically oriented specialist impenetrable. They may learn how to use some of the facilities by memorizing the operating instructions but they have little appreciation of how information is organized within the system, the processing mechanisms, and so on. In some systems this can lead to over 60 percent of the computing power being wasted. This waste may grow as systems become more complex unless a model of the system is presented which clearly explains to the user the limitations, as well as the scope of the technology. For example, if the human–computer dialogue can take place using a limited form of natural language vocabulary and grammar, it should be made clear to users that they still cannot communicate with the computer with the same freedom as they can chat to colleagues.

(3) *The system's expectation of the user.* As has already been asserted, there is no such thing as *the* user of a system. There are many types of user and individual users change over a period of time. Systems should therefore have the ability to be tailored to particular *profiles* that define the tasks to be carried out by a particular user. The more knowledge the system has about the user and his or her tasks, goals and understanding, the better should be its ability to adapt its behaviour to match the varied requirements of different user needs.

Convivial human–computer partnerships

A key aim of software ergonomics is to develop systems that are symbiotic and convivial. Symbiotic systems combine human skills and computing power to carry out a task more effectively than it could be done by the human or computer alone. Convivial systems give users the power to adapt the system. Knowledge-based systems will help to profile systems in a deeper way than by simply specifying and adjusting the values of particular *parameters* (variable factors, such as the size of a file). With knowledge-based convivial systems, users will be able to create new programs and adapt designs without needing specialist training.

Symbiotic systems exist in many different areas. For example, computerized axial tomography is a computer-controlled scan-ningtechnique which can present three-dimensional X-ray images of the body. It operates as a partnership between the computer, which performs an immense amount of mathematical calculations, and the doctor, whose experience and visual perception enable the information to be interpreted in ways which discriminate between subtle differences in aspects of the image. In financial forecasting, a knowledge-based system can perform calculations, advise the user of errors, explain the origins of particular data and generate proposals according to constraints formulated by the user in an 'intelligent' dialogue, as would take place in discussions with knowledgeable colleagues.

Balancing on the trade-off tightrope

While there are a number of clear principles and trends for guiding software ergonomic design, choosing the best solution in a particular case is often like walking a tightrope. As the system progresses, the balance needs to be restored as different forces come into play.

Even when there seems to be a clear-cut advantage in a particular technique, the details of the implementation must be carefully examined. For example, in early text processing systems the following instruction may have been needed to replace a word four lines down and six characters to the left of the current position of the text pointer with the five-letter word 'green':

(4n6fsi"green")

Such a command has all the characteristics of poor ergonomics: it is complex, hard to remember, liable to cause errors and is difficult to relate to what is actually happening.

A more direct and preferable form of performing this type of editing is to use human visual abilities to move the cursor directly to the point where text is to be deleted, changed or inserted. There are, however, many ways of controlling the cursor. On some personal computers, two keys need to be pressed for each movement, such as the control key and the I, J, M or K key, which bear no obvious relation to particular movements. Generally, however, there are special control keys with arrows to indicate the direction moved by the cursor when that key is pressed on its own. From an ergonomic point of view, the cluster of keys should be arranged so that they are easy to access and their positioning should indicate their function (top key for upward movements, left-most key for left movement, etc.)

In other areas, the pros and cons can be more finely balanced. For instance, with the principle of WYSIWYG (what you see is what you get), the user does not have to keep transforming what is on the screen to the form it will take in printed hard copy which is obviously a benefit. On the other hand, the user may have to do more work when directly manipulating a format than if separate formatting software was being used to translate the screen information to printed form. It may also be too costly or impractical to have a printer that gives the same functions as the screen, and *vice versa*, although this drawback is likely to diminish in time.

Another example of a design conflict arises from the need to have systems that allow the manipulation of various information objects, such as text, graphics, programs, mail messages, and so on. There should be a uniformity and consistency in interactions handlingdifferent functions but there should also be provision to manipulate specific objects in particular ways, which are not needed for other types.

Help systems

The extent to which a system helps the user is an indication of the degree to which the computer is being used to filter, summarize and diffuse information selectively rather than merely adding more data to a world already overloaded with information.

When a person looks for assistance from a colleague or from a computer, it is to answer questions like: 'How can I do X?', 'What happens if . . . .?', 'Why did Y occur?', or 'Can I undo the effects of Z?'. On many systems, the help facility is initiated by a special HELP key or typing in the command HELP. Unfortunately, the computer's response is often to present a lot of information, much of which is irrelevant to the question in the user's mind. Finding the answer may be time consuming, if it is there at all. It is as if a colleague responded to a question such as 'Who is responsible for signing this requisition form?' by presenting you with a manual containing the full organization chart.

To be able to answer requests for help in an appropriate way, the system should have some knowledge about the dynamic context in which help is requested. The user should be able to describe to the computer what is wanted and the system should also offer an explanation based on an informed model of the user. The help facility should not be intrusive, giving advice when the user does not want it and getting in the way of other work being carried out. Given that users can be unaware of about 60 percent of the functions of some systems, the help service may need to be *active*, volunteering advice that is relevant and unintrusive. Most help systems, however, have been *passive*, activated only on the user's initiative. The development of suitable active aids is a complex task which needs to be done well or not at all.

Menus: making the right decisions

One of the major lessons from human–computer communication research is that there are no optimal solutions, only trade offs. The variety of interrelated issues that affect the user and the task being formed means that solutions need to be approached systematically but with sensitivity to the particular circumstances in question. Prescriptive formulae applicable to all systems are not possible or desirable. The nature of the trade offs that need to be made can be illustrated by examining the pros and cons of menu-based interactions.

A menu is a list of alternatives which appears on the screen, similar to the items on a restaurant menu. This reminds the user of the options available at a particular stage, from which one or more can be selected. Selection may be done by keying in the number associated with the desired item(s) or pointing to it with a mouse or using a touch-sensitive screen. Ideally, the menu system, like a help service, should be aware of the dynamically changing context in which it is being used. This means that it can intelligently select information valid in that situation to limit the possibility of the user making an error by selecting an inappropriate option. The menu can also be employed as a means of reminding the user of options that can assist exploring unknown parts of the system.

Alternatives to menus include command and natural languages. Command languages make available a number of commands and instructions, usually within a very restricted format. Natural languages allow theuser to interact in a way which is similar to human languages, although usually with a limited vocabulary applicable only to particular tasks. Where a small set of alternatives exist, menus can be an effective alternative or supplement to command languages. Where it is necessary to construct a complex phrase to make the user's needs clear, say, when making an enquiry of a database, command and natural languages are generally better.

The selection of a suitable system is often a matter of 'horses for courses' – different users have different requirements. Provided the words used in the display are meaningful to the user, menus provide particularly valuable assistance to new and casual users because they do not rely on memorizing commands, limit the amount of typing (and so avoid and minimize the likelihood of errors), and constantly remind the user of the options available. On the other hand, more experienced users often complain about menus although they can be an effective means of reducing the complexity of sophisticated systems. If the user knows what to do, it is a waste of time to request the menu, wait for it to appear, and then to look through it for the appropriate option. In these cases, the user would prefer a command or natural language to express his or her requirement directly.

Once it is decided that a menu approach is suitable, there are still many open questions in relation to the technology with which it is implemented, as well as the groups of users and the sets of tasks for which it is applied. Managers must avoid regarding this openness as a reason for dodging the issues and attempting to find simplistic answers. Careful thought should be given to weighing up factors relevant to particular circumstances, including the following aspects:

(1) *Technology used*. Managers and users often have to make the most of systems already available rather than obtaining a more suitable technology. To be really effective and efficient, with the minimum chances of error, menus should operate with multiwindow systems and pointing devices. A traditional single-window screen has all its other information wiped out when the menu is presented and relies totally on keyed responses. Nevertheless, if the user has no other feasible option, the content and structure of menus should be carefully considered to make the best use of a traditional keyboard and screen VDT.

(2) *Number and order of menu items*. Too many items are confusing, too few can limit the range of choice unnecessarily. Elements in the menu can be ordered alphabetically, by functions or randomly. The optimum number and order depend on the tasks involved and the experience of the user;

these may need to be adapted for different users and applications.

(3) *Hierarchical menus.* If it is necessary to trace a path through a number of menus to get to the desired point, the user should be given the opportunity to go directly to the place needed, otherwise he or she has to re-tread a tedious path through the networks of menus. Provisions should also be made to limit the chance of the user getting lost in the hierarchy and providing help if the user is in doubt as to what to do next.

(4) *Presentation and positioning.* In multiwindow systems, the menu may be ever-present or only pop-up when required. Decisions also need to be taken on how close the menu should be to the window(s) of information to which it relates, and whether it should always be in the same place.

(5) *Icons.* When it is appropriate to use icons in menus rather than verbal descriptions.

(6) *Default values.* A decision is required as to what action the system takes if the user fails to specify one or more of the number of items expected to be selected on each occasion the menu is activated.

(7) *Conviviality.* The extent to which users are allowed to modify the system, for example, by extending the items in a given menu, choosing default values or deciding where to position the menu. Too much choice can be confusing, too little can mean the system is too rigid for necessary local adaptations.

Future improvements to user performance

This chapter has shown that user performance can be improved not just by providing new interfaces to the system but also through a combination of increasing the understanding of the user and the knowledge built into the system. There are, however, important issues which need to be investigated in future research into human–computer communication:

(1) *User training.* We have started to live in a world where people are likely to learn new skills several times in their working lives. One of the aims of software ergonomics is to cut the training load by creating systems which are easy to use, helpful, and forgiving of mistakes. Short periods of hands-on training with well designed systems should be a

cost-effective alternative to investments in formal training courses or trying to invent mythical 'ultimate' interfaces which require the user to act totally naturally (*see* Chapter 9).

(2) *Genuine productivity improvements.* There is a limit to the gains in productivity that can be made by simply carrying out existing operations at a faster pace. A broader analysis must also be made of work and organizational procedures and structures (*see* Chapters 5 to 10).

(3) *A firmer theoretical foundation.* The application of computer-based technology on a wide scale amongst non-technical users is still in its infancy. It is, therefore, to be expected that research into human–computer communication, which must draw on real experience as well as experiment, is in an embryonic stage. Technological developments have also moved much faster than present psychological and behavioural research, and have been given much more support. In the future, an ergonomic methodology should emerge which is more systematic, more detailed and more reliable than is possible at present.

(4) *Managing technological innovation.* New technologies, such as graphics and multiwindow screens with a pointer device, give the designer increased scope for creating enhanced interfaces before clear guidelines have been established even for the much more limited older technologies. Increased technological power and sophistication can make interfaces far better than before, or make things much worse because designers and users are unable to master the new-found possibilities.

(5) *Identifying real limiting factors.* At present there is a general awareness that there are some limits to human and computing abilities. This needs to be explored further.

The first phases of computerization, from the 1950s to the 1970s, were dominated by the view that people, work procedures and organizations had to re-orientate themselves to behave in ways most acceptable and appropriate to the computer's mode of behaviour. The advent of low cost office systems, personal workstations and home computers has changed this. With good ergonomics, computers will cease being logical but rigid and insensitive dictators. Instead, they will become supportive, knowledgeable, helpful and adaptive partners and aids, as indicated in *Figure 3.2*.

Figure 3.2 User-centred versus computer-centred systems (based on a design by Peter Hajnozcky in Zürich)

Recommendations

(1) Managers must play an active role in the design and implementation of systems to ensure they achieve the results desired by the organization as a whole and by each group and individual. This means having a good understanding of the issues involved in human–computer communication in order to act effectively, as follows:
   (a) Provide guidelines and requirement specifications to systems designers.
   (b) Create a working environment which is more supportive, less stressful and more productive than existing systems.
   (c) Select the right computer systems for themselves and other users of the technology.

(2) In order to gain acceptance of the technology amongst all managers, professionals and staff, the system and its application should be designed to be genuinely usable and useful in practical work situations.

(3) Managers should not expect to obtain foolproof ergonomic guidelines which will inevitably produce an optimal solution: there is no such thing. The process of developing and assessing good human–computer communication should be viewed as an attempt to balance trade offs between what is known of different users' needs and of the technologies available. The following are desirable characteristics for any computer-based system:
   (a) *Adaptability*. Computer systems should be able to evolve, grow and change to meet different and changing needs, preferably under the direct control and navigation of the user(s) most involved.

(b) *Knowledgeability*. The more a system knows about the behaviour of users, the tasks to be performed and the limits of its own capabilities, the more effective it is in interactions with users.

(c) *Helpfulness*. The system should assist the user to sift out relevant and useful information, provide prompts and advice on how to exploit computing capabilities to the full, and should limit the possibilities of making errors.

(d) *Forgivingness*. The user should be allowed to make mistakes without causing the whole system to collapse. The system should be friendly and helpful in informing the user of the causes of errors or breakdowns and the user should have the ability to retrace steps to undo some errors.

(4) System design should be user-centred, starting from the user on the outside and moving inside to the more technical requirements.

(5) More and more managerial and professional work will be carried out through personal workstations. It is therefore important that workstations not only have the ability to carry out the required functions (now and in the future) but also that these functions are integrated in a consistent framework.

(6) Knowledge-based and expert systems should be understood and carefully examined because they provide the most promising route for resolving many of the problems that have previously existed in human–computer communication.

References

1. Armbruster, A., Ergonomic requirements, in Otway, H.J. and Peltu, M. (eds), *New Office Technology: Human and Organizational Aspects*, Frances Pinter, London; Ablex, Norwood, N.J. (1983)
2. Jensen, S., Software and user satisfaction, ibid

Bibliography

The following publications are also relevant to topics discussed in this chapter.

ACM Computing Surveys, complete issue on interactive editing systems and document formatting systems, **14**(3) (1982)

Balzert, H. (ed), *Software Ergonomie*, Teubner, Stuttgart (1983)

Card, S.K., Moran, T.P. and Newell, A., *The Psychology of Human–computer Interaction*, Erlbaum, Hillsdale, N.J. (1983)
Feigenbaum, E.A. and McCorduck, P., *The Fifth Generation: Artificial Intelligence and Japan's Computer Challenge to the World*, Addison-Wesley, Reading, Mass. (1983)
Infotech State of the Art Report, *Man/Computer Communication*, Vol 1 and Vol 2, Infotech International, Maidenhead (1979)
Moran, T. (ed), The psychology of human–computer interaction, *ACM Computing Surveys*, **13**(1) (1981)
Simon, H.A., *The Sciences of The Artificial*, MIT Press, Cambridge, Mass. (2nd edition, 1981)

4

Decision Support for Managers

Lawrence D. Phillips

Introduction

Making decisions is a crucial management task, particularly where it involves the allocation of some resource. In order to improve the effectiveness of managers, therefore, computer-based systems should provide aids to decision making. A wide variety of financial modelling, information retrieval and other computer-based systems have been sold for many years under the umbrella title of *Decision Support Systems* (DSS). In practice, however, they have generally failed to get to the heart of how most decisions are taken: that is, on the basis of personal experience and subjective judgements. While acting as a useful tool for many management tasks, they have been of relatively narrow relevance to key decision making processes.

This chapter indicates how computer-based decision support systems can be improved to meet the needs of managers, particularly senior executives, more satisfactorily. It explores the nature of *decision technology* techniques. These accept that there can be no wholly objective way of reaching the best decision, so they aim to provide technological assistance to the person ultimately responsible for the consequences of a preferred course of action. The type of work activity at different levels in an organization is analysed to provide a framework within which to identify the kind of decision support that is most appropriate to managers at a particular level.

Improving the quality of decisions

When asked 'How do you take decisions at work?' managers give a variety of answers, such as 'I choose as I did the last time I was faced with a similar situation' or 'I gather enough information so that the best option is obvious', or 'I weigh up the pros and cons and then choose the alternative that, on balance, comes out best'. A friend of mine in the insurance industry, Roger Miller, has noticed that managers often refer to some part of their body in trying to explain how they make decisions:

'You get a gut feeling for what is best'.
'It's a seat of the pants affair'.
'You feel it in your fingertips'.
'You either have a nose for this sort of thing or you don't'.
'We just suck it and see'.
'You have to play it by ear'.

Sometimes a wet finger would be raised in the air. The one part of the body that is rarely mentioned is the head.

These answers indicate that most people regard experience and intuition, value judgements and personal preferences as vital ingredients of decisions. By their nature, these elements are considered to be subjective, inaccessible to words and incapable of analysis. It is therefore commonly thought that the decision making process should remain an essentially human activity. This is the correct conclusion but the wrong reason for it. Decision making can be substantially improved by the application of *decision technology* which provides a way of systematically bringing together all ingredients, including the subjective ones, to provide an effective recipe for actions.

A technology to assist decision makers

Decision technology has three components: people, information technology and preference technology. The people involved are primarily the owners of the problems to be solved, the managers faced with a choice. They contribute the necessary experience, intuition and knowledge that are crucial in working towards a solution of the problem at hand. Information technology consists of the computer-based systems that handle the storage, processing and analysis of relevant information and providing software modelling assistance to determine possible future consequences of pursuing different alternatives. In addition, of course, computers provide all the other office information services discussed in Chapter 2, such as word processing and electronic mail.

The third ingredient, *preference technology*, is less well known. It is a computer-based technique that helps to clarify subjective value judgements made when evaluating possible consequences of different courses of action, the time and risks involved, and the trade offs between various objectives.

More than information is needed

Most key management decisions take the form of questions like: 'Is a possible 20 per cent return on investment for this venture twice as good as a possible 10 per cent return and is 40 per cent twice as good as 20 per cent?'; 'How much do we prefer a dollar now to one received in a year's time?'; 'How much better is a definite one million dollar profit than a 50–50 chance of going for double or nothing (is a bird in the hand really worth two in the bush)?'; and 'Should we sacrifice short-term profitability to capture an increased market share in the hope that profitability will be achieved in the long term?'.

Answers to questions like these must, in the end, be provided by people. There is no completely 'objective' way of determining, for example, how much better one level of return on investment is for one company than another, or what discount rate should be applied to expected cash flows in business plans, or how much risk a company should accept in new ventures, or how relatively important different objectives are when a decision is being considered. Computers can help with these issues by providing relevant information to reduce uncertainty and constructing models as a guide to future behaviour. By itself this is insufficient. Preference technology is needed too.

Managers often waste time and resources using new office technology to gather more and more information in the hope that eventually they will have sufficient facts to make the decision obvious and reduce all risk. At best, however, databases and other computing services can make the manager more sure about what has happened or what might occur and thus may lead to taking a decision or searching for a new alternative. Before this happens, however, preference technology should be available to assist in the formulation of a lucid picture in the problem owner's mind of the real issues at stake.

An example of preference technology is the MAUD software developed by my colleagues Patrick Humphreys and Ayleen Wisudha. It helps people faced with a decision made difficult by having a number of objectives, some of which are in conflict. This occurs when an individual chooses a house or changes a job, or a company has to select a suitable location for a new plant or develop a strategic direction for the next ten years. You open a dialogue with MAUD by specifying alternatives that you are examining or might like to consider. From then on, MAUD takes the initiative by engaging you in a series of interactions to help clarify your objectives, set priorities and assess the options.

MAUD seems to be most useful in the early stages of considering a problem, when aims are still unclear and new possibilities are still being invented. No two sessions with MAUD are ever the same and many users take away the results of an hour's interaction, consider them, then return for one or more sessions. Gradually, MAUD helps to translate a fuzzy problem into a more structured and manageable one. This is done purely on the basis of the information in the problem owner's head without any reference to other information sources or databases.

Decision support systems defined

Decision technology is centred on the human problem owner supplemented by information and preference aids (*see Figure 4.1*). Added knowledge is provided by information technology which helps to overcome uncertainty. The making of value judgements is

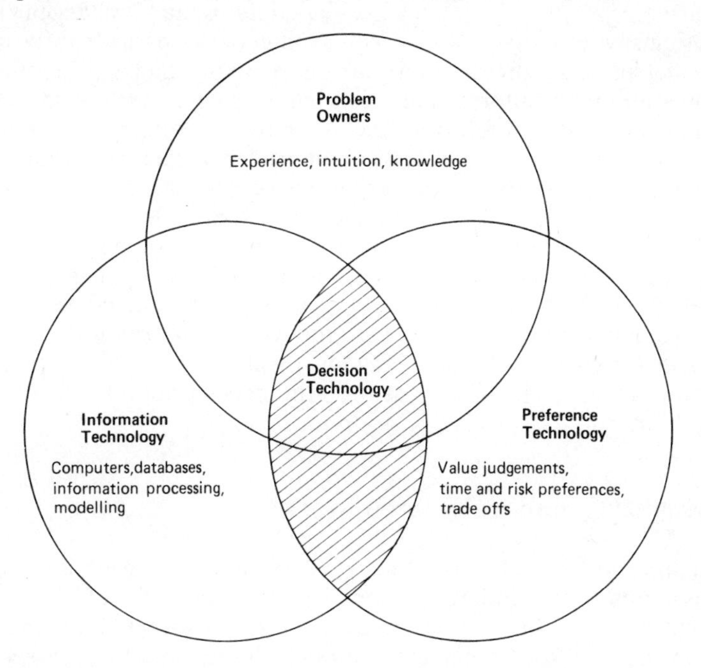

Figure 4.1 The components of decision technology

helped by preference technology, which helps people to clarify their value judgements. Only when these three ingredients are combined can the resulting brew provide adequate nourishment for the problem owners.

Leave out the problem owners, and you have an artificially intelligent system capable of, for example, recognizing signatures and rejecting unauthorized ones, but unable to respond flexibly to the shifting nature of problems faced by managers. Leave out the preference technology and you have an expert system that can make available to problem owners the collective knowledge of many experts on a particular topic, but is unable to help with ill structured problems, particularly those in which value judgements are made (*see* Chapter 3 for more on expert systems). Omit information technology, and problem owners may use the preference technology to construct value judgements based on fantasies rather than facts.

Many computing services and software packages lay claim to being 'decision support systems' although they lack any preference technology. They are, at best, extended information management systems with perhaps more facilities than in the past for software modelling and presentation of information, and a smoother integration of information retrieval, display, processing and modelling capabilities. Carried away by marketing zeal, some vendors have given the 'decision support' label to a lot of products, including the simplest spreadsheets (*see* Chapter 2), which has begun to devalue the meaning of the term. Once preference technology is explicitly incorporated, decision support takes a qualitative leap and becomes much more useful to top managers. I believe, therefore, that a true decision support system should be defined as: *any system that helps the manager to form preferences, make judgements and take decisions*. I will use this meaning in the rest of the chapter. The focus is on the person, not on computers and software.

Discretion and rule-based work

In order to get a job done, managers usually need to exercise some discretion while following overall rules. The type of decision support system appropriate to different levels within an organization depends on the balance between discretion and rule-based work in particular job roles. The importance of maintaining a strong element of individual autonomy after computerization is also explored in Chapters 5, 6 and 10.

Work is usually directed towards achieving a goal by fulfilling a need, although neither the goal nor the need may be explicitly recognized. For example, a sales manager may sense that sales are below target even before he or she has seen the month's figures and may take corrective action immediately. In exercising discretion and taking decisions within prescribed limits, employees are expected to complete their work within a reasonable time according to company policy, procedures and rules. These rules can be clearly defined so that the employee can learn them; following the rules then becomes automatic. The real work comes in deciding how to accomplish the assigned task within those limits and in balancing the quality of work against the speed of completing it. Tasks differ in the extent to which personal judgements can be made or predefined procedures have to be followed.

Typically, the proportion of discretionary to rule-based content becomes greater as one climbs the executive hierarchy. Top managers find that a substantial portion of their time is spent in forming preferences, making judgements and taking decisions: the essence of exercising discretion. Thus, to be useful, decision support systems for top managers must be particularly good at aiding discretionary activity.

Stratification of work within organizations

In order to judge the effectiveness of decision support systems it is helpful to examine the nature of discretionary activity, not just at the top but to all levels in the organization. The work of Elliott Jaques on *Stratified Systems Theory* ([1,2]) provides a useful framework for these considerations. As a result of widespread research, he and his colleagues have discovered a common structure for all organizations, large or small, public or private, located in the East or the West, providing goods or services. This structure has up to eight levels or *strata*, with the boundaries between strata representing qualitative shifts in the nature of work within each level (*see Table 4.1*).

Associated with the boundary between each stratum is what Jaques calls the *time span of discretion*. This indicates the amount of time an individual would be expected to work unsupervised at the longest task in a job. It is the time it would take a manager to be sure that an employee was not satisfactorily balancing pace and

Table 4.1 Basic structure of work in organizations and associated decision support systems

Time span	*Stratum*	*Organizational level*	*Main activity*	*Capabilities of Decision Support Systems*
	VIII	Super corporation	Shaping society	
50 years				
	VII	Corporation	Providing overall strategic direction	
20 years				
	VI	Corporate group of subsidiaries	Creating strategy and translating it into business direction	
10 years				
	V	Corporate subsidiary and top specialists	Redefining goals and determining field of operations	Articulation of principles guiding goal setting
5 years				
	IV	General management and Chief specialists	Creating methods of operation	Selecting from types, e.g. generating new decision support systems
2 years				
	III	Departmental managers and Chief specialists	Organizing programmes into systems of work	Restructuring within fixed structure, e.g. establishing new criteria
1 year				
	II	Front line managerial professional and technical	Generating programmes of work	Altering judgement on a variable within a fixed structure, e.g. 'What if?' models
3 months				
	I	Office and shop floor	Doing concrete tasks	Judgement within fixed structure, e.g. with information retrieval service
1 day				

quality in exercising discretion. For example, jobs at the office and shop floor typically have time spans of less than three months. If a job has many tasks associated with it, then some tasks may have to be completed today, but others can take longer. A typist may have to turn out a finished document today, but may also be responsible for the maintenance of the typewriter and photocopier, tasks that allow a longer time for exercising discretion.

If you ask a person holding a job at any stratum who that person's real manager is, someone at the next higher stratum is usually mentioned. People at the same level may be referred to as the 'supervisor' or equivalent, but the real boss is to be found one level up. The discontinuities between strata are also associated with shifts in the type of work. Problems are generally dealt with in a more abstract way at higher levels. An individual promoted across a boundary generally experiences a major increase in the weight of responsibility. For promotions within a stratum, the change in responsibility merely means 'more of the same' but promotions across boundaries cause an experience of 'more and different'.

The shift in the way discretion is exercised from one level to the next alters the nature of decision support required. A system that provides adequate support for stratum II, for example, will be found wanting at stratum III.

Types of job in each stratum

A full explanation of what occurs at each level would need to describe the complete socio-technical system involving the individual's relationships to other people, to the social system as a whole and on the physical and technical resources available. For the purpose of this chapter, however, it is sufficient to indicate enough about the nature of work at each stratum to derive the main implications for decision support systems.

The following are brief summaries of the types of job at each level. They are related to jobs rather than people because an individual's capacity to exercise discretion may be more or less than that required to do the job. If it is more, then the person feels underemployed; and if less, overwhelmed. The specific jobs mentioned are taken from industry and commerce, but it is important to remember that a similar stratification can be found in all types of organizations.

(1) *Stratum I: Office and Shop Floor.* Covers jobs made up of tangible tasks with a time span up to three months. The

individual does distinct, practical tasks which are largely accomplished by following predefined rules. Discretion is exercised in deciding how the rules are to be carried out. For example, a secretary must type a letter to a certain standard, but can exercise judgement in how it is to be done, or a machinist must turn out a part but can decide how a slightly misaligned tool can be employed to finish it. Output that results from work at this stratum is concrete and can be completely specified beforehand.

(2) *Stratum II: Front line managerial, professional and technical.* This is the lowest level at which the 'real' manager is found. The manager knows everyone in the group and oversees their work, solving problems, determining priorities and setting the rules and procedures to be followed. This requires an ability to think about concrete tasks and to imagine how they might come out if performed differently, applying 'What if?' mental analyses. Discretion is exercised in putting together a programme of work, in solving problems to maintain the programme, and in changing the programme as circumstances demand. Time spans vary from three months to a year. Some work programmes have to be planned as much as a year in advance.

(3) *Stratum III: Departmental management and principal specialists.* At this level we are talking about the manager of, say, a department whose members can recognize one another. Working life has become too complex for the manager to keep track of all the tasks for which she or he is responsible. It may even not be possible to imagine all the areas of responsibility at one time. With a time span of one to two years, the manager must be aware of *trends* in work activities and problems so that tasks can be organized into systems of work that will produce the desired output. Discretion is exercised in redirecting and retraining people, modifying equipment and facilitating work flow to improve efficiency and reduce costs. The focus is still on tasks concerned with directly providing tangible outputs, but the manager must also be able to conceptualize the tasks and objectives in an abstract way, and to scan the tasks in her or his imagination.

(4) *Stratum IV: General management and chief specialists.* Here we typically find the sales, production or R&D manager of a business unit. The move up from Stratum III is characterized by a shift of focus from direct output tasks to methods of operation. The sales manager, for example, is concerned

with how to organize a group of salesmen so they can get on with selling well; the production manager's main worry is obtaining and organizing technology to assist plants to run effectively; the R&D manager's prime interest is planning a programme of research to make potential new products. Specific problems dealt with at this level have implications for broad policies and procedures. Given the two to five year time span, managers are anticipating new technologies, equipment and methods, as well as preparing new procedures. They exercise discretion by instituting training programmes and proposing changes in anything from new technology to the structure of the organization, all with an eye on major corporate goals such as improving profitability and service.

(5) *Stratum V: Corporate subsidiary and top specialists*. This is the level of the managing director of a business unit. The time span of five to ten years indicates that discretion is exercised in deciding the general direction of the business within policies that are partly set from above. The manager is free, however, to reopen objectives that had previously been set and to close goals that had been left open. Not only can the manager define the field of operations for others at lower strata, but can also redefine his or her own arena of work within the limits set higher up. For example, the manager of a snack food company in a larger group was able to establish a new venture in the confectionery market because he was worried that certain trends in the snack food business were likely to lead to a loss of profit in about five to seven years. Much of the discretionary work at this level is concerned with creating and evaluating alternative medium term plans for the company, allocating necessary financial, human, physical and information resources, and with providing input for strategic planning which starts at the next level up.

(6) *Stratum VI: Corporate group of subsidiaries*. This is where longer term strategies begin to be formulated. Typically this level contains the director responsible for the collective performance of several business units in a corporation. This may include profit-and-loss accountability for a territory in a multinational group, or it might cover adequate provison of specific products, services or functions. With time spans between ten and twenty years, these jobs require attention to the world at large. The directors look at the changing, even turbulent, environment to detect possible impacts on the

activities for which they are accountable. They must work together as equals striving for consensus, while below this level relationships are usually that of manager-subordinate, although stratum VI directors can also work as the colleagues of stratum V managers. Discretion is exercised by creating a strategy based on analysing actual performance in the context of the broader environment and then translating that strategy into business directions. A major problem is determining the allocation of resources across different units to provide maximum corporate benefits for the least cost. This can be a complex and difficult process because there is usually much uncertainty about the future. In addition, conflicting objectives lead to different solutions, depending on whether a short or long time perspective is taken.

(7) *Stratum VII: Corporation*. We have now come to the top of most bigger organizations, typically the chief executive officer of a large corporation. Like the stratum VI director, this individual also scans the world noting economic, social, technical and political developments as they relate to the corporation's business. The chief executive officer, however, exercises discretion in providing strategic direction for the organization as a whole, anticipating paths of development for existing businesses and creating new businesses to meet needs that will be felt in twenty to fifty years.

(8) *Stratum VIII: Super corporation*. Generalizations about this supreme level are difficult to make. It is the realm inhabited by the Thomas Watsons and John D Rockefellers who create the IBMs and Standard Oils of the world that determine, decades later, the kind of world the rest of us will live in. These stratum VIII individuals do not just plan their business in relation to what is happening around them, but help to shape the future of society. Once they have made their mark, they can turn their businesses over to be run by stratum VII directors.

Making decision support systems more effective

Although brief, the above descriptions of jobs at different levels in Jaques' organizational strata illustrate clearly how individuals progressing up the executive hierarchy will experience abrupt changes in the discretionary content of their jobs when they move between strata. These shifts have not been taken sufficiently into account in computer-based management information and decision support systems, which is a major reason why I believe these systems have been of relatively limited use to top management. To see why this is so, it is instructive to examine the linkage between Jaques' strata and the capabilities of decision support systems.

Where support is available

Computer-based decision support systems are readily available for strata I to III.

At stratum I, the individual is doing distinct, tangible tasks and is following rules much of the time. Judgement is focused on the task at hand. Any external aids assist to implement judgements *after* preferences have been formed. As such, they are not what I would call decision support systems because they do not help the user to form preferences, make judgements or take decisions. They are tools and there are very many available at this level. For example, the user of an information retrieval system decides what information is wanted then, within the fixed structure of the system, selects commands to extract the required data. A word processor makes available many document production options from which the user can choose, unaided by the system in making the judgements. As explained in Chapter 3, an intelligent knowledge-based system can provide a better service if it has some understanding of the user's needs and the context of the dialogue but, at this level, it would still be a working tool not a decision support system.

At stratum II, true decision support enters. The front line manager at this level must handle abstract tasks, think of alternative ways of solving a problem and imagine possible solutions. These 'What if?' analyses can be helped by a decision support system whose structure is fixed, say embodied in a software model, and which allows judgements to be altered on one variable at a time, at the least. A *sensitivity analysis* program, for example, allows its user to try a whole spectrum of possible judgements, displaying the results over that range. A more sophisticated stratum II system would also suggest which variables might be worth investigating and what ranges of judgements could give different results. This would help the manager to form preferences and make judgements in support of the type of work typical at this level. There are many stratum II decision support systems available, although they are not as plentiful as stratum I tools.

A stratum III system still works within a fixed structure, but allows room for restructuring of the basic model and generation of new criteria. A manager at this level requires decision aids that help to evaluate alternative ways of organizing tasks and creating systems of work. Such evaluations can only be done by assessment against a number of criteria and the support systems should be flexible enough to allow new criteria to be generated, not merely adding to and deleting existing ones. Few decision support systems allow this restructuring to happen. Spreadsheet software, for example (*see* Chapter 2), does not suggest when a different layout might prove useful; software handling inventory control does not signal the possible need for a new product category; an information retrieval system does not indicate when the database should be reorganized.

Examples of stratum III decision support systems are some statistical analysis programs that examine errors and then provide messages that can be of great assistance in building a more satisfactory model, usually a reorganized version of the same type of structural model. The MAUD program discussed above also helps the user to think more deeply about what criteria are relevant to the problem at hand, thus facilitating the creation of new criteria.

Complexity at the top

Most computer systems used by managers in the mid 1980s generally work within fixed structures, and at most facilitate 'What if?' analyses on one variable at a time. Programs that allow the user to change several variables to new values without providing any help to advise when or how sensitivity analyses should be carried out are essentially level I systems. At levels higher than stratum III, effective computer systems, which handle the full complexity of discretionary activities in an integrated way, have not yet become available. There is doubt about the possibility of ever producing such aids at the highest levels. Nevertheless, there are ways in which better support can be provided for senior executives, as shown in the next section.

Managers at stratum IV need to cover a number of subsystems involving a mixture of types of problems. Each subsystem has its own characteristics and structure. A stratum IV decision support system therefore needs to be able to handle concepts that encompass a variety of structures, whereas systems below this level can operate within a single structure. A production manager concerned about the increasing age of the company's plants, for example, would require a system which, amongst other things, would help to:

(1) Model his or her uncertainty about future demand for the company's products.
(2) Take account of financial considerations such as capital outlay, operating and transportation costs.
(3) Incorporate non financial objectives such as flexibility of operations.
(4) Evaluate alternative options for improving plant efficiency.

I know of no stand alone computer program or integrated system in the mid 1980s that can bring together all these different considerations in a coherent manner.

Discretionary work at level V is concerned with complete fields of operation. A decision support system for these executives should help to articulate the principles that guide the setting of goals. There are no computer programs that can do this and I doubt that any will be seen for a long time. The reason is that goal setting has been studied for many decades by psychologists. While they have made some progress, the state of knowledge is still far from providing practical principles that can be embodied in software to serve decision makers with multiple goals. As for strata VI to VIII, it is not even clear what would constitute a useful decision support aid to handle such complex discretionary work.

Many top managers do, of course, make valuable use of computer aids even though systems are not available to handle all their discretionary needs. Work at all levels is made up of many tasks, some with longer time horizons than others. Those activities with the shorter time spans are the ones for which adequate decision support systems are available now. The provision of up-to-the-minute performance details through a stratum I type information retrieval system, for example, can be of great benefit to the highest levels of management by giving them an accurate and timely picture of what is occurring in the organization.

A stratum V managing director, say, may find nothing that can help him or her with setting goals, but may make effective use of software modelling and sensitivity analysis aids from level II. These could question the current strategic direction by providing a model of the company that can be used to test assumptions about the impact on future profitability of factors such as inflation, commodity prices, manufacturing costs and competitive pressures. A level I or II system can therefore be used in a stratum V (or above) way but still remains in the lower strata because it is not capable of directly aiding the discretionary activity of higher level managers. That is why I query the claim made by vendors that their relatively kow level aids are 'decision support systems for top managers'.

Towards support for top managers

The traditional notion of a decision support system is to have the manager interacting directly with the computer-based system. This has been adequate for carrying out tasks with a direct output, classified in *Table 4.1* as strata I to III. A different approach is needed above stratum III. This is because the shift in level of abstraction encountered in moving to the senior management levels (stratum IV and above) requires managers to rely much more heavily on judgement and intuition. In addition, they need

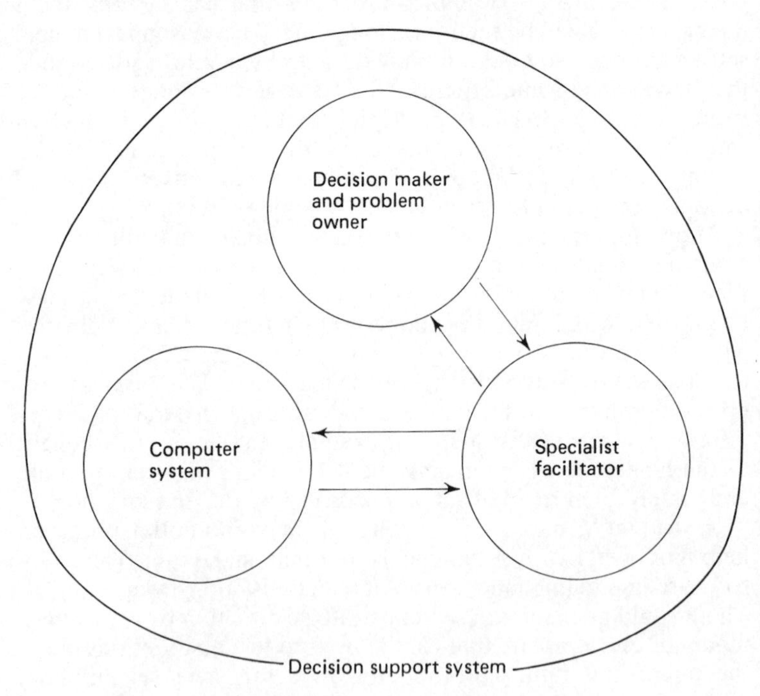

Figure 4.2 Decision support systems for top managers

to deal with a variety of problems of different structural types. To help these senior managers, a decision support system must have three main parts (*see Figure 4.2*):

(1) *Decision makers and major problem owners*. The people who have information and preferences relevant to the problem and who have some responsibility for it.
(2) *Computer systems*. Hardware and software that facilitate modelling and sensitivity analyses; decision makers and problem owners do not interact directly with the computer system but they monitor its output.
(3) *Specialist facilitators*. Experts in problem solving techniques who help the problem owners to formulate and structure the problems, express preferences and make judgements in quantitative form; the facilitator does not, however, tell the problem owners *what* to think.

It is the integration of these three elements which is needed for true decision support for top executives. Computer modelling is used to put together all the pieces of the problem in one framework and to show the problem owners the implications of their judgements. The specialist provides the flexibility that is needed to represent the different aspects of the problem with different structures. The problem owners contribute the vital ingredient: content.

Decision conferencing

It *is* possible to provide first-rate support for top managers, including executives at strata VI to VIII. One approach which has been used successfully in a number of organizations is *decision conferencing*. This is a two-day problem solving activity that occurs in a face to face group. Four rules govern the decision conference:

(1) *The decision maker must be present*. This ensures that the individual's view of the problem is represented and keeps the group from being side tracked or from solving the wrong problem.
(2) *All major problem owners must be present*. This encourages a variety of viewpoints to be expressed and prevents only 'yes men' from attending.
(3) *No papers are allowed in the room on the first day*. This prevents formal presentations, reading from reports, passing on written information and other actions which obscure the real problem. Experience has shown that the actual problem

is more likely to emerge if everything initially comes out of the heads of the problem owners and decision makers. Helping the problem owners to express their preferences and judgements is a major task for the specialist facilitator, and is one of the reasons why this individual is a necessary part of top-level decision support systems.

(4) *The problem must be live.* There should not be any retrospective analyses, in which hindsight biases are so great that participants cannot think themselves back to the situation they faced at the time, or hypothetical problems, where preferences and judgements will be ill informed.

The initial couple of hours on the first day of a decision conference is spent in a free discussion of the problem, the issues of concern, and the main objectives. The facilitator uses her or his knowledge of decision technology to help model the problem. While this model is being created by the group, it is implemented on the computer system. The specialist helps the group to stick to the task at hand, to develop a structure for the problem, to assess judgemental quantities and to interpret the results from the computer. On the second day the results of manipulating the computer models are compared to the participants' intuitions. When discrepancies occur, as they inevitably will, the model may be revised or intuitions changed and the process repeated. Eventually, the group is helped to a deeper understanding of the problem and, usually, a crisp solution and implementation plan emerge.

Experience with decision conferences for top executives has shown that one of the main benefits is that the group develops a shared understanding of the problem. This brings home to them that decision making in the past has been made more difficult because the group lacked a mechanism for evolving a common understanding, let alone a commitment to subsequent action. Participants usually leave the conference with similar appreciations of the problem, an agreed plan of action for what to do next, and a commitment to do it. Not all participants may agree with all the details, one or two problem owners may even be in substantial disagreement, but at least everyone knows where they stand and why.

The process is open and fair and all points of view can be represented. The conference can be regarded as a real decision support system for top managers because it brings together the three elements identified at the beginning of the chapter (*see*

Figure 4.1):

(1) *The problem owners*. The conference brings together the different perspectives of participants who contribute their experience, intuition and knowledge.
(2) *Preference technology*. The decision technology specialist establishes a framework within which participants can meaningfully express their value judgements.
(3) *Information technology*. The computer system helps to bring all the elements together in a systematic way. In short, decision support for top managers differs fundamentally from systems for lower level managers by the necessary inclusion of specialist services. Thus, top level decision support is based on both computers *and* services.

Recommendations

(1) Recognize that exercising discretion is the key aspect of a senior manager's job. This includes assessing uncertainty about the future, judging the value of possible consequences of decisions, formulating time and risk preferences, and making trade offs among objectives. These are responsibilities and tasks that can ultimately be undertaken only by a human decision maker.
(2) Do not expect computer systems to automate senior managers' discretionary activities.
(3) Be wary of claims made for 'decision support systems'. True ones help the manager to form sound judgements, clarify preferences and take decisions, not just to extract information and manipulate relatively limited models.
(4) Understand the underlying stratified structure of organizations and the way in which the mix between discretionary and rule-based activity changes significantly when moving between strata. The vast majority of computer systems are aimed at satisfying the more rule-based tasks common at the lower strata.
(5) Seek and evaluate new decision support aids which genuinely help top managers in the exercise of discretion as well as relieving them of rule-based tasks. Recognize that true decision support for top managers requires the services of specialists in problem solving. Hardware and software are not sufficient.

References

1. Jaques, E., *A General Theory of Bureaucracy*, Heinemann, London (1976)
2. Jaques, E., *Free Enterprise, Fair Employment*, Crane Russak, New York; Heineman, London (1982)

Bibliography

The following publications are also relevant to topics discussed in this chapter.

Brown, R.V., Kahr, A. and Peterson, C., *Decision Analysis for the Manager*, Holt, Rinehart and Winston, New York (1974)

Checkland, P., *Systems Thinking, Systems Practice*, Wiley, Chichester (1981)

French, S., Hartley R., Thomas, L.C. and White, D.J., *Multi-objective Decision Making*, Academic Press, London (1983)

Humphreys, P.C., Levels of abstraction in structuring decision problems, *Journal of Applied Systems Analysis*, in press (1984)

Keeney, R. and Raiffa, H., *Decisions with Multiple Objectives*, Wiley, New York (1976)

5

Management use of new office technology

Niels Bjørn-Andersen

Introduction

New office technology provides a wide range of facilities of direct use to all levels of managers. Such capabilities do more than just make managers increasingly efficient in their existing jobs. They cause fundamental changes in the ways in which management work is carried out and to the very nature of management jobs and roles. There will be changes in job content and in the numbers of management jobs available. Interpersonal relationships will alter between managers and their secretaries, colleagues, bosses, subordinates and technical specialists.

This chapter takes a systematic look at the impact of new office technology on the role of managers. It provides an informed evaluation of likely changes that managers will be faced with when computer-based systems are introduced. It starts by examining the importance of information as a management resource before looking in detail at possible consequences for the nature of management work. Broader psychological and social impacts are discussed, insights provided for the direction of appropriate technological developments, and advice given on how to train managers for the future.

Information as a resource

Information plays a vital role in all management work. Managers need to gather data on sales, accounting, financial performance, the effectiveness of support services to customers and clients, economic and business trends, and so on. Computer-based information retrieval, processing and communication clearly assist in getting that information and communicating the results of decisions. In helping managers to make decisions, computer systems will play an increasingly significant role in in three main areas:

(1) Problem awareness and problem definition.
(2) Analysis and evaluation of the problem and its possible solutions.
(3) Choice of a particular solution and communication of the decision.

Clarifying and defining the problem, and utilizing managers' expertise to make qualitative judgements are critical areas of decision making but are complex, subjective tasks. There are many computer-based tools to assist managers to sift through large volumes of information and to test hypotheses successfully wherever quantifiable data and solutions are applicable. It is in the crucial area of decision making based on instinctive managerial skills that computers have been least helpful in the past (*see* Chapter 4).

Time spent on actually making a choice is likely to be reduced if computers have been used to gather, analyse and evaluate information. More efficient ways are also available for producing reports, letters, memos and visual aids to present and explain decisions. The most widespread application of new office technology has been to improve the *forms* of presenting information: text documents can be laid out attractively without corrections, slides for presentations can be created automatically from a workstation, and so on. There is a real risk, however, that this can lead to an over-emphasis on form rather than content, particularly where the originator of material (the *principal* or *author*) also produces the output.

Rate of acceptance of computer systems

General acceptance of the use of computer-based systems by managers has been slow. One of the reasons has been that vendors have been over optimistic, frequently promising that imagination sets the limit on what can be done, not the technology. So, in the late 1960s, many managers bought data processing equipment in the belief that it would provide comprehensive *Management Information Systems* (MIS) to solve all management problems with a single service. Most attempts at developing such integrated systems failed. Managers were disappointed. Realizing these difficulties, the buzzword from vendors then became *Decision*

Support Systems (DSS). These also fell short of their vendors' claims (*see* Chapter 4).The 1980s have seen yet more promises, this time that *office automation* will place all necessary information services at managers' fingertips and expert systems will give them added brain power. New office technology has much to offer but there is no guarantee that it will be successful; knowledge-based expert systems have an important role to play but are not a universal panacea.

There have been other reasons for managers' slow take up of computer systems.

(1) *Systems have not been cost effective*. Many systems did not deliver the financial benefits expected of them. For example, while word processors led to increased keystroke productivity, the same documents were typed over and over so many times, because of the ease of making changes, that there were few ultimate benefits. Managers have also often been provided with too much information. John D. Meltion, president of the Blue Cross & Blue shield in Texas has commented, 'You can get so damn much information with computers that you get into this trees-and-forest stuff.'
(2) *Resistance to keyboards*. Most managers have avoided having typewriters on their desks. A reluctance to use keyboards, because it signifies a lowering of status or through sheer laziness, has kept some managers away from computer-based systems. This is changing. Fewer managers have personal secretaries. More managers have had hands-on experience of microcomputers and have survived, and even enjoyed, the experience. There have been developments in human–computer communication, such as the mouse pointer, which provide an alternative to the keyboard as the main form of input (*see* Chapters 2 and 3). 'User friendliness' is a key issue in determining management acceptance. William J. Weiss, chairman of Motorola Inc, for example, tried three different systems and concluded, 'I found you need a lot of familiarity with the machine to do things beyond the very simple. It is cheaper and more efficient to hire an expensive assistant who can do that.'
(3) *No clear cut case for computerization*. Managers have not usually perceived a vital need to have their own jobs computerized. Computers are obviously more useful for tasks that are carried out according to predefined routines, but these may just be a small proportion of some managers'

jobs. Little independent research was available, before the 1980s, which unambiguously identified substantial savings that could be made by applying computes to management jobs.

Managers can have a considerable say in the introduction of new office technology. If they do not see a new system as personally beneficial to their own performance, they will not bother with it. Unlike most secretarial and clerical staff, many managers are in a position to say no to new technology.

The nature of computer impact

There is frequent talk about the computer impact on this, that or the other. Two important factors should be remembered when thinking what this impact may be on management and organizational life.

(1) *The application is more important than the technology*. The same items of hardware and software can have different impacts depending on how they are applied, particularly because of:
   (a) The degree of individual control allowed over developments.
   (b) The type of human–computer communication chosen (*see* Chapter 3).
   (c) The implementation strategy followed (*see* Chapters 7 to 9).
   (d) The degree of authority and discretion given to the local manager to change and modify the system to meet specific needs. The more influence exerted by the local manager, the more beneficial will the consequences be to the organization.

(2) *Technological change may be inevitable, but there is no inevitability about the consequences of pursuing a particular computer application*. The particular course followed by a specific application is the end result of choices made by people, deliberately or implicitly, regarding the division of labour among employees, management style, skills required by users of the technology, and so on. The final system mirrors the values of those who are most influential in the system's design and development, be they managers, computer specialists or particular users. The *scientific management* techniques that underly assembly line automation, for

example, are a technological expression of the belief that work is most efficient when subdivided into its discrete, uni-skilled tasks which can be measured and monitored, whereas socio-techncial designs have a higher regard for individual and social satisfaction and motivation[1].

Managerial redundancy, redeployment and career prospects

The main anxiety of managers faced by new office technology, as for any other employees, is whether their jobs are threatened. Until the late 1970s, computerization was used primarily to improve productivity at clerical levels, which has often meant reducing the number of people needed to carry out the same, or more, work. Then evidence began emerging that traditional data processing systems were leading to some middle managers being made redundant or being moved to other jobs (*redeployed*).

Much of the information gathering and transmission carried out by middle managers can be performed faster, cheaper and more effectively through an integrated information service. For example, when top management used to have a query about a cost calculation, they would have to wait for a few days for others to sift through the data and feed back an answer. Now, the senior executive can sit at a personal workstation and find up to date answers directly and immediately. Many organizations have used such computerized services to cut down on management staff. A Danish radio and television company, for instance, reduced the number of production planners from 35 to 11 in a couple of years because of a new computerized production control system. Alexander F. Giacco, chairman and chief executive of Hercules Inc, has claimed that the introduction of computer systems cut corporate staff from 25 to 14 between 1978 and 1982. Xerox Corporation has laid off 13 managers, equipped them with workstations in their homes and made them self employed subcontractors.

Computer information systems can also make it possible to devolve more decision making, thereby strengthening the position of operational level managers, such as those who are face to face with customers or clients. Many managers have used new technical capabilities to reinforce their position in other ways, say, by using 'What if?' modelling and information retrieval systems to generate significant and identifiable extra earnings to the organization. For example, Fred P. Hochberg, senior vice president for marketing at the mail order company Lillian Vernon Corporation used his computer to study order trends, plot sales curves and track the time taken for customers to respond to mail shots. As a result, he was able to work out the best week to post new catalogues, thereby saving the company $100 000[2].

By the early 1980s most evidence of the impact of coputers on management jobs had come from traditional data processing applications because there had been insufficient direct experience of new office technology. A study by management consultants Booz-Allen, however, indicates that office systems will also lead to savings in management resources. Booz-Allen estimates that managers spend as much as 25 per cent of their time on unproductive tasks, such as waiting for information or making photocopies. Based on an assessment of future office technology, they expect that managers and professionals could save an average of 15 per cent of their time through more automation.

The number of management positions in an organization is therefore likely to shrink, at least in the short term, through the increased use of computer-based systems. There are likely to be fewer organizational layers between top executives and middle managers, with fewer direct promotions but more redeployment and lateral moves. The managers who are most likely to succeed are those who make best use of computer aids in decision making. In the longer term, of course, organizations that use computer systems to improve their overall performance will generate new jobs, although it is impossible to predict the actual numbers and whether new jobs will balance or exceed those which are lost because of the technology.

The changing content of managerial jobs

There are three areas in the content of management jobs which are likely to feel the main impact of computerization:

(1) *Structuring, preprogramming and formalization*. Increased standardization and quantification of work tasks have grown with the use of computers, primarily because the specification of data formats and decision rules is a prerequisite for writing software.

(2) *Seduction by computerizable aspects*. There can be a tendency to put more and more emphasis on those aspects of a task

or problem that are most suitable for handling by computer-based systems.

(3) *Performance monitoring*. Most computer systems at a clerical level encompass some kind of performance measurement, such as the number of transactions carried out and mistakes made, which is recorded and passed up the hierarchy. Management jobs could also become subject to increasing surveillance by the computer.

Freedom to exercise discretion

The standardization required by computers does not inevitably lead to increased centralization and a reduction in freedom for local managers. Traditional data processing applications, however, have tended to follow this course. For instance, in a large, five-country study of management information systems in organizations operating in fields as diverse as electronics, mail order, medical care and air transport, it was found that the degree of discretion allowed to individual managers was universally reduced. Some of this loss was caused because the human–computer communication allowed only a restricted interaction following prescribed routines. A more significant reason was the pressure on managers to improve overall efficiency.

Even when an organization officially attempts to decentralize, systems are often designed with the implication that maximum productivity is achieved by using computers as a control technology directed by top management to limit the autonomy of decision makers lower in the hierarchy. For example, a Danish bank began an exercise in what was meant to be decentralization. At the same time, a new computer-based planning and control system was introduced. This specified the type of customers who could receive loans, the nature of loans that could be given, conditions the customer had to meet, and so on. Lending officers were then closely monitored to see if they followed the predetermined guidelines. They felt that all their autonomy has gone and saw themselves as being reduced to the level of supermarket cashiers.

In another case, consultants to a Norwegian shipping line recommended in the mid 1970s that each ship should be made an autonomous profit centre to improve effectiveness and the quality of life onboard. Meanwhile, the computer department was pursuing the implementation of an information system that put central control of all shipping activities in the company's Oslo headquarters, even to the extent of having central handling of detailed maintenance, staffing and food provisions on each ship. At the time, nobody in the organization seemed to be aware of the conflict between these two organizational strategies.

The way microelectronics has made local computing power more feasible opens the possibility of genuine decentralization of decision making. Software can be tailored to the requirements of an individual manager or department while still conforming to external corporate needs. Private local files and financial models can be maintained as well as having shared databases and decision support aids.

Top managers need to make a deliberate strategic decision to use computing to encourage genuine decentralization and to reverse the trend towards applying technology to increase structuring and formalization of management roles. Thomas J. Peters, co-author of the best seller *In Search of Excellence*[3], has perceptively commented:

> Managers' obsession with numbers and checks and balances is being challenged by CEOs (chief executive officers) with an equally obsessive determination to create atmospheres in which entrepreneurs can flourish. Indeed, after limiting decision making to the inhabitants of top floor offices for much of the past two decades, companies are now frantically trying to push it down to those who are closest to the market place, giving more autonomy to plant managers, sales people and engineers – and bypassing middle levels completely . . . . if you look at the way truly decentralized companies outperform centralized companies, you've got to say it is a trend that has got to force itself on even the most reluctant CEOs[2].

Turning people into machines

The Danish philosopher Piet Hein has neatly encapsulated one of the great risks of computerization: 'A lot of people are worried about machines getting more and more like humans. I am worried about human beings getting more and more like machines.' American computer scientist Joseph Weizenbaum has also cogently argued against the danger of putting too much emphasis on work elements that are most amenable to computing applications and forget the qualitative aspects[4]. There are five areas where this danger is most acute.

(1) *Quantification of data*. The drive towards computerization is often based on an assumption that it is possible to quantify

most, if not all, relevant data for decision making and other work activities. Trying to reduce everything to digits, however, loses a great deal of vital qualitative information.

(2) *Formalization of communication*. This is closely associated with the growing worship of numbers and quantified data. As discussed in Chapter 3, human–computer communication is generally far less rich than when people communicate with each other. Knowledge about how people use a variety of gestures, signals and intonations of voice, and an understanding of the context in which the communication is taking place ensures that, as Humpty Dumpty says in Lewis Carroll's *Through The Looking Glass*, 'When I use a word it means just what I choose it to mean, neither more nor less.' The subtleties of human communication and interaction are also important in the way people evolve their ideas and preferences. More than just extra information is needed to make better decisions.

(3) *Commitment and alienation*. Direct person to person communication is an important element in creating commitment to an idea, a project or a whole organization. An increased reliance on electronic communications may, therefore, lead to a reduced level of commitment within an organization, resulting in less likelihood of the organization achieving its goals. Social contact between people is a vital motivational factor in office life. It aids the growth of an individual's job satisfaction by enhancing feelings of a common interest in the organization, and promoting work effectiveness. If managers spend most of their time interacting with a workstation, rather than people, they can lose touch with what others are doing and begin to feel isolated, alienated and dissatisfied.

(4) *Rule-oriented bureaucratic behaviour*. There are two main ways of deciding what to do in a particular circumstance, such as deciding on a new investment proposal or responding to a customer's complaint. Either the problem is solved by searching for the rule to apply irrespective of consequence, or by first considering the likely implications of a course of action. The programmed nature of software makes computers suited for rule/norm-oriented behaviour, which can encourage static and bureaucratic responses. Acting by considering consequences is based on lessons learnt from past experiences and can be more imaginative and sensitive to particular local circumstances.

(5) *Information overload*. Managers can be provided with too

much irrelevant data.

Monitoring managers' performance

The relatively unstructured nature of much of their work has made managers' performance less susceptible to measurement and surveillance by computer systems than clerical jobs. Nevertheless, computer-based systems are being used to identify outstanding and substandard management achievements. Increased central co-ordination and control through computer networks can result in managers along the line having to follow more precise evaluation criteria. Their own and their unit's performance can be relayed more quickly up the hierarchy so that more and more of an individual manager's activity is spent explaining deviations, trying to avoid further budget constraints, and so on.

Middle managers want to see what the penalties are before they are willing to exercise personal discretion. Making mistakes and learning from such experiences should, however, be a desirable and necessary element in developing management skills. Managers will become inhibited and refuse to use their initiative if they know that their every use of electronic information services can be recorded. The results of such monitoring may be counterproductive even if, as a Danish department store claimed, it was meant 'only for self control so that managers could compare their own performances with that of others.' Managers are likely to respond either by avoiding the service or, if they are forced to use it, by shifting their attention from the real business objectives towards optimizing the expected performance criteria. This can make it difficult to follow the reasonably sensible tactic of monitoring all activities over a short period because managers may adapt their behaviour to make it seem better than it really is.

Keeping computing tabs on managers can take a number of forms. Computers can, for example, automatically count the number of transactions performed, such as how many messages are sent by electronic mail, plus details of the time each was sent and the quickness of response. One service that has created some management resistance has been the electronic diary. If others can have access to the diary, the individual may feel vulnerable to detailed analyses of their behaviour and to having their time organized directly by their superiors. An electronic diary may be acceptable if it is implemented in a way that protects privacy and prevents others from finding out and manipulating its content.

Lost in a sea of information

As has already been noted, having too much information can make it difficult for managers to see the forest for the trees. This was particularly noticeable in the early data processing era where huge mountains of printed output were dumped on managers' desks and rarely used. With increasing access to more databases and the availability of electronic mail services, the dangers of being flooded by too much information have been increased. That is why one aim in human–computer communication is to provide knowledge-based systems that help to sift through data before presenting it to the user (*see* Chapter 4). As long ago as 1967, management consultant Russel Ackoff commented that 'it is a fundamental mistake to think that managers need more in information. They need less.'

In my own experience of an electronic mail system, I have found that it is so easy to send messages to everybody that too much information accumulates in our electronic mailboxes, so many messages never get looked at. A broader illustration of the problem is the fact that the Royal Danish Library made as many Danish acquisitions between 1960 and 1984 as in its total previous history between 1400 and 1959. Information may be exploding but there is a danger that rubbish is expanding faster than the amount of valuable information.

Changes in interpersonal relationships

New office technology is likely to change the relationship between a manager and her or his secretary, subordinates, superiors, technical specialists and colleagues. All of these interactions will be altered by new communications media, such as electronic mail, teleconferencing and electronic diaries. There are many transactions, however, which are unsuitable for these new media, particularly where problems, information exchanges and decisions have a high degree of complexity and the outcome depends on the kind of rich communication possible only when people meet. Electronic mail is inadequate, for example, when having a discussion to clarify a message to persuade someone or to sell them something, or when delicate negotiations are involved. Videoconferencing may greatly facilitate communications for busines-like meetings among people with existing working relations. In other circumstances, it may be less effective than face-to-face meetings. Direct human contact provides an opportunity to establish personal ties, helps commitment to a decision and opens up a dialogue that can lead to further business.

The ease of organizing meetings can be improved through an electronic diary system. This type of service can, however, cause some management resistance, as has already been indicated. It enables meetings to be scheduled automatically without the manager's knowledge. This does not take account of the fact that deciding whether or not to attend a meeting involves some negotiation. For example, the time for the meeting may be free but there may be insufficient time beforehand to prepare the necessary material. Managers who find themselves attending more meetings than before, or being forced into meetings they do not want to attend, begin to defend themselves by indicating that time slots are 'occupied' when they are really 'free time' that can be used to read, think and get on with work that is felt to be more important.

The manager–secretary relationships

The most visible impact of new office technology for many managers is the changing relationship with his or her secretary. Many professionals and some managers have started to do their own word processing. A secretary may do the initial text input, based on handwriting or dictation, with the principal author (the manager or professional) doing the final editing. Many managers prefer the reverse method: they do the initial input and leave the final editing to the secretary. Increasingly, the author does all the work, from input, through editing to final output, with the work evolving as the author interacts at the workstation.

In general, new office technology is likely to reduce the amount of traditional secretarial services required, such as typing, filing, getting information and photocopying. Some of this saving in labour will be reflected in a reduction in the number of secretarial posts. For those still at work, decisions will have to be taken on how work is divided between the manager and secretary and how secretarial support services are organized.

Secretarial work could be organized, for example, as *administrative support groups*. In these, a number of secretarial/clerical staff provide a service to a group of managers and professionals and help decide how to introduce and use new technological options. This opens up opportunities for more varied workloads, enhanced career prospects and more job flexibility. There are many organizations, however, that prefer having word processors in a central pool because it requires less equipment and fewer staff. Microelectronics and improved telecommunications services are reducing the cost advantage of such pools. There is also clear evidence that such pools can have a detrimental effect on the relationship between the author and typist, employee motivation, and the quality and overall effectiveness of the work. If secretarial support is reduced too much, managers may spend a lot of extra time doing relatively trivial clerical tasks, like making photocopies, which negates much of the cost benefits of the word processors. Having pools for some tasks with decentralized support groups for other activities can prove to be successful[5].

Manager–subordinate relationships

Computer-based information technology has a tendency towards increasing formalization and structuring of management work, as explained above. Much information transmitted from a manager to subordinates can be carried out via electronic communications and by the rules programmed into software. The need for personal contact is therefore reduced. This occurs both in highly centralized organizations and where decentralization is aided by distributed computing power. Information systems can also do some performance monitoring.

This means that managers will need to spend less time communicating with, watching over, helping, guiding and instructing subordinates. This reduction can be be of benefit for both parties. It gives the manager more time to get on with more strategic activities rather than getting bogged down in operational concerns. Subordinates can be allowed to do their work with less intervention from their boss. On the debit side, managers can lose the important social and business benefits of keeping in personal contact with staff, and subordinates may be dictated to, and supervised by, the computer.

If managers do spend more time on investigating important medium and long term issues, they may eventually be able to revitalize contacts with subordinates and others within a new framework. Instead of constantly focusing on day to day problems, such contacts could become more broadly based, with more attention given to the exploring of ideas than meeting deadlines.

Manager–superior relationships

Managers are likely to be more enthusiastic about the changes brought by new office technology to their interactions with subordinates than to the organizational visibility introduced by the new system in relation to their own bosses. This new visibility can take many forms. For example, in a large chemical plant, the technical director obtained a computer-based information service that kept him in direct touch with the status of the work flow. He was informed immediately if there was an interruption to any production process. This seemingly attractive management information service proved to have some vital flaw. As soon as he was informed on his VDT that something had gone wrong, the technical director phoned the production engineer in charge. This was a waste of time because the engineer had also just heard about it and was trying to investigate the cause. Eventually, a time delay was built into the system to allow the engineer a chance to investigate the cause of a problem before being badgered by the director.

Information systems give senior managers the option to have access to information that was previously controlled and filtered by a manager who acted as the communication channel linking the department to the outside world. A great deal of information can therefore be made visible directly to top managers or to outside agencies. Some government departments, for example, use computers to gather data on, say, the performance of hospitals or universities. This information can then be used to judge performance against quantified criteria on which financial allocations are made, and to check adherence to guidelines on staffing levels, work load per doctor/nurse/professor, and so on. This type of 'X-ray vision' into the numerical bones of an organization's working is a key element in the increased performance monitoring which, one way or another, is usually a consequence of new office technology.

Making a manager's day to day activities more easily observable by superiors could create controls which can be relatively easily manipulated to allow people to get away with a minimum amount of work, provided they follow the rules and meet the quantified targets. This is more likely to occur if the performance information is fed directly to those high up the hierarchy where aggregations and comparisons become detached from their context and lose real meaning.

In order to maintain healthy relationships between managers and their superiors, explicit criteria should be built into information systems based on the provision of:

(1) Generalized, not over detailed, performance controls.

(2) A high degree of decentralization and local autonomy within the corporate framework.
(3) Infrequent, in-depth investigations of particular departments or units carried out in co-operation with the unit.

Manager–colleague relationships

The potential strains introduced into manager–superior relationships by new office technology do not exist between managers or professionals at the same (*peer*) level. Electronic mail systems, in particular, can facilitate and further improve contacts between people in different locations within an organization or between individuals in different organizations. The growing availability of networks within academic and scientific communities has shown the way in which contacts made, say at a conference, can be consolidated and developed through exchanges of information by electronic mail. Teleconferencing also has potential for such communications.

The mere implementation of an apparently desirable capability for communicating with colleagues does not lead automatically to a fully satisfactory application. I have already mentioned how I have experienced information overload on one electronic mail system. On another network, this time an experimental one linking a few fairly small groups around the world, I encountered another difficulty. At the time, my own interests were concentrated on work other than that involved in the network, so I rarely bothered to check what was in my electronic mailbox. In the end, colleagues started using the ordinary post to send me photocopies of what they had sent electronically. This illustrates the importance of considering the motivation and commitment of individuals to innovations that must be relevant to real needs, as well as, perhaps, being technically interesting.

Manager–specialist relationships

Computerization can have a profound effect on the relative power balance between computing specialist and operations/line managers. For example, a computer-based production control and scheduling system was introduced in the component assembly plants of a Danish electronic company, primarily as a tool for the production planners, a staff function which reported directly to the production manager. The system gave the planners far more influence than the foreman and plant managers who previously had been the main influence. Within two years of introduction, one planner became the manager of a small plant and the head of central planning was promoted to technical director. Meanwhile, three plant managers were dismissed and replaced by only two newly recruited managers because the new system simplified the job of being a plant manager.

Three main reasons helped the technical specialist to gain more power:

(1) The computer system monitored the work flow and no change in daily production could be made until the computer system ascertained that all components were available. Planners had direct personal access to this computer data. Foremen in charge of human resources, however, were unable to support their own arguments with such hard facts.
(2) Only the planners had the expert knowledge needed to operate the computer systems and to change its assumptions about production routines.
(3) The up to date knowledge provided by the computer system meant that planners were the first to be able to evaluate the consequences of major changes in component deliveries or customer orders.

This type of development has been typical in office as well as production work, particularly when technical specialists use their potent computing aids to increase efficiency through rationalization and cost cutting. As the *gate keepers* of the technology, the specialists get more power because either the new systems are incomprehensible to others or access to the technology is kept largely the preserve of the technical high priest. As often happens, however, the revolution eventually starts eating its own children. Many managers have become unhappy that the number of planners, systems designers and computing specialists has escalated. The availability of cheaper and easier to use computing systems has undermined the monopoly previously enjoyed by the technical specialists. As I have already pointed out, it has also given top managers the ability to keep in direct touch with operational levels, thereby enabling them to eliminate some middle level staff.

General Electric of the US, for example, cut its corporate strategic planning staff in the early 1980s from 60 to 25 in order to extend the authority of its general managers. The NCR Corporation moved its engineering staff out of its headquarters and placed them in operating groups to correct troublesome gaps in the product line and overcome other development problems. The era when it was thought beneficial to have specialists and 'planners' separated from business specialists and 'doers' is gradually on the wane.

The new heroes who are beginning to inherit control are line managers, particularly those capable of understanding and manipulating computer-based systems and who can steer technical specialists towards corporate goals. Operational managers are in the best position to know how to analyse real requirements, then devise and implement effective plans that will meet actual working needs. Planners and technical analysts are generally too remote from how the organization really functions.

Many technical specialists need to learn managerial skills to cope with the human and organizational consequences of their new computing aids. An engineering design department, for example, will probably need no urging to introduce new technology; in fact, the demand may be for too much technology. Once introduced, however, computer-based systems can lead to changing job patterns, such as more home based work and more contact with colleagues outside the immediate workplace through workstations linked to communications networks. Administrative support staff in technical departments are also likely to be reorganized. The professional in charge will therefore need sharp management skills as well as technical ones, to handle the possibly turbulent transition successfully.

Psychological impact on managers

The changes in job content and interpersonal relationships discussed above will have a significant impact on the pyschological and social well being of the individual manager. The nature of the impact will depend on two main aspects: the *direction* of change and the *rate* of change. I have already indicated some of the many managerial changes that can occur which may be positive or negative depending on the route followed in particular circumstances. The speed of innovation is also important.

Once, not so long ago, people expected to be in the same job or same career progression for a considerable period, possibly a whole working life. Now, it is likely that an individual will hold a few jobs and be frequently required to learn new skills. Even within the same job, the character of the work done can change completely within five years because of technological and other developments. Computer-based systems have been a motor for changes that have travelled at an unprecendently fast rate across a broad front. This makes it tough for managers to keep on top of the situation. Experience counts less than it did. The individual must be in a continuous 'unfrozen' state, ready to adapt to every new challenge that arises, rather than being able to 'freeze' their positions once they have learnt their way in their new job. Similarly, organizations must also remain in a state of continuous flux.

The manager under pressure

Many managers will thrive in the dynamic environment stimulated by new office technology. They will seize the opportunities opened up and help to ensure that computer-based systems are applied in useful ways. Other managers will be unable to cope or will be in organizations which apply technology in an unimaginative, restricting manner. The following are the main ways in which managers could be adversely affected.

(1) *Stress*. Living in a state of uncertainty and change, unable to enjoy the security usually obtained through experience, can cause stress and tension in itself. Computer systems can add strains, for example when:
   (a) An answer is wanted quickly from a computer and it takes a long time to respond, sometimes even seeming to go dead.
   (b) The computer system fails at a critical moment and an incomprehensible or unhelpful error report is provided.
   (c) The manager feels there is a discrepancy between the computer figures or proposals and the actual situation but does not have the technical knowhow to challenge the 'objective and logical' computer data.
   (d) The manager is unable to meet the performance figures programmed into the systems on the basis of 'average' expectations throughout the organization.

(2) *Job satisfaction*. The trend towards applying computers to increase the structuring, control and monitoring of managerial tasks, explained earlier in the chapter, is likely to lead to a decrease in motivation and satisfaction at work. The individual may feel less identification with the organization and commitment to the job.

(3) *Privacy*. More and more aspects of managers' work are being measured and computerized for others to evaluate. The result can be that managers feel their privacy has been

eroded and are no longer willing to use their own initiative and imagination, becoming supreme bureaucrats sticking to the very letter of corporate rules and procedure, in case 'someone up there' observes a deviation from the norm.

(4) *Alienation*. The magnitude and rate of change induced by new office technology has caused many managers to become alienated. They begin to sense they are caught in a computing web, with senior management monitoring every twitch. Managers can therefore cease to believe they can control how their job is changing and no longer feel part of an integrated working community in which work can be a means of self expression.

The negative spiral

Changes in stress levels, job satisfaction, and other aspects of job content and personal relationships can interconnect into a negative spiral ending in some managers being unable to cope (*see Figure 5.1*). For example, a negative change in interpersonal relationships, such as reduced contact with subordinates, can lead to job dissatisfaction, which in turn generates stress and feelings of alienation. The result is that managers are less able to fulfil their responsibilities. This may lead to redundancy or a further twist down the spiral loop.

This negative spiral can be broken and turned into a positive one by applying technology so that it improves some of the elements in *Figure 5.1* or by providing training to assist managers to cope with the impact of new systems.

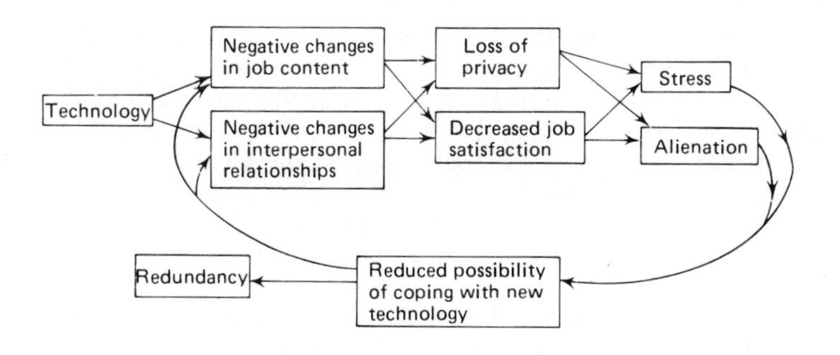

Figure 5.1 A negative spiral of computer impact

Directions for appropriate technology

The impact of a computer cannot be predetermined, but the likely course of development can be gauged according to whether the system designer has a technical or a broader human and organizational perspective, and the extent to which the design task is allowed to extend beyond purely technical considerations. Four main outcomes are possible (*see Table 5.1*):

(1) *Deterministic impact.* Where technically oriented designers stick to a technical brief, the available technology will totally shape the type of system produced.
(2) *Contingent impact.* This occurs when designers with a broad organizational understanding are constrained to tackle only technical problems, so that the final outcome is dependent on developments outside their remit.
(3) *Accidental impact.* The unexpected consequences that happen when technical designers are allowed to specify organizational issues, such as job definitions.
(4) *Chosen/planned impact.* This occurs when there is a coherent, flexible and well monitored organizational strategy within which computer-based systems help to meet planned corporate objectives, such as increased local decision making through a move towards decentralized management structures.

In practice, the impact is usually contingent or accidental, with few systems chosen through a comprehensive master plan. The full benefits of new technology, however, can come only from a rethinking of the way people work and how the organization operates. The development of computer-based systems therefore requires knowledge about organization and job design, how to involve users in shaping the system, training, phased implementation that allows for learning from experience, and other skills not specific to any particular technical option. Focusing purely on technicalities can mean that an apparent short term success turns out to be a long term nightmare.

Are expert systems the answer?

In the early 1980s, the Japanese government embarked on its Fifth Generation Computer project[6]. Its ultimate aim is to produce systems that are usable by everyone and much technical attention has been given to its espousal of artificial intelligence techniques in

Table 5.1 Factors influencing impact of new office technology

	Organisational change outside design task	*Organisational change inside design task*
Designer employing technical perspective	(1) Deterministic Impact	(3) Accidental Impact
Designer employing organizational perspective	(2) Contingent Impact	(4) Chosen/planned Impact

general, and expert systems in particular. While expert systems are beneficial in some activities (*see* Chapter 3), there is a danger of attempting to pack too much intelligence into the computer without considering the impact on people and organizations.

Consider, for example, an expert system used in hospitals to help diagnose ailments by 'interviewing' the patient and coming to a conclusion that should be as accurate as an experienced doctor. Say, however, that a doctor who is with the patient disagrees with the expert system and overrules it. If the patient is subsequently harmed and brings an action for damages, the doctor will be vulnerable to charges of ignoring the computer. On the other hand, if the doctor follows the expert system's recommendation, he or she will have the alibi of 'blaming the computer' if the patient comes to harm. The system could therefore lead to a *de facto* automation of diagnoses because doctors may be subtly constrained to follow what the computer says and to disregard their own judgements. It also means that inexperienced doctors will have fewer opportunities to learn for themselves how to assess a patient's condition.

Guidelines for the office of the future

The aim of new office technology should be to form a symbiotic partnership between the user and the computer in which the weakness of one partner is balanced by the strengths of the other. Working with computer-based systems can then become a challenge, not a surrender of human initiative. There is no single route to a successful outcome, but some themes have been developed in this chapter and Chapters 3 and 4 which offer guidelines on desirable characteristics that should be aimed at when designing and developing new systems (*see Table 5.2*). These embody a set of socio-technical design principles that I call a Scandinavian model of the office of the future, but which has its roots and flowering in many countries. Systems designed along these lines have generally provided better quality and more effective solutions for customers/clients and employees, as well as having also improved efficiency.

Table 5.2 Desirable characteristics for an office information system

Desirable characteristics	*Comment*
No continuous monitoring	Systems should not monitor the activities of managers every second. If they do, managers might work more efficiently, but they are likely to be less effective and creative
Assume user has knowledge	Systems should not treat the user as a dumb being. They should exploit the user's substantial knowledge of how the task is to be performed
Allow high discretion	Computers should give users more discretion and autonomy in doing their job, not less
Possible to modify	Systems should be modifiable by users, who should be trained to do so effectively
Understandable structure	Users should be able to appreciate how they are organised, without having to become experts on technical aspects
Assist learning	Systems should enhance skills and stimulate users to learn better ways of performing their jobs
Support intuition	Computers have traditionally supported logical, rationalizing human abilities. It is vital that they also respect and assist other important human qualities, such as intuition, creativity and emotions
Enhance social contact	New office technology should maintain and improve informal social contacts, rather than inhibit them.

Training to meet the managerial challenge

The speed of innovation in office jobs, working skills and technology requires that training and education for managers is an absolute necessity, not an optional nicety. It should be provided in an environment that allows training to succeed, such as having some degree of job security and a close link between training and real jobs. In this context, it is interesting to note that in Japan managers in big companies virtually have job security for life, with promotion achieved mainly on the basis of age. This has been an important factor in enabling Japanese management to adapt to the multi-skill area of electronic information technology.

Few managers will need to know the bits and bytes of computing. Systems are generally becoming much easier to use and to program by non-experts, although they may still lack some desirable human–computer communication features. The key skills for which training is needed include:

(1) A general understanding of the basic principles and applications of information technology, particularly the notion of software control.
(2) The ability to decide whether a problem is suited to being solved by computer.
(3) How to formulate problems in a manner appropriate to computerization.
(4) Sufficient knowledge about systems analysis and design to direct the development of new systems.
(5) Knowledge of available technical options to help evaluate systems.
(6) The ability, where necessary, to be able to modify installed systems.

Probably the greatest demand is in acquiring the skills of problem identification and definition that are becoming more important than problem solving as such.

Awareness and the ability to cope

Managers need to be trained in an awareness of the new opportunities offered by computer-based technology and in how to cope with subsequent changes involved in introducing and managing the systems. *Awareness training* is often regarded as synonymous with the concept of *overcoming resistance to change*. This should not be so. The aim is not for the elite in charge of the change to persuade and manipulate others to accept new systems unquestioningly. Instead, managers should be informed and educated in a manner that enables them to participate positively in the shaping of the system.

The wide availability of low cost microcomputers has provided a major boost to management awareness of new office technology. Many managers have home computers, possibly bought initially for their children. The Firestone Company has encouraged this trend by setting up a computer store near its headquarters and offering employees discounts for such computers. Within organizations, personal computers have been made available in workshops, information centres (*see* Chapter 9) and directly on managers' desks. This can break down myths about the difficulty of using the technology and give an appreciation of its potential. Personal computers, however, can give a distorted impression of computing because they emphasize particular styles of programming and relatively simplistic database management and software modelling techniques. A broader perspective of information technology developments should, therefore, be provided.

Training managers to cope with the *consequences* of technological developments is far more complicated. Many organizations take the easy way out and concentrate only on explaining the *how* rather than the *why* of new office technology. Instead of providing the necessary training to develop existing managers, organizations often rely on getting rid of employees who fail to cope and employing younger people with appropriate qualifications. This wastes existing expertise and talent. It also plants the seeds of future problems. As Walter K. Joelson, chief economist at General Electric of the US has put it, 'How to get rid of unwanted workers is the name of the game now. But in seven to ten years time it will be tough to find the people we want to hire'[2].

Most organizations, unfortunately, give low priority to the retraining of managers. Unless there is a fresh and realistic reappraisal of future skills requirements, backed by systematic new training initiatives, scarce human talent will be wasted, now and in the future. In the end, we will all lose if a short sighted attitude is taken to preparing managers to succeed with new office technology.

Recommendations

(1) Formulate strategic organization objectives to guide the

development of new office technology to meet the required goals regarding the nature of work. Do not allow the technology to push the organization in directions it does not wish to go.

(2) Encourage individual users and departments to participate in the creation of systems. Such developments should not be left primarily in the hands of technically oriented specialists because the systems have a direct impact on the nature of managers' jobs, which is essentially a human issue.

(3) Take specific steps to understand the potential negative impact of new office technology on managerial jobs and undertake practical initiatives to avoid them, particularly in terms of the tendency of computer-based systems to:
   (a) Increase structuring and formalization of individual jobs.
   (b) Make people do those things computers are best at, in a way that optimizes computer, not human, performance.
   (c) Increase detailed performance monitoring.

(4) Use new office technology to enhance interpersonal relationships and job satisfaction. The commitment and effectiveness of managers are often dependent on the establishment of good relationships with others and a self-motivated desire to want to 'get on and do the job.'

(5) Give high priority, backed by appropriate resources and authority, to training programmes that increase managers' awareness of the potential of computer-based technology and assist them to handle the change to new systems.

(6) Consider redeploying existing staff, supported by necessary training, if it is necessary to reduce the number of managers because their work is made superfluous by new information systems. The experience of existing managers is a valuable resource that should not be wasted.

(7) To cope with the high rate of job change induced by new technology and to avoid the spectre of being one of those managers who loses her or his job because they cannot cope, individuals should take the initiative to learn enough about the technology to be able to:
   (a) Critically evaluate different proposals for new systems.
   (b) Independently formulate requirements for new systems.
   (c) Have hands-on experience with some form of computing in an environment where experimentation is possible without being watched by others or disciplined for making errors.

(d) Develop small scale, 'user driven' software using a fourth generation language (*see* Chapter 3).

References

1. Mumford, E., Successful systems design, in Otway, H.J. and Peltu, M., *New Office Technology: Human and Organizational Aspects*, Frances Pinter, London; Ablex, Norwood, N.J. (1983)
2. Special Report, A new era for management, *Business Week*, 34–58 (25th April 1983)
3. Peters, T.J. and Waterman, R. H., *In Search of Excellence*, Harper and Row, New York (1982)
4. Weizenbaum, J., *Computer Power and Human Reason*, Freeman, San Francisco (1976); Penguin Books, London (1984)
5. Pomfrett, S. M., Olphert, C. W. and Eason, K. D., Work organization implications of word processing, paper for *Interact '84 conference*, Intenational Federation for Information Processing (IFIP), London, September 1984
6. Simons, G.L., *Towards Fifth-Generation Computers*, National Computing Centre, Manchester (1983)

Bibliography

The following publications are also relevant to topics discussed in this chapter.

Blauner, R., *Alienation and Freedom*, University of Chicago Press, Chicago (1964)

Michael, D.N., Some long-range implications of computer technology for human behaviour in organizations, in Etzioni, A., *Readings in Modern Organizations*, Prentice-Hall, Englewood Cliffs, N.J. (1969)

Mintzberg, H., *The Nature of Managerial Work*, Harper and Row, London (1973)

Mumford, E., *Job Satisfaction: A Study of Computer Specialists*, Longman, London (1972)

Nylehn, B., Frihagen, T. and Halgunset, J., *Edb-systemer og Mellemledere*, Institutt for Industriel Miljoførskning, Trondheim (1982)

6

Managing the Changing Organization

Michel Crozier and Francis Pavé

Introduction

The application of computer-based information technology can lead to complex organizational changes which need to be carefully managed. New procedures and information flows appropriate to the technology can require fundamental changes to work procedures and social interactions. The power and authority exercised by particular individuals and groups in the organization may alter. Informal arrangements developed to facilitate the smooth running of an organization can be disrupted.

This chapter discusses how managers can develop strategies to cope with these organizational and technical changes to achieve successful innovation in office work. It explores the advantages and problems of attempting to use computers to respond to the growth of organizational complexity. The key stages in the evaluation and development of systems are identified. Advice is given on how to achieve a harmonious evolution of social and technical aspects, illustrated by examples of actual responses to new computer-based systems.

Coping with complexity

Many forms of bureaucracy, covering a variety of management and administrative methods, have been developed in an attempt to handle the complex interactions within any organization or social group of a substantial size. Public and private bureaucracies, however, have proved to be incapable of controlling such organizational complexity and, in fact, may contribute to its increase. The arrival of computers in the 1960s appeared to offer a means of making traditional bureaucratic practices work. In action, however, computers have often tended to compound bureaucratic inefficiencies and inflexibilities.

The use of digital information as a management tool is nothing new. Six thousand years ago the fabulous wealth of the Mesopotamian states was kept under control by applying the invention of the earliest techniques of numerical symbols and accounting. This pre-dated the development of cuneiform writing. Now, computer manufacturers have fuelled the belief that, at last, people have been given a fully effective means of dominating the extraordinary amount of data generated by the diversity of economic, social and cultural activities in society. One would have expected private and public bureaucracies to welcome the computer as a valuable helpmate. However, experience has shown that they felt threatened by the new technology and refused to make any substantial changes in their ways of operation.

Hierarchy, distance and secrecy

The classical bureaucratic approach which still infuses administration and management styles in most organizations is based on a *hierarchical* structure in which *formal* rules control the activities of the whole organization within a consistent framework. In reality, *informal* ways of handling day-to-day actions have been developed by individuals and groups to enable the organization to adapt continually to circumstances unforeseen in the formal procedures.

The ability of local units in the organization to modify or bypass formal procedures helps the organization to evolve by learning from experience. It also gives important motivational incentives to local management and staff, who have a degree of power and authority to negotiate how best to meet unexpected needs. This autonomy has been made possible because there has usually been sufficient remoteness of the local unit from the centres of hierarchical control. Informal arrangements have generally been kept secret and separate from official procedures. For example, in every office there are informal interactions between people, from chance meetings to organized discussions, which are used to gain a feel for opinion on a subject before formal reports are written and meetings held to decide policies.

The combination of hierarchy, distance and secrecy has enabled even large bureaucracies to maintain corporate coherence while allowing for the adaptability needed to keep in touch with 'grassroots' needs.

Programming the organization

People carry out office work in an environment where there is a great deal of uncertainty and ambiguity. They must use intelligence and imagination to interpret information that is often incomplete; to reach decisions when many factors are unknown; and to respond to the unexpected by adapting established procedures or creating innovative solutions to new problems. People learn from experience and apply that knowledge so that the organizations in which they work can progress in a world that is continually evolving and changing.

Most computers, on the other hand, have no innate intelligence and no imagination. Detailed sequences of program instructions must be fed into them before computers can act. These instructions must be unambiguous, exhaustive (nothing can be left to chance), and consistent, allowing no contradictions within their internal logic. Faced with any conflicting propositions, the computer allows for no grey areas or middle-road compromises: the computer must decide that one is 'true' and the other 'false'. (Note that knowledge-based systems and artificial intelligence techniques aim to develop software that is better able to handle ambiguity and uncertainty, *see* Chapter 3.)

As the price of computer hardware has fallen and the range of capabilities has expanded (*see* Chapter 2), it has become clear that the main challenge posed by computers relates to the constraints imposed by the predominant role of software in controlling all applications of the technology. The formal model of the structure and functions of an organization need to be made explicit (*transparent*) so that programs can be written. Once embodied in software, the computer can insist that anyone using it must follow the rules precisely, monitoring or prohibiting any deviations.

Software is likely to define and control an increasing range of organizational activities. Computers will also speed up the flow of information. By making procedures transparent, opportunities for developing effective informal arrangements may become limited. Senior managers can be brought into closer direct contact with operational levels in the organization, bypassing some middle management. Organizations may no longer be able to operate on the basis of distance, secrecy and a relatively slow movement of information. Software therefore has a major impact on the personal and social activities of an organization.

Success in introducing new office technology depends on marrying the logical information-handling power of computers to how their users actually behave, not how the formal organizational procedures expect them to act. The development of software requires expertise in understanding and expressing human and social needs, as well as the ability to produce the necessary code. Yet too often the creation of computer systems is viewed as a mainly technical process.

Creating an effective computer system

The process of computerization is one of continuous evolution. It cannot be neatly divided into independent and consecutive stages, as is frequently done when presenting computing developments from a technologically oriented perspective. There are, however, phases in the creation of a computer-based system which can be categorized as primarily concerned with social and organizational issues, while others properly belong more in the technical domain.

These stages are:

(1) Human and organizational aspects.
  (a) *Feasibility studies* investigate options open to the organization in the future, leading to decisions which extend far beyond the realm of computing. Each study is unique, rooted in the situation prevailing within a particular organization. They include analyses which give an insight into likely costs and benefits associated with any investment decision.
  (b) *Systems analysis* defines a *functional model* of the organization: the functions carried out and the relationships between them. It specifies the chronology and logic of the procedures and information flows to be computerized and establishes what human and material resources are needed to achieve the desired objectives.

(2) Technical developments.
  (a) *Systems design* specifies computer requirements in minute detail, such as calculations performed; type and volume of information (customer/client records, letters, reports, etc); type and frequency of information transactions (answering questions, updating files, etc).
  (b) *Program writing* produces the full and coherent sequence of instructions which computer hardware can understand and execute.
  (c) *Program testing* finds out how the software will operate

when applied to live operational applications. Seeks logical errors (*bugs*) in the code and tries to eliminate (*debug*) them before live operation of the software begins.

It should be emphasized that this is not meant to represent discrete stages in a linear sequence of events. There are many overlaps between stages. The result of one stage can influence previous ones. The live system will be subject to continuous modification because further bugs are found or the specification is altered for organizational and functional reasons. (The term 'systems design' is sometimes used to encompass what here has been called systems analysis *and* systems design. Chapter 7 examines the planning process from a different perspective which incorporates the phases described here.)

When computer logic meets the real world

The first phase (feasibility studies and systems analysis) is similar to that which would have been carried out even if computerization was not involved. The second phase should produce a program which is a logical, symbolic transcription of the organizational model developed during systems analysis. In practice, it is never so. The model of the organization as embodied in the software has its own logical rules and vetting of internal consistency which differ from the reality that underlies it.

The software is therefore a logical version of an organizational analysis that is itself an abstraction of the tangible reality in which work is actually carried out. This can be regarded as a form of *hyper-reality*, a concept derived by analogy from the art movement which rejected the emotional subjectivity of painting and took photography as the 'objective' image of real life. Working from the photographic source, the artist creates an image which is regarded as being even more objective, 'more real' than the photograph.

With computerization, the real world is initially subjected to a functional analysis which is then tested, stripped-down and re-rationalized according to the rules of computer software. A transition is made from how things are, to a functional view of how they should be, then to a purely abstract, mathematical model of information-handling behaviour. The computer becomes an essential tool in attempting to subject organizational activity to a process of strict rationalization.

The testing phase is the critical moment in creating a computer system: the point where computer logic comes face to face with the reality it represents and aims to assist. It is a time of great emotional intensity for the computer expert or team. If the program fails, it must be re-worked. As problems in the software often have their roots in analysis and design, the re-working affects earlier phases. In this somewhat insidious way, technical questions are allowed to affect social factors. As the human agent responsible for presenting organizational models to the software and for writing and testing program code, the computing expert now possesses the key to the reality which the software will expect its users to follow, as specified by its logical procedures.

Potential hazards of computerization

Before computerization, people could easily adapt any formal organizational model to the social realities of working life. The model did not need to have a rigid logical backbone and could be relatively imprecise. Such 'fuzziness' made it easier for the model to be adapted to meet unexpected circumstances. People could absorb, distort or digest the formal functions and interactions expected of them to create more pragmatic informal methods, when necessary. Such is the inevitable consequence of everyday power-play within an organization.

Computer software, however, requires the organizational model to follow logical and mathematical rules, expecting it to be consistent, exhaustive and non-contradictory. The process of analysis and programming results in an improved organizational logic, *hyperfunctionalism*. This has many advantages because it provides a systematic framework in which to examine and understand how the organization works. Together with the information-handling aids provided by computer-based systems, this can lead to great improvements in efficiency and effectiveness.

There are, however, some dangers inherent in this process. The relentless logic of computers allows no grey areas. It can reveal various arrangements between individuals and groups as being totally 'irrational', although they may play an important role in oiling the wheels of working life. The programming of work procedures into the software may make social control more meticulous and more rigid.

The result may be a bug-free program but there is no guarantee that the software is a good representation of reality. Quite the contrary: the hyper-rationalist approach engendered by the nature of computer systems assumes a social organization that is transparent, unambiguous and totally unrealistic. Observations of the use of computer-based information systems have shown that the logic of the computer system is all too frequently ill-suited to the needs of the human systems they purport to govern. Transparency and the need to satisfy logical criteria can inhibit the adaptability necessary to an organization's survival.

Another major issue with computerization is its all-pervasiveness. Too often, however, computerization is regarded as primarily a technical activity. When analysing costs and benefits in feasibility studies there has been a tendency to focus on the changes related to the introduction of the technology itself, although there is no means of distinguishing the disturbances which arise as a direct result of computerization from those which arise from other changes in work processes, information flows and organizational responsibilities (*see* Chapter 8).

Innovations in the use of computer-based systems can reverberate across all organizational boundaries. The analyst must go beyond a problem's technical limits in order to make the underlying procedures more explicit. For example, if one starts with the objective of computerizing the management of a manufacturing production line, it quickly becomes clear that the first step is to understand fully how the whole workforce is occupied and how information and work methods relating to production interact with other parts of the organization.

The systematic analysis of information requirements can create an impetus which encourages attempts to integrate all the factors which are associated with them. It is this inevitable process which has induced computer specialists to conceive, and sometimes design, vast integrated systems whose only achievement has been to demonstrate that in practice they do not work. Chapters 7 to 9 discuss how to overcome these problems by managing the introduction of new technology in a carefully planned, but flexible and evolutionary manner.

Reactions to computerization

During the development and introduction of computer-based office systems, technical specialists and management decision-makers often encounter problems which they refer to as *resistance to change*. This is a somewhat simplistic view of a variety of organizational reactions to the new systems. Errors constantly arise if the only sociological dimension taken account of during feasibility studies and onwards is a narrow concept of 'resistance' by people and groups.

Our own work has identified three major types of reaction; this does not claim to cover every possible response but highlights the variety and complexity of the factors involved:

(1) Outright rejection of the computer system and the organizational arrangements it implies.
(2) Acceptance of computerization without any significant changes in the organization or in behaviour patterns.
(3) Modification of the computer system according to the evolving needs of its organizational context, leading to acceptance by all protagonists, improved social cohesion and better communications within the human environment.

These responses are illustrated by the following three case studies. Similar experiences have been identified in most other applications of computer-based systems.

Rejection of a miracle

When interviewing a computer specialist there is one question which usually uncovers a deep-rooted hurt: 'Have you ever had to abandon a project which was on the verge of becoming operational?' The specialist is likely to turn pale and launch into an indignant attack on the unfairness and obscurantism of those who failed to take advantage of the computer miracle that had been offered to them. The expert's personal dignity has been punctured by a social system that has rejected her or his model of reality.

The clearest example of this in our experience was a nationwide company which decided to optimize its vehicle fleet. The computer team worked night and day to construct a beautiful program. Its technical elegance was admired by other specialists. Everything worked perfectly on the computer.

Then came the time to go live with the system. At that point, after some hesitation, the drivers went on strike. The key problem was that, in the enthusiasm for pursuing the logic of the computer, it had been forgotten that managing a vehicle fleet also means managing the drivers of the vehicle. The bargaining and negotiation processes previously developed by the social system were unable to withstand the introduction of a new computer model of reality (*see* Chapter 10 for a fuller discussion on the impact of computers on bargaining and negotiations).

The transport company decided to withdraw the 'miracle'

program for all time and to hide it in the deepest recesses of collective memory. It was agreed that, all things considered, the firm was working quite well without it. Such an outcome has occurred frequently in the computing Chamber of Horrors.

Bypassing the computer

All too frequently, feasibility studies fail to take account of two key elements in social reality: freedom and power. The computer specialists tend to accept the formal view of the relationships of power and authority within the organization and incorporates these assumptions into the software. When the freedom of individuals or groups is restricted because their actions are subject to organizational transparency and computer monitoring, there is usually an attempt to circumvent that transparency. The possible consequences of this is illustrated by the case of a production scheduling and central system developed for a small French factory.

The key organizational protagonists involved were the work-scheduling and production departments. The schedulers saw the installation of the system as a means of bringing production under proper control. They believed that the monitoring of work in progress would ensure that all relevant information would be available so that an exact picture of what was happening in the workshops could be examined via the computer system, whenever required. In practice, the transparency imposed by the system remained for only a few months following the startup of the computer system.

Individuals in the scheduling department and workshops could not stick to their preprogrammed procedures because they were faced with *ad hoc* demands that obliged them to make exceptions from what should happen theoretically. The scheduling department, for example, had regular negotiations with customers which resulted in the need to reschedule jobs continually, lengthening and shortening delivery deadlines. Works supervisors, under continuous pressure from management to increase productivity, were obliged not only to ignore production standards (such as the re-use of offcuts, short cuts on production tolerances, and so on) but also to interrupt work in progress for their own supervision of unscheduled damaged jobs. The situation eventually came full circle with the scheduling staff in and out of the workshops making visual checks on the progress of orders while customers waited on the telephone.

The protagonists in this system reconquered their freedom of manoeuvre by, quite legitimately, juggling the data. The attempt to introduce transparancy and a hyper-rational way of working was a total failure. Computerization was effectively bypassed, leaving the same patterns of work and social behaviour as before. All those concerned re-established their power to renegotiate, at short notice, the progress of individual orders and the consequent daily workload.

Shifts in the balances of power

The establishment and exercise of power by various groups and individuals is a vital aspect of the behaviour of all organizations, but the underlying complexities have defied all attempts at computer modelling. This failure is illustrated by the attempt to swing the balance of power between the scheduling department and workshops in the previous example.

The aims of computerization were not only to model the organization of work, and hence of the predictability of workshop activities, but also to give the scheduling department more power. The workshop staff, however, established areas of ambiguity to protect themselves from over-detailed inspection, particularly when justifying actions performed in the pursuit of productivity. Paradoxically, the initial consequence was that the scheduling department was trapped by its own planning, which became too predictable. Using the justification of 'customer service', the schedulers also began to adopt a non-conformist approach so as to re-establish their negotiating position. In the last analysis, neither side accepted being subordinate either to each other or to the hyper-rational software model of the organization.

This situation is common when introducing computer-based systems. Computer modelling can attempt to crystallize a balance of power in favour of one side or another, but the protagonist whose power is being diminished will feel it necessary to obtain sufficient freedom to act independently. This freedom gives the opportunity to negotiate local arrangements, which gives the organization flexibility to adapt to changing circumstances and is also an important motivational force for individuals. By refusing to be shackled by a system which took their decisions for them, those involved widened their room for manoeuvre. The relationships and interactions between the schedulers and workshop staff also ceased to be regulated and closed, returning to being negotiated and open.

The collective power of a group is built on its ability to negotiate arrangements which differ from the predetermined model. This power is based on the exploitation and manipulation of relevant uncertainties. That is why any model which purports to give a full account of human activity and to control it is doomed to failure. Human systems are woven from exchange in negotiation. Computer logic is incapable of resolving the problems inherent in governing such systems: reality is always more complex than an abstract model of its behaviour. The process adopted by the schedulers and production staff of introducing vagueness and uncertainty into the computer model was worthwhile and rational because it enabled them to regain control over parts of their territory.

How to master the technology

The analysis of the previous example highlights some problems that can occur. Modelling, planning and computerization can also lead to improved management and act as a catalyst for enhancing teamwork. This is illustrated by the working of a computerized budget control system in the French division of a multinational corporation which we have had the opportunity to study. At first, the system seemed to be a failure, but on investigation it was found to be a considerable success. The main reason for this success was that sufficient automony was given to local managers, within a corporate framework built on the computer system.

The computerized budget management service, which was based on centralized mainframes, had originally been set up to take over the lengthy and tedious task of preparing the annual budget and its monthly status report. The aim was to facilitate the work of the budget control department and to allow managers to test the likely consequences of different decisions so as to optimize production requirements to meet various market hypotheses and, consequently, to obtain the most effective operation of manufacturing plants. The reality was somewhat different.

Despite computerization, the process of preparing the budget remained as lengthy as before; the testing of market hypotheses and their repercussions had to be abandoned. During the development of the computer system much time was wasted searching for errors, waiting at terminals when the mainframe processor became overloaded with work, and coping with computer breakdowns. Nobody took responsibility for the vast quantity of figures produced by the computer in printed reports and managers seemed to give them just a cursory glance.

The positive effects came from a radical change in the attitude of executives towards budget management and the way in which the system was allowed to evolve over a period of time without trying to impose the initial, imperfect model. The computer system resulted in a change of the *nature* rather than the quantity of work needed to draw up and follow through a budget. Instead of spending the bulk of budgetary work gathering and producing data, the work switched to tracking down errors and reprocessing information. Although this was also time consuming, the logical requirements for data consistency imposed by the data management software resulted in a demand for greater accuracy of information.

In the days of manual budget preparation, almost anything went and the whole budgetary control system lost credibility. The benefit of the new, accurate and more rational approach introduced by the computer was to provide better control, based on more reliable figures. Previously, when managers failed to meet targets set for them, and could find no other explanation, they could assert that the figures were wrong. That is why budget management was not taken seriously. Computerization prevented managers using this excuse; executives now allowed themselves to be directed by management by objective techniques. The preparation and follow-through of the budget allowed dialogue, bargaining, negotiation and agreement amongst participants. Teamwork was encouraged amongst all managers involved by holding meetings which became the final legitimation of the collective process.

Importance of evolution and local autonomy

The turnaround in the computer system, from an apparent failure existing in a vacuum to a beneficial influence working in the mainstream of corporate activity, did not occur overnight. It was the result of a long evolutionary period. In the first phase, a large degree of liberty was allowed in the way particular departments and establishments pursued computerization. This left the mechanisms of producing and distributing budgets unaffected. When all units had established a computer system in their own way, a process of centralization was begun, initially involving divisions in the company and, subsequently, Head Office. After five years, the transition was made from a local management system to one which was centrally defined.

Head Office used the computer to categorize the systems previously operated by individual executives and to define the structure of the overall budget and the individual budget lines. As usually happens with a centralized system that has to apply to everybody, the budgets received by local management were too broad and imprecise to allow them to analyse discrepancies properly and to take appropriate actions to correct them. Instead of rejecting or bypassing the computer system, as in the previous examples, these executives developed a two-level response. At the corporate level, they used the central computer system as a standard reference to facilitate communication and agreement throughout the organization. At the same time, as centralization proceeded, parallel unofficial systems developed locally; for example, using decentralized computer hardware which escaped the attention of corporate administration.

The two apparently conflicting information systems within the corporation worked well together. The official, unchallenged system was a vital tool in structuring corporate identity. The unofficial, dissident system allowed local management to tune the figures in the budgets to their circumstances. The actual numbers in the budget reports were relatively unimportant in themselves, which is why the printouts from Head Office were not widely used at local level, but they were the mainstay of corporate meetings that interpreted variations from budgets and identified problems. Individuals at all levels had to account for and justify their actions according to a commonly agreed form of thought-categorization, terminology and measurement required by corporate headquarters and implemented by the computer.

Marketing, technical and financial experts were thus able to communicate beyond the boundaries of their own specializations. Head Office received the information it needed, namely a detailed understanding of what was going on in each unit, which dovetailed with each step up the hierarchical ladder. In this way, the corporation had achieved one of the prime purposes of computerization: the ability of executives to evaluate the real situation and for the organization to be capable of effectively managing its own complexity. The computer gave Head Office staff the means of formulating corporate policy and to have its point of view accepted as the common basis for all management decisions. At the same time, and crucial to the success of the system, corporate policy was sufficiently flexible to leave some freedom of manoeuvre at the grassroots.

An example to follow

This short case study is provided as an example of technology being mastered in a way that benefits all aspects of the organization. It shows how a social system can react positively to a technological system; how technology can play a governing role but is yet governed. The computer system is in control in the sense that it provides the common framework for intra-organizational communications and establishes a number of restrictive, logical rules for the structure and exchange of information. The system itself is, at the same time, controlled by the individuals who use it without being totally subordinated to it.

To achieve this, Head Office used its managerial power to lay down rules to be applied universally. Wisely, corporate management regarded these computerized procedures as an incentive to improve co-operation and communication rather than as an attempt to regulate human activity in a bureaucratic way. The computer was not seen as an all-encompassing solution to every problem but as an aid to help people to resolve difficulties in their own ways. The system was, of course, unable to dispense with all conflicts, but the budget management system became an effective means of settling disputes that arose.

Initially, the computer system shifted the balance of power away from Head Office, while individual units developed their own system. By judicious use of the computer once the centralization process began in earnest, power flowed back to Head Office. The side-by-side existence of official and unofficial systems subsequently allowed a reasonable balance to be maintained between the individuals and groups involved, with a better integration of their various rationales.

A strategy for coping with change

The examples provided above, each typical of a particular type of reaction to computerization, show there can be no guarantee about whether a particular system will be a success or a failure in live operation. Any management strategy to cope effectively with the change induced by computer systems calls for an approach which takes account of the confrontation between the hyper-rationality of formal software models and the actual behaviour of the organization. Traditional methods of developing organizational models are too imprecise when tested against the criteria of logical consistency and exhaustiveness required by computers. On the other hand, analyses made by computing specialists are too partial, too analytical and too fragmented to be adequate.

A broader systems approach must be adopted which takes account of the variety of relevant human, organizational, economic and technical factors and which understands the need for continuous adaptation of the system based on lessons derived from actual experience.

Maintaining flexibility

The hyper-rational approach of the computer specialists may appeal to those managers whose habitual reasoning instinct is to try to identify understandable, concrete solutions and to simplify a reality which is naturally complex and frequently impenetrable and inconsistent. The process of computerization seen from a technical viewpoint often aims to reduce, or remove, uncertainty and to provide 'objective' answers to many of the apparently intractable challenges faced by managers.

Such an approach may be adequate when dealing with tasks contained within *closed systems* which operate within set boundaries and follow predictable, pre-determined rules. The social activities involved in running an organization, however, form an *open system* which is in a constant state of internal flux as well as interacting with a variety of external agents, such as clients and customers, the competitive marketplace, global economic determinants and government legislation. Any attempt to translate this ever-changing picture into a totally transparent model of how an organization behaves is doomed to failure. The very notion of organizational transparency is a myth which can give birth to its own software chimera if there is a literal implementation of the organizational and communications models generated by computer specialists.

The example of the small provincial factory where schedulers and production staff bypassed the computer illustrates what happens when that rationalist monster meets two fundamental factors in social organization: the freedom of the individual and the constant quest by individuals and groups for greater power within the system. The case of the French subsidiary of the multinational organization indicated how a harmonious accommodation can be reached between formal corporate constraints and the need for informal local adaptation. Head Office showed enough intelligence to tolerate a dissident information system beyond its control. Such a dissident system is an essential factor in the social and technological success described.

If the centralization had been too restrictive and inquisitive, the impetus engendered by the computerization would have been broken and the ultimate goal of a decentralized system would have been missed. Individuals would have taken refuge behind print-outs and the entire operation would have sunk beyond hope. The key message of this success, and others like it, is that managers must not be content with a simplified, purely functional, technocratic approach to computerization. Despite their consistency and mathematical validity, computer models fail to take account of social dimensions. In order to develop an analysis which allows a better understanding of the subtle interplay between individuals and tasks, the dynamics of the operational system must be considered, as well as the static structures and relationships.

Adapt to survive

Irrespective of the type of computer system installed, those involved in it participate in a learning process. Managers must be prepared to have the initial project distorted, reoriented and redefined several times over. That is why one of the indicators of success in the management of change is the introduction of feedback mechanisms to adjust and correct the route being taken. Accepting that systems are subject to dynamic change is at the heart of the innovation process. It means using knowledge acquired from real experiences, from mistakes as well as positive consequences, as a way of keeping that dynamic movement on course so as to obtain the desired objectives.

If an organization seeks stability, it will never dominate its environment. Like any living organism, organizations must adapt to survive. It is the survival of the organization that must be the driving force, not the survival of a particular computer system, which should be only the means to an end. The rejection and burial of the computer system by the transport company in the earlier example illustrated this point. In other cases, the individuals may counteract a system which they perceive as working against their interests through a longer trial of strength or through a gradual paralysis. A computer system which is managed in a way that fails to give local freedom for adaptation can lead to the collapse of the whole organization.

Our example of successful computerization came about primarily because the organization was willing to evolve the system in the light of experience rather than because of any special management foresight or technical brilliance. To some extent, the happy outcome was fortuitous. No thought had been given initially to the broader consequences that would arise. By gradually accepting the dynamics of computerized budget management, executives discovered increased room to negotiate their own objectives and points of view. People reacted individually, rather than collectively, without really analysing the whole situation or fully mastering the complexity of their own system. A happy system of human and technical interactions was eventually constructed on the basis of almost incidental happenings which resulted from relying on negotiation as the motor for consensus.

The radical change in attitude that took place over a period of time was effective because all those involved were given the opportunity to draw lessons from their experience and to apply that knowledge to optimizing their situation. Centralization, the natural tendency of all head offices, proved to be an ideal way of integrating corporate activities throughout the organization. Dissidence was tolerated so long as it did not jeopardize the entire corporation, which allowed sufficient flexibility to satisfy individuals.

How to achieve success

A successful strategy for managing innovation in office systems must be based on knowledge of how individuals and social systems act. It must accept a dynamic picture of organizational life and use real experience as the basis for managing human groups. Such an approach plays little part in the functional models of organizations developed by traditional analytical means and is even less influential in the hyperfunctional software models of organizational behaviour.

The success story we have analysed indicates that chance can lead to a desirable outcome, provided the organization is sufficiently flexible. This is not meant, however, as a justification for managers 'flying blind'. The final result of any process of innovation may be unpredictable, but a strategic long-term plan is a vital element in steering the course of change. The strategy must itself be innovative, taking a fresh look at all the factors affected during a period of rapid change. It must be an open strategy which willingly accepts the need for its own change and adaptation.

Recommendations

(1) A long-term strategy must be developed to handle the complex human, organizational, technical and economic issues which arise during the process of technological innnovation in information systems. This strategy must have the following characteristics:

(a) *Comprehensive*. It must attempt to cover all relevant aspects and avoid concentrating on narrow technical and short-term economic issues.

(b) *Flexible and evolutionary*. The strategy (and the organization) should be regarded as a living organism undergoing dynamic change according to the influences on it from its operational environment.

(c) *Responsive feedback*. The control mechanisms for adapting the strategy (and the organization) should include the effective implementation of lessons learnt from real experiences.

(d) *Step-by-step planning*. Carefully phased plans should be formulated to allow the system to be developed in stages, allowing time for adjustments if necessary. The plan must ensure that systems are compatible and interlock where necessary. Trying to computerize many activities in a single integrated system is to be avoided.

(2) Regard the development of a computer system as consisting of two main phases:

(a) Human and organizational aspects: feasibility studies and systems analysis.

(b) Technical issues: systems design, program writing and software testing.

These phases, and the stages within them, do not form a once-off, linear, chronological progression. There is a considerable degree of overlap, interaction and feedback between them on a continuing basis. Controls must be established to avoid allowing computing specialists to dominate the process by independently reshaping previous phases in order to solve program faults during testing.

(3) Managers must have a good understanding of the opportunities and limitations of computer software. They must appreciate, in particular, why programs require logical consistency, unambiguity and exhaustiveness, where such techniques can be applied to assist organizational actions, and the types of activities where such techniques are

inappropriate.

(4) Treat the existence of informal operational procedures and informal communications networks as a positive influence and make allowances for the co-existence of official formal systems and informal dissident arrangements.

(5) Encourage freedom for local negotiations and bargaining, provided it does not seriously conflict with corporate requirements.

Bibliography

The following publications are relevant to topics discussed in this chapter.

Ballé, C. and Peaucelle, J.L., *Le Pouvoir Informatique dans l'enteprise*, Edition d'Organisation, Paris (1972)

Crozier, M. and Friedberg E., *Actors and Systems: The Politics of Collective Action*, University of Chicago Press, Chicago (1980)

Lussato, B., *Le défi informatique*, Editions Fayard, Paris (1981)

Nora, S. and Minc, A., *L'informatisation de la Société*, Documentation Francaise, Paris (1978): English version: *The Computerization of Society*, MIT Press, Cambridge, Mass (1980)

Pavé, F., Le katangais et le financier ou les limites de l'audit informatique, *L'Informatique Professionnelle*, (8) (December 1982)

Vitalis, A., *Informatique, pouvoir et Libertés*, Economica, Paris (1981)

7

Planning for Successful Innovation

Peter G. W. Keen

Introduction

Before new systems are introduced, managers need to create a strategy to co-ordinate the complex behavioural and technical aspects of office technology. Analyses of organizational and user requirements, as discussed in the rest of the book, focus on *what* new information systems should do. A more technical 'engineering' approach, which has often driven the planning process in many organizations, is mainly concerned with *how* computer-based systems work and the kinds of technical solutions that are most appropriate. In addition, there is the *why* of office technology: why, in terms of business effectiveness, efficiency, quality of life, and so on, new systems justify the risks and investments involved.

This chapter presents an approach, based on practical experiences, which will assist organizations to be imaginative and effective in developing methods to integrate the why, what and how. It explains that a clear vision of the 'why' should drive the 'what' and 'how'. The way such a vision can be built is discussed in detail and the responsibilities of top management are explored. In addition, advice is provided on how to proceed from an overall image to develop the more specific, well structured and carefully phased plans needed to turn that vision into reality.

The purpose of planning

Office technology is associated with computers. Most managers are aware of how hard it has always been to design, introduce and use computer-based systems, so it is not surprising that senior executives often feel uncomfortable about how to play a positive role in preparing for new office systems. This anxiety can be exacerbated because office technology plans must cover many types of technical developments and risks, including project management, the selection of vendors and the phasing and integration of a variety of items of hardware, software, databases and telecommunications. Without strong pro-active direction from management, there is a tendency for the process of change to be driven by technical considerations and an engineering view of office systems.

To be effective, strategic planning must begin with a *vision*, a concrete picture of a desired and attainable future, which lucidly explains why changes are to take place. The lack of technological understanding amongst many managers and the resultant uncertainty has, however, meant that organizations often have fog instead of vision: a blurred and ambiguous picture of the future that office technology is intended to help create. It does not make sense to base complex and expensive plans on fog. There may be no tidy, well-defined experiences to draw on in building a concrete picture of the future, but it is possible to define a sharply focused strategy that systematically helps people at many levels of the organization to shape a vision.

Change in office work should not take place on the basis of a rigid predetermined view of the organization and how it functions (*see* Chapter 6). In the past, however, most organizations have adopted pre-structured, formalized methodologies for strategic planning, such as IBM's widely used Business Systems Planning (BSP). Many organizations evolve their own schemes, which may sometimes be effective, but often become bureaucratized, unimaginative exercises in numbermanship. Pre-structured methodologies emphasize the *procedure* that needs to be followed: steps to be taken; methods to be used; output documents to expect from each stage. They blur the difference between plans and planning. Having a plan does not necessarily indicate effective planning. The object of planning is to think through carefully:

(1) What needs to be accomplished and why.
(2) How to get it done.
(3) The resources required.
(4) The decisions, roles and responsibilities needed to carry through the process from inception to everyday use.

An adventure into the unknown

Computer-based office technology is relatively new and application of it can be risky and unproven. The planning process must therefore be one that stresses *learning and communication*. The people who develop the plans have to learn about the real meaning of 'productivity'; technological opportunities and constraints; and potential uncertainties and dangers. They need to explore comparable experiences in other contexts, such as data processing, as well as the still relatively limited experiences, so far, of office technology. Above all, they must learn how to anticipate and manage the complex and dynamic political, social and technical changes involved. Then, when a vision has been developed, the rest of the organization must be convinced of the reason why the required investment is needed.

A clear picture must be provided of the pay offs, costs, timing and phasing of a project. Everyone involved in the implementation must be helped to understand, to believe and to commit themselves to what can only be described as an adventure into the unknown. If the plans, however precise and detailed, do not communicate and convince, people may choose to opt out of the trip. If the planners have not mapped out the terrain and learned to be reliable and credible guides, the brave explorers may soon get lost, fed up – and then give up.

The spectrum of change

The journey to the office of the future can follow a number of paths for different applications, from a radical strike in a new direction to relatively modest operational improvements in current activities. The following summarizes the characteristics of the four main routes.

(1) *Radical*.
   (a) Explores an uncharted business, technical or organizational area.
   (b) Involves major new technological and resource commitments and risks.
   (c) Is an act of faith with no guaranteed pay off.
   (d) Has a strategic impact on the organization's future direction, if successful.

   For example, installing integrated voice and computer data workstations and an international telecommunications network to be used as the basis for major improvements in customer service, information access and managerial productivity.

(2) *Innovative*.
   (a) Builds on current capability and experience.
   (b) Requires a significant increase in the type and degree of

technological and resource commitment.

(c) Has a significant risk in implementation, but is based on a proven concept.

(d) Provides substantial benefits to the organization, if successful.

For example, installing a major electronic mail capability which replaces many functions previously handled via telephones, secretaries, telex, etc.

(3) *Incremental.*

(a) Is the 'next' step in technology or application development.

(b) Requires an increase in the scale but not the type of commitment to a technology or its application.

(c) Has some degree of risk.

(d) Gives a clear and measurable *Return on Investment* (ROI), if successful.

For example, adding electronic mail facilities to existing word processors and microcomputers.

(4) *Operational.*

(a) Is a 'better' way of handling some current activity.

(b) Substitutes new technology, equipment or procedures for existing ones.

(c) Has a limited and manageable risk.

(d) Contributes directly to the *bottom line*, mainly in terms of cost/staff displacement or avoidance, if successful.

For example, upgrading a voice PABX to reduce costs and increase the convenience of use.

At one end of this spectrum, where office technology merely extends existing tools and procedures in an operational change, the planning is usually relatively straightforward and can be handled by pre-structured procedural methods. For example, operational enhancements, like upgrading stand alone-word processors to communicating ones or installing a local area network to link microcomputers, usually require little, if any, organizational change and do not demand any corporate policy changes. By contrast, a radical move generally affects many aspects of jobs, relationships, people's sense of competence and autonomy. This can create substantial doubts about costs, benefits and risks and can lead to major disruptions in work activities during installation. That is why the planning process for radical change needs to be more broadly based, with effective learning and communication at its heart.

This chapter focuses on innovative and radical moves because they are the ones that pose the greatest challenge to managers responsible for planning new office systems and to the functioning of the organization as a whole. The full planning sequence for such moves start with the definition of the vision and ends with an operational proposal that begins the implementation sequence (*see Figure 7.1*). The remainder of this chapter examines the planning elements in detail. Good planning does not, of course, guarantee effective implementation. Turning plans into actual systems is explored more fully in Chapters 8 and 9. The planning/implementation phases described in *Figure 7.1* are similar to, but not precisely the same as, the main phases discussed in Chapter 6 and can be regarded as a compatible but different perspective on the same issues.

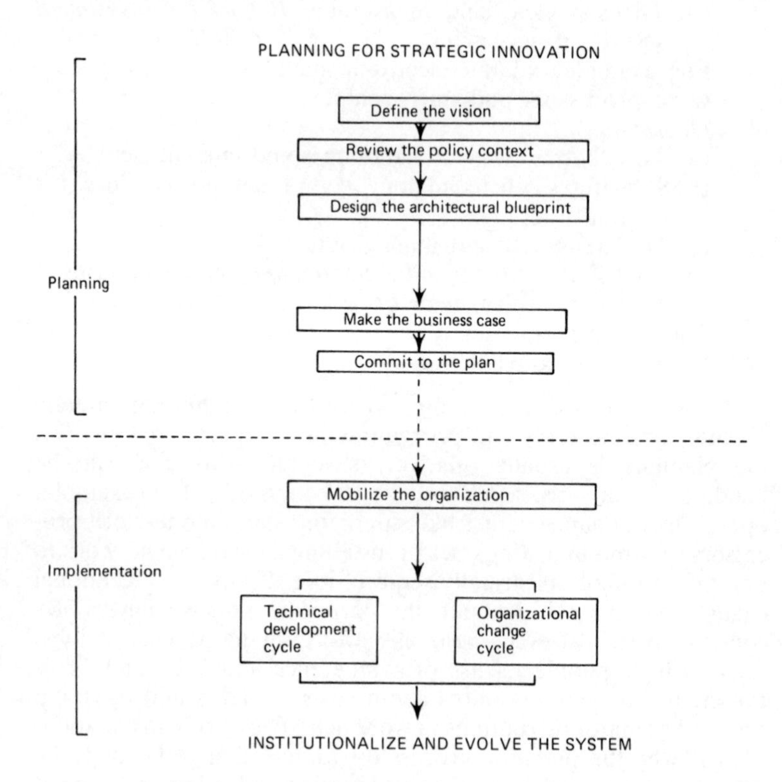

Figure 7.1 The planning process for radical and innovative changes in office technology

Questions that must be answered

The vision which needs to be defined for office technology should be a practical view of the future which attempts to highlight specific goals and opportunities. Office technology is a means to some organizational end; we must get a clear idea of that end *before* an attempt is made to define the means. The planners should avoid starting with ideas about the need to introduce particular functions, such as teleconferencing or electronic mail. The top priority for managers in charge of planning is to get answers to the following types of question on behalf of the whole organization:

(1) How do we see our organization in five to ten years in terms of factors such as products, competition, markets and organizational character?
(2) What are the key trends in the economic, political and social environment that we have to respond to?
(3) What are our main priorities, opportunities and problems as an organization?
(4) What is special about us: what do we want to build on and do we need to rethink our direction in any area?
(5) What do we mean by being 'more productive' a decade from now?
(6) What are our critical *success* factors: the five to ten things we simply have to do well to meet our aspirations and expectations?
(7) What are our critical *failure* factors: the aspects in which we cannot afford to slip?
(8) Where and how can new office technology help us to make our vision a reality? The answer to this defines where the result falls along the spectrum from radical to operational change described above.

The term *vision* does not mean 'fantasy'. In order to motivate people, the vision must be transmitted to others as a tangible, vivid reality. Vagueness will blur the picture, increasing the likelihood of scepticism, misunderstanding, uncertainty and ambiguity. The more radical or innovative the proposal, the harder it will be to convince people to 'sign on' and commit themselves to it and therefore the greater will be the need to have a clear-cut vision.

What a vision looks like

The following is a simplified, fictitious example which indicates the flavour that a vision should take.

The Vision of Company XYZ

We see ourselves in ten years in an industry where a number of existing firms will have gone under. Only the ones that really get their operations and costs under control will survive. We do not expect to be innovators but to market a small line of high quality products.

We will be a leaner organization, more reliant on automation in all areas. Our people are more skilled technically than in most companies like ours and work together well. We have a reputation for making tough decisions and being a good firm to work for. These are the strengths we must build on: when we consider being 'more productive' we must achieve improvements in our smooth organizational machine through being technically efficient and well run with good staff relations and communications within the company . . . .

Our key critical success factors are quality assurance and cost control. Our critical failure factor is how we handle the painful necessity of cutting head count: we must not damage the morale of our people but we must hold our costs down, starting now.

New office technology for us means integrated information management. We have too many paper chasers, people tracking down records, getting answers to customer inquiries, cross-checking between marketing and finance, production and warehousing and so on. In ten years' time we must be an organization of skilled people where all documents are electronically created, distributed and accessed. Virtually all our people will, by then, be doers and they will not waste time chasing paper. They will be able to get information immediately about the guts of the business: customers, products, production and delivery. We see new office technology changing the way we handle our work flows. We will use the workstation instead of administrative staff to keep tight information control with no spare bodies shuffling files.

This would be a fairly tough minded company. 'Running lean' and the containment of costs are the ends which identify and validate the means; office technology is used as a strategic aid, particularly in relation to information management and professionals' productivity. Other types of business would have different emphases, perhaps focusing more on the competitive marketplace or, for a public organization, government policy directives.

The planning group

The first step in planning is to bring together a group to define the vision. This group is of crucial significance. It should include the following types of people.

(1) *Business thinkers*. Managers or staff who are known as forward thinkers and who have a clear and practical understanding of the industry or activity in which the organization operates. They must be credible to the rest of the organization, not wild-eyed romantics or ideologues, because the vision they shape must be adventurous but believable.
(2) *Opinion leaders*. Respected individuals to whom colleagues naturally turn for advice. They must be of a status to be influential in gaining the support of the decision makers responsible for subsequent approval of the plans; the more radical and innovative the project, the more senior will be the level at which it has to be justified. Opinion leaders must help to create a link between the planners and the people who can turn the plan into action who are either *doers*, senior managers who can act on the plans, or *vetoers*, managers and staff whose support may not help but whose active or passive opposition can be an effective veto.
(3) *Office technology thinkers*. People who not only understand, and can talk intelligibly about, the nuts and bolts of the technology, but who are also able to relate the technology to broad organizational objectives. Like business thinkers, they should combine practicality with creative imagination.

In addition to people from within the organization, an outside consultant may be used as a catalyst. If this is required, the consultant should have relevant experience, be credible within the organization and, as with the rest of the group, mix practical know-how with creative inventiveness.

The role of top managers

It has become a platitude to say that top management commitment is vital to the success of any computer-based system. To be effective, such commitment must be more than just a memo or pious statement of goodwill. It must involve actions which speak to their subordinates louder and more concretely than words.

Delegation cannot be regarded as a strategy. If senior managers never go to planning meetings themselves or overdelegate the whole change process to middle-level managers without a clear mandate and with vague goals, the credibility of the whole office technology project will be undermined.

Senior executives must set the policy context within which change takes place. Absence of explicit, clear and suitable policy can be remedied only at that level. For example, only senior managers can provide the necessary incentives and guarantees to overcome the justifiable anxieties of many in the organization who will be faced with the need to change the way they work, to build new skills, and to help to implement complex cultural and technical change. Senior executives can implement a policy of no compulsory redundancies, with any cut in head count made through attrition by not replacing those who leave voluntarily or through retirement. Only top managers can also make training more pervasive and available at an early stage, and give everyone in the organization a real chance of influencing the design and use of the system in a positive way, not just through token and passive 'consultation'.

It is therefore important that the group or individual responsible for office technology planning should have access to the actual policy and decision makers. I have explored the direct responsibilities of top managers in office technology in more detail elsewhere[1] and my recommendations can be summarized in five key actions.

(1) Decide who is to lead office technology developments and back the authority of this leadership strongly.
(2) Write a clear business message which explains why the organization is committing itself to change, the opportunities and problems it relates to and the steps and responsibilities involved.
(3) Give people in the organization a concrete picture of what work life will be like after new systems are introduced, with a realistic idea of when these changes will occur.
(4) Provide incentives and guarantees to allay anxieties.
(5) Make a real and visible commitment to the project.

Creating the policy context

A vision needs to be carried into action through a policy context established by senior managers. This policy is concerned mainly with *who* decides rather than *what* is to be decided. A group or individual from within the organization must be given a clear *mandate* to establish its authority and responsibility in carrying out a *development contract* to plan and implement the project. The policy set by top management should give overall directives for this contract in terms of the:

(1) Authority of the office technology leadership.
(2) Accountability of that leadership.
(3) Criteria for planning.
(4) Organizational base for implementation.
(5) Key planning constraints and assumptions.

In many cases, the lack of such policy has blocked office technology planning. For example, the data processing department may often be given responsibility for office technology but lacks the authority to establish company-wide standards. On the other hand, some organizations have allowed each division to follow its own office technology route with nobody clearly in charge of long-term interactions, despite the fact that everyone emphasizes its importance. There has also often been an imprecise definition of 'productivity'. Data processing departments tend to view productivity in terms of operational efficiency. Some departmental line managers focus primarily on how computing systems can substitute technology for people costs, while others think in terms of the extra value to the organization that can be added by the new system.

Such problems are well known. Attempts to bypass them or simply to pretend they do not matter frequently result in political fights or impede the ability of office technology planners to go much beyond single, well-defined applications. The establishment and use of authority cannot be made by diktat and involve a great deal of effective negotiations between interested parties (*see* Chapter 10 for a discussion on the impact of technology on management negotiations and bargaining). The degree to which existing policies need to be revised will depend on where the change falls in the radical–operational spectrum discussed earlier. A radical move invariably requires new mandates to establish the necessary authority, for office technology and innovative changes are likely to strain current arrangements. Incremental and operational changes, however, should be capable of being handled within existing policy.

Matching authority to accountability

Extreme problems are likely to occur, particularly of a political nature, if any gap opens between the degree of authority established for the office technology leadership and the level to which it is held accountable for achieving the goals of the system. A radical vision for office technology requires a high level of accountability because the unit in charge has to address functions that are vital to the long-term success of the organization, has to cross traditional organizational boundaries and will affect many areas and jobs. If it lacks comparable authority, ambiguity and conflict will be stirred up.

There are four ways in which levels of authority and accountability can be combined in office technology leadership (*see Figure 7.2*).

(1) *The whipping boy* is found when a major office technology initiative, demanding a high degree of authority, is directed by leadership with low authority who gets caught in the middle and is unable either to resolve conflicting user demands or force the pace of change.

(2) *The information janitor* occurs where an organization pays lip service to office technology but there is really minimal commitment (low authority) and little expectation (low accountability) by top management who, nevertheless, assign a person or unit to create an office technology plan.

(3) *The monopolist* is typical of many old style data processing managers. They want high authority to give them complete control over the use of information technology in the

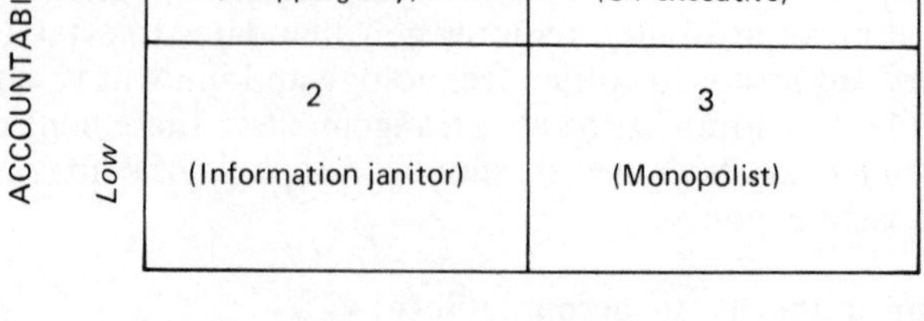

ACCOUNTABILITY	AUTHORITY: *Low*	AUTHORITY: *High*
High	1 (Whipping boy)	4 (OT executive)
Low	2 (Information janitor)	3 (Monopolist)

Figure 7.2 How accountability and authority for office technology can be combined

organization, but want their accountability to be confined to a narrow range of mainly technical issues. They frequently oppose end-user computing and microcomputers. If put in charge of office technology, they generally want to address the issue in their own purely technical terms and impose their own view of 'productivity'.

(4) *The true Office Technology (OT) executive*. A radical or innovatory move in office technology can be carried out successfully only if the OT executive in charge has high levels of authority and accountability. The individuals must have organizational credibility, managerial skill and a reasonable level of technical skills – plus the ability to persuade senior managers to give them the mandate to do the job.

The nature of office technology leadership

The most common types of office technology leadership have been the monopolists and whipping boys. The creation of a genuine and effective OT executive requires a person with the appropriate abilities who has the authority/accountability combination summarized in *Figure 7.2*. This must be complemented by a balance between organizational and office technology leadership styles which can be combined in four ways (*see Figure 7.3*):

OT LEADERSHIP

ORGANIZATIONAL LEADERSHIP	*Passive,reactive*	*Active, innovative*
Active, innovative	1 (Footdragger)	4 (OT executive)
Passive, reactive	2 (Loser)	3 (Missionary)

Figure 7.3 Types of leadership of office technology projects

(1) *The footdragger* is found where the organizational leadership is active and innovative, but the office technology leadership is passive and reactive, such as when a data processing group committed to a mainframe-based view of office technology lags behind the business vision.

(2) *The loser* occurs where both leaderships are passive and reactive, so the organization as a whole will lose the benefits of office technology. Its survival will be endangered because it lacks both the business vision to cope with a harsh and competitive economic environment and the technical vision to exploit the opportunities provided by computer-based systems to improve efficiency and effectiveness.

(3) *The missionary* is the result of an office technology leadership which has the required vision but has to persuade a passive and reactive management to open their eyes and expand their horizons and commitments. This is the most difficult leadership role, and the missionary could end up also as the whipping boy (*see Figure 7.2*). Having innovative and radical plans is pointless unless they grab top managers' attention and are backed by policy commitments.

(4) *The OT executive* should be active and innovative in a generally active and innovative managerial environment in order to be really successful.

In the initial wave of office technology applications, footdraggers and missionaries have probably constituted the majority of office technology leaders. The footdraggers are a blockage and are also often DP monopolists. The widespread and increasing use of microcomputers and word processors, together with at least pilot project experience of broader office systems, is likely to mean that line managers will begin to press for more action which will cause the footdraggers to be bypassed or replaced.

Defining the vision

The first phase of an office technology planning cycle is to define the vision. This involves three main steps:

(1) Locate and form into a planning group the thinkers and opinion makers who have access to those who decide policy.
(2) Discuss the vision.
(3) Produce a Vision Paper and communicate its messages widely.

The Vision Paper is a key strategic document in the planning process. It is the vehicle for discussing and building up the detailed vision and also provides a practical focus for the planning group. The whole process of developing the Vision Paper should take from about one to three months, starting with an initial one-day meeting that aims to draft the essence of the vision, as illustrated earlier in the case of the fictitious Company XYZ. The final paper should be brief, about ten to twenty pages. Although it has strategic significance it should avoid discussing strategy as such but should instead stress goals, opportunities and key decision areas. The social and computing themes highlighted in Chapter 6 should be united harmoniously by having:

(1) *Organization vision.* Where the organization is heading, what it should become and the targets of opportunity where office technology can be a significant aid.
(2) *Technical vision.* Where the technology is moving, what proven pay offs can be identified and how the technology can contribute to, complement or even add to the business vision.

Aims of the Vision Paper

Managers should ensure that the Vision Paper addresses itself to the relevant topics. This can be done by requiring it to have a number of section headings and items to be dealt with (*see Table 7.1*). The content, themes and tone of Vision Papers will vary greatly between organizations in terms of technology, applications and objectives (*see Table 7. 2*) in comparison with the earlier vision of Company XYZ. The implicit aims of the Vision Paper include:

(1) *Political.* Consensus can be built early on by bringing together thinkers and opinion leaders to create a succinct, but powerful, document that highlights the central issues, particularly broad organizational ones, *before* detailed planning begins.
(2) *Cultural.* After being produced, the Vision Paper should be circulated widely and followed up by detailed interviews across and down the organization. It becomes the vivid, concrete image which others can use as the springboard for depicting their own more detailed requirements relating to the management of change, providing education and training, maintaining morale, avoiding disruption, responding to resistance, creating incentives, and encouraging meaningful

Table 7.1 Outline of the contents of a Vision Paper for a private company

Executive section headings	*Content outline*
Summary	Our vision for office technology
The marketplace	Trends in our industry; competitive pressures; customer trends; strategic role of information technology
Our company	Strengths; plans; priority opportunities and problem areas; aspects where office technology can play a strategic role
Office technology	(1) Key components, such as networks, proven databases management techniques and workstations (2) Key applications and pay offs in main and related activities of the organization (3) Implementation issues, such as the impact on people, jobs, relationships, the need to manage change carefully, to sustain commintment and genuine involvement and to provide adequate education and support
Our vision for office technology	(1) Strategic priorities (2) Long-term (five to ten year) goals (3) Strategic organizational issues (4) Strategic technical issues (5) The next steps

involvement for all parts of the organization. It can be likened to the Rorschach ink-blot test where people react to a generalized shape. The Vision Paper can be held up to a range of people who can be asked to respond through fairly simple questions like: 'This is how we see office technology over the next five to ten years. How does it strike you? What would you like to see in terms of training, resources, etc? . . .'

(3) *Managerial*. The Vision Paper highlights key policy decisions. For example, in *Table 7.2*, the central question for the bank involved is who will have the mandate for defining the communications infrastructure. Currently, telecommunications functions are fragmented and split between corporate

Table 7.2 Summary from a Vision Paper for an international bank

Vision requirement	*Summary of content*
Strategic priorities	Integrated network Focus on professional workstation and multiservice administrative workstation
Longterm goals	One workstation per employee at all levels Elimination of paper *hand-offs* where a document, such as a customer order or enquiry, is handed on to many people, creating multiple steps leading to delays and the likelihood of errors in processing the information Full-scale integrated customer information base First-rate communication between customers, branches and head office Use of efficient internal operations as a competitive edge in customer service Become a low-cost banking operation via office technology
Strategic organizational	Establish the mandate for office technology Co-ordinate between the office technology group and users Manage the transition to a new era of work Define funding and pay back measures
Strategic technical	Build an integrated private communications network Define high priority workstation applications and phasing Begin move to integrated customer text/data information base Define pilots for advanced applications: videoconferencing and intelligent Optical Character Recognition (OCR) Define policy in main risk areas: technology, vendors and government and industry regulations
The next steps	Review the vision, involving senior management, users on the office technology 'frontline', supervisors and staff Take policy decisions Establish and carry through the planning process

data processing, administrative services, and international and retail banking divisions. There has been no precedent in the bank for centralized communications planning, which includes defining the network architecture, technical standards and the phased progress towards a fully integrated service (*see* Chapter 2). The Vision Paper flags the areas where senior management must make a policy decision to allow the planning and implementation to be successful.

Creating the commitment to the policy

The Vision Paper sets the agenda and opens up the planning process. It is a critical first step but too easily neglected. It makes no sense to go on to create a more detailed policy until a mechanism like the Vision Paper has established:

(1) *The rationale* for an office technology strategy defined concretely and simply.
(2) *A shared reference point* that people at all levels and in all functions of the organization can use to provide their responses and inputs.
(3) *The key policy issues* which must be addressed.
(4) *An understanding amongst senior management* and other 'doers' and 'vetoers' as to the strategic context for office technology and the key policy issues.

The Vision Paper is the first cut at defining goals and pay offs. The second step is to clarify the policy context in terms of the leadership mandates discussed above. This leads to the next major phase in the office technology planning cycle, creating the policy commitment (*see Figure 7.4*). The first three steps (comprising Stage I, defining the vision) have already been described. So far, the senior policy makers have not yet been brought into the process, although thinkers and opinion leaders who have access to them were included from the start in the planning group. The next move is to use the Vision Paper to contact *doers* (step 4), the top manager executives who make decisions and policy, and the *frontliners* (step 6), the users who have to live with the new systems, and whose attitudes and actions will determine their effective use.

There is little point in defining a grand vision if the potential users find it unappealing, unhelpful and disruptive. Innovation requires a constant two-way learning and communications effort

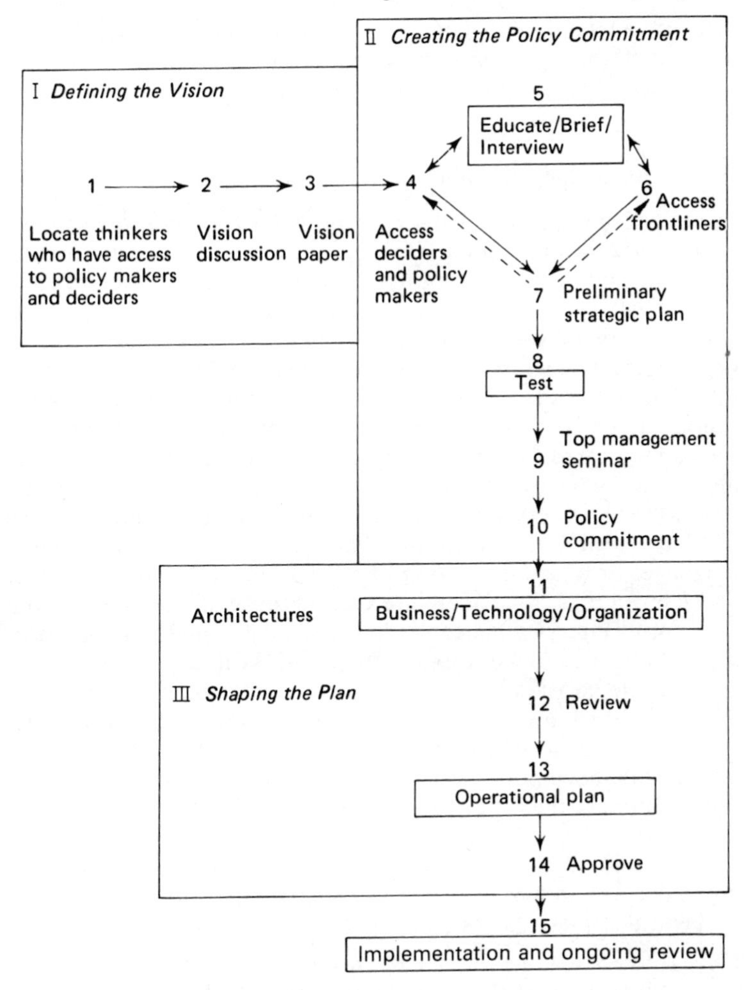

Figure 7.4 The office technology planning cycle

which moves:

(1) *Top-down* from the definition of the vision, to the establishment of the policy context to a commitment to the plan.
(2) *Bottom-up* through eliciting opinion, experimentation, and communication upwards to acceptance of the plan.

The office technology planners must get out into the organization and use formal workshops and informal interviews to educate people and brief them about the vision and its implications (step 5).

Interviews to help learning and communication

Interviewing managers and staff can be a useful way for planners to learn about what people want and for them to communicate the vision around the organization, clarifying any unfamiliar ideas and terms. Data gathered in the interviews give a range of information which planners can draw on to create as rich and clear an organizational picture as possible. This information should be incorporated in the Vision Paper and, in future discussions on the vision and on consequent plans, how to implement them and how to manage organizational change. The interviewing process can also form the basis of meaningful education so that technical, professional, supervisory, clerical and managerial people are able to share common perceptions and concepts using a common language. Provided the Vision Paper is sufficiently coherent, clear and relevant to people's self interest and sense of excitement about the future, interviewing can help build some degree of consensus and willingness to be committed to the vision.

Valuable information can be gained by interviewing about 25 to 30 people, each for around an hour, in a carefully structured way. A list of topics to which answers are needed should be sketched out at the beginning, with the interviewer leading off with a question to get the other person talking. Generally, the topics can then be covered as the interviewee presents his or her ideas, rather than forcing the interview along a predetermined path. If there are any gaps, the interviewer can ask specific questions at the end.

Typical topics and organizing questions include:

(1) *Jobs*. What makes it easy for you to do your job? What makes it hard? Do you see any aspect of what we cover in the Vision Paper as helpful to you in your work and likely career path? Will any of it hamper you?

(2) *Technology*. How comfortable and knowledgeable do you feel about office technology in general and about what we are doing or plan to do? What information or education is needed?

(3) *Messages to the top*. What messages would you like senior managers to get about the application, impact or implementation of office technology?

Table 7.3 Extracts from actual interviews reviewing office technology progress in a company

Job role	*Comment*
Senior DP Analyst	It's not my job to see that they use it . . . . I'm a technical man. 'X' is the Division Manager: it's his job.
User Manager	I would spend a lot more time on the design of (the office technology project in progress) if I knew what was going on. My level of expertise is so low that I probably wouldn't contribute much. I'm afraid of computers. I just don't know much about them.
Supervisor	We had a meeting and when senior management announced the user team (to work with the office technology group) I just about died. That person just wasn't competent or skilled enough to represent us, so why was he chosen? I was told he was the only one we have available!
Line Manager	I suffered with delays on getting reports for so long. I'm like a kid with a new toy. I think I am typical and once you get through people's initial suspicion, I'm sure this will take off. But it hasn't because nobody is really in charge.
Salesman	There is no doubt that our clients will benefit from anything that speeds up paperwork. I get embarrassed when they phone up day after day waiting for documents.
Line Manager	Well over 50 percent of my staff still resist computers. I worry about any effort to accelerate the introduction of technology.
Office Technology Project Manager	How can you make people less reluctant? When you are in front of it (a terminal), you feel some fear. In a business like ours, where unemployment is high, the fear is doubled. Most managers and staff in operations do not have university degrees. The only way to make them comfortable with technology is through hands-on training, *now*! It's expensive to make equipment available for people to play with – but it's worth it.
Senior Planner	It's absolutely clear we need office technology and, if anything, the vision is too conservative. I'm sceptical much will happen because top management will not push the needed resources behind it. The short-term will drive out the long-term.

In interviews in a real organization (*see Table 7.3* for some sample quotes), the results were presented to a senior management briefing in a way that protected anonymity. They helped to make abstract issues very concrete and brought home to the people at the top the need for an effective policy with clear business messages that workers on the frontline (salesmen) and at the coalface (secretaries and clerks) could relate to. Above all, it convinced them of the need for a strong, pervasive education plan.

The preliminary strategic plan

Steps 4 to 6 in *Figure 7.4* use learning and communication as a means of ending up with a preliminary strategic plan (step 7) which extends the vision to include:

(1) *A summary of the strategic goals* for office technology.
(2) *The rationale* for the strategy, such as the economic and organizational opportunities, pressures and/or problems motivating it, and the expected areas of pay off.
(3) *The priority applications* and operational measures of benefits and of 'productivity'.
(4) *The key technical decisions* and investments needed.
(5) *A tentative list of policy issues* that will need reviewing, particularly who is in charge of:
    (a) Managing the technical infrastructure.
    (b) Defining the timing and details of individual applications
    (c) Co-ordinating the overall plan.

Some of these elements in the preliminary strategic plan will be essentially restatements or enlargements of what is already in the Vision Paper; others will be new aspects highlighted in steps 4 to 6. Together, they provide the basis for creating awareness amongst senior executives, which can then be translated into top management policy, that in turn must be translated into meaningful commitment.

Once a plan has emerged, key elements in it should be tested to establish its practical implications (step 8). The process, summarized as steps 4 to 8 in *Figure 7.4*, is *iterative*, in that the cycle needs to be repeated a number of times to gradually sharpen the definition of the main elements in the plan. This can take from about two to six months. If it is to be effective, it must involve a dialogue on organizational and business issues between planners and key decision makers, possibly via the thinkers and opinion leaders in the planning group. At the same time, technical questions need to be refined in order to assist in the eventual transition to the third major phase, Stage III, shaping the plan.

The pivotal point

A crucial stage in the planning cycle is to persuade top management of the importance of the project and to get their backing. This can be achieved effectively by holding a seminar for senior executives (step 9) which becomes a pivotal point in the whole planning process. In order to have a fair chance of enticing top managers to such a seminar, the previous steps must have been executed sufficiently well to have communicated a clear picture of the potential and practical value of office technology to the overall health of the organization.

The seminar should take about two to three days. It should highlight policy issues and brief managers on the nature of office technology, application opportunities, the management process to deliver office technology successfully, and the details of the preliminary strategic plan. The outcome of the seminar should be an operational definition of the participants' commitment to office technology.

As discussed earlier in the section on the role of senior managers, this commitment should result in practical actions which involve establishing the authority and accountability of the mandate for the office technology development contract; the writing of a clear business message; presenting people with tangible pictures of their office life after computerization; offering incentives and guarantees to allay anxieties; and providing visible evidence to the rest of the organization of their own belief in office technology as managers and users of the new systems. A seminar to achieve these important objectives can be difficult to design and must be taught well (*see Table 7.4* for the outlines of the contents of a seminar). When it succeeds, it provides the organizational base for launching office technology with a full understanding of all the issues and the informed, active backing of senior managers and frontline users.

Finishing off: from planning to plans

At the start of this chapter it was stated, perhaps over-assertively, that pre-structured procedural methods of planning for office technology 'can become bureaucratized, unimaginative exercises

Table 7.4 Outline of topics for a senior management seminar in office technology

Topic	*Items to be covered*
Overview of office technology	Proven applications with a high pay off: (1) Text handling (2) Communication (3) Professional and managerial productivity
Problem areas	Overselling Need for support infrastructure Managing organizational change
Vision for office technology	What is happening in our industry and marketplace What we mean by *productivity* High priority opportunities with office technology Business pay-offs
Summary of main types of computer-based systems	Workstations Communications Applications
Management issues	Policy options and needs Writing the business message Managing change Education and support
Next step	Phased action plan

in numbermanship'. To some extent, this type of approach is actually required in the final phases of shaping the detailed plan (steps 11 to 14 in *Figure 7.4*), which shifts the planning process from vision, learning and communication to methodology, technique and design. The 'vision' development opens out the planning cycle. This is subsequently refined through policy development to set the criteria for establishing an overall architectural framework that sets the bounds within which the final operational plan is developed with precise definitions of the phasing, funding and milestones for the project.

The planning process recommended in this chapter should make it relatively easy to define the detailed plan because it pulls in people at all levels in a dialogue that relates technical to organizational issues and *vice versa*. Defining the vision for office technology gives something worth shaping the final plans for. Creating the policy commitment provides some likelihood that the plan, whatever it is, will be organizationally feasible and that the office technology leader does not become a forlorn missionary or harassed whipping boy.

The architectural blueprint

The notion of an 'architecture' to define an overall blueprint is being used increasingly in data processing, office technology and telecommunications. It can be regarded as analogous to a city plan which establishes general building regulations, defines major boundaries and highways and sets standards and guidelines. A good architecture allows for freedom, initiative and flexibility at the local level, which provides a basis for expansion and enhancement in adapting to growth and change in an evolutionary way.

Neither organizational nor office technology designs can be regarded as fixed and static (*see* Chapter 6). The exact applications, volumes and types of use of technical building blocks cannot be pre-defined. It can be a dreadful mistake at this stage to fix in stone a single design, which is often obsolescent before implementation. Inflexibility is the Achilles heel of office technology plans. For this reason, above all, the focus needs to be on *architectures* in shaping the plan, not a particular design: architectures that provide the blueprints which can cover a range of specific designs and applications.

Three types of architecture need to be covered. The flavour of each of these is provided by the following questions, which represent just a small fraction of the issues involved.

(1) *Technical*. What is the telecommunications and data infrastructure? What operating systems environment is assumed? How will the need for integration, interconnection, compatibility and expansion be met? If this is to be a multivendor environment, what are the criteria for vendor selection?
(2) *Organizational*. What new mechanisms for planning and co-ordination must be put in place, such as steering committees? What are the likely organizational changes that need to occur to turn the office technology plan into action or that will be created by the introduction and use of office technology? What education is needed – and when?
(3) *Business*. What is the basis for costing, internal pricing, capital investment and business justification? What are the

expected levels of funding? How will costs be recovered? Over what time frame?

There is no quick or simple cook-book for building the architecture. Solid, substantive effort is required. The process becomes more formal than in earlier stages and often needs special expertise to carry out, expertise which may need to come from outside the organization.

Why have an organizational architecture?

A technical blueprint is relatively easy to understand because it can be defined reasonably accurately. The idea of an organizational architecture, however, may seem a little strange. Why not just refer to it as an organizational *structure*, *process* or *plan*? Using the term 'architecture' is a useful reminder that the aim is not to create a specific organizational design, but a framework which can then be used to develop specific tasks and structures depending on dynamically changing needs.

An organizational architecture is an important aid to handling the complex tasks of assessing the real costs and benefits to the organization and of implementing systems successfully. This is more fully discussed in Chapters 8 and 9. The need to consider the organizational architecture and the issues discussed in Chapter 6 is important, but is often overlooked and may require some major commitments by senior managers. This is another reason for holding the formal top-management seminar that gets across what has to happen to make office technology work behaviourally and managerially, as well as technically. The key features of an organizational architecture should include:

(1) *Leadership*. The mesh between authority and accountability discussed earlier (*see Figures 7.1* and *7.2*).
(2) *Formal liaison roles*. Establishing people at the project level who can bridge the culture gap between technicians and users. These are business-oriented analysts or user representatives who are 'hybrids', fluent about business and literate about office technology, or the reverse.
(3) *Education and support*. A sustained commitment to education and training as a mobilizing force to lead implementation, rather than follow it, is vital. Without a formal education plan, any office technology strategy is incomplete because the new systems involve new concepts, skills and technology that demand careful preparation beforehand (*see* Chapter 9).

The way ahead

In the past, office technology has been dominated by technocentric naivety. Technical plans too easily substitute for planning and are often divorced from the realities of organizational life. The approach presented in this chapter shows the way ahead to successful innovations in the office through co-operation, communication and organization. Once the vision is clear and once policy is explicit and commitment real, the rest of the planning process is relatively routine. If the steps to define the vision and obtain policy commitments are omitted, no amount of technical expertise can help to provide the necessary clarity, thrust and authority to carry through the changes effectively. Expertise is essential, but in the correct place within the planning sequence. The real issues determining the course of office technology are not technical: they are concerned with vision and policy.

Recommendations

(1) Recognize that successful office innovation can be obtained only through managing all aspects of change: social, technical and business.
(2) Crystallize the strategic objectives that drive office technology in a vision of a desired and attainable future that will enhance the overall health of the organization.
(3) Define the vision, starting by setting up a planning group including imaginative, practical and credible individuals from the organization, to produce a Vision Paper.
(4) Top management must give real, visible commitment to office technology, by taking firm decisions that ensure the leadership of office technology has an appropriate mandate and that the organization is working towards common and well charted goals to which senior executives are seen to give personal attention and support.
(5) Obtain a commitment to the policy through a process of learning and communications which refines the Vision Paper to a more specific strategic plan. All levels in the organization should feel their views have been taken seriously in producing the plan.
(6) Develop architectural blueprints that cover organizational, technical and business requirements and set the general

framework within which specific choices can be made to help the system and the organization to adapt to changing needs.

(7) Establish and sustain an education and training plan that prepares, at the earliest possible stage, all people in the organization to use, supervise and manage new office technology.

(8) Produce the detailed operational plans in a systematic, structured way that translates the architectural blueprint into actual working systems.

(9) Monitor the implementation of the plan on a continuing basis and establish a new planning cycle when the next radical or innovative change is required.

Reference

1. Keen, P. G. W., Strategic planning for the new system, in Otway, H. J. and Peltu, M., *New Office Technology: Human and Organizationl Aspects*, Frances Pinter, London; Ablex, Norwood, N.J. (1983)

Bibliography

The following publications are also relevant to topics discussed in this chapter:

Keen, P. G. W., Information systems and organizational change, *Communications of the ACM*, **24**(1), 24–33 (1981)

National Economic Development Office (NEDO), *The Impact of Advanced Information Systems: The Effect on Job Content and Job Boundaries* (two volumes, Summary and Appendix: Case Studies), NEDO, London (1983)

Rockart, J. F., Chief executives define their own information needs, *Harvard Business Review*, **57**(2), 81–93 (1979)

Zuboff, S., The psychology of computer-mediated work, *Harvard Business Review*, **60**(5), 142–152 (1982)

8

Assessing Costs and Benefits in Systems Design and Selection

Janine E. Nahapiet

Introduction

Many computer-based systems have failed to meet expectations because the managers and specialists who shaped them formed their judgements on narrow economic and technological calculations. The process of making assessments of the full range of benefits and costs of new office technology requires a deeper exploration of the role of information and communications within enterprises. It must go beyond relatively simplistic evaluations of functions performed by a system, the face-value costs of hardware and software, and the staff resources that can be saved by new systems.

This chapter discusses how assessments can be undertaken most effectively. It identifies the main costs and benefits of new information systems and reviews two main approaches to their evaluation, emphasizing the influence of decision makers' beliefs, assumptions and perceptions in determining the final outcome. The purposes of planning and evaluation are investigated and guidelines offered on how to evaluate the potential of new office technology.

Benefits of new office technology

There are four characteristics of computer-based systems that can generally improve the work performance of individual users and the enterprise as a whole:

(1) *Wide accessibility*. Microelectronics has broken the barriers that kept early data processing systems at a distance from most of their users. Computer-based systems now have:
(a) More robust and compact construction, no longer

needing special operational environments.

(b) Cheaper hardware, bringing powerful systems within the range of most organizations.

(c) More varied software at reasonable prices.

(d) Easier to use facilities, even by non-specialists, although the full human–communication goals specified in Chapter 3 may not be met.

(2) *A broad range of information handling*. New office technology can handle text, graphics, voice, illustrations, printed characters, and so on. Traditional data processing systems were restricted mainly to numerically oriented information in highly structured files and activities.

(3) *Co-ordination and integration of many activities*. The work of geographically separate people, particularly in data collection and communication, can be facilitated by using services such as electronic mail, teleconferencing and corporate databases. For example, information on customers' orders can be collected directly from portable computers carried by salesmen or from workstations in many offices. This data can be pooled to provide a common, up to date information source that can assist with speedier and more effective handling of customer transactions by sales, distribution, manufacturing, accounts and other departments. It could also be possible, with systems that can handle images as well as text, to link all parties to a new product development in a network that gives access to the latest drawings and specifications of new products or buildings.

(4) *High versatility and flexibility*. Computer-based systems can evolve to meet changing user needs. A word processing system, for example, can produce high quality documents efficiently. When linked to a database it can generate personalized letters automatically for selective mailshots. The database, of course, can be of great help in extracting information to assist decision making, in providing answers to customer queries, helping monitor cash flows, and in many other activities. End user languages (*see* Chapter 2) can make it reasonably easy to create new ways of analysing data or presenting results.

Improved organizational performance

The above capabilities provide a rich and fruitful source that can be drawn on to enhance and extend the performance of an organization in terms of:

(1) *Increasing efficiency in existing activities*, such as making improvements in typing productivity by using word processors or making savings on travelling by exploiting electronic mail and teleconferencing facilities.
(2) *Stimulating new activities*, say by having better ways of communicating with customers or providing new services or products.
(3) *Winning new business and beating competition* as a result, for example, of having access to more up to date information or better communications with customers and clients.
(4) *Encouraging a fresh look at management methods*, for instance, by reconsidering the degree of centralization or decentralization.

Important choices about management structure and the control of organizations influence the selection, design and installation of new office technology, such as the extent of local autonomy allowed to managers. As a direct result of the new systems, new jobs may be created, for example, an *information manager* to co-ordinate all information systems and technology. Responsibilities between sections and departments may be reallocated, say, in redefining the roles of data processing, administration and telecommunications functions. More indirectly, new patterns of monitoring and control of work can be established through the availability and distribution of computerized information. Work procedures can become more transparent and jobs more structured and preprogrammed (*see* Chapters 5 and 6).

Organizational and job changes are not predetermined by the technology. The wide accessibility, flexibility and variety of computer-based systems can be used to tighten control or foster creative independence, to support centralization or encourage decentralized structures. Managers should be aware that *computer systems design implies organization design and job design*. Explicit or implicit preferences for particular forms of management and control held by those involved in specifying and introducing the technology will be influential in deciding how the enterprise and the people in it operate.

A word of warning

The full benefits, theoretically available with new office technology, may not always be realizable in practice. Vendors often exaggerate potential benefits by stressing minimum prices and maximum performance. To achieve the required performance, however, it is usually necessary to have more than the minimum hardware and software facilities. In many cases, systems also prove to be more limited or rigid than expected. With database systems whose structure must be predetermined, users may find it difficult to adapt the system once it has been set up. You should always explore how a system will operate in an actual working environment; it is better to talk to others who have used a product, rather than rely on the manufacturer's demonstration or paper specifications.

Identifying the major costs

The price the organization has to pay in seeking the benefits of new information systems includes visible expenditure and costs that are less immediately apparent.

Visible costs

Direct costs are incurred in a number of key office innovation activities:

(1) *Purchase/rental of hardware and software*. Capital expenditure is required for:
   (a) All items of hardware and software. This includes apparently trivial items, such as floppy disks and power supplies, that can add up to a sizeable sum when required in significant volumes.
   (b) Changes to the physical environment, such as modifications to the buildings to accommodate systems, buying new furniture, lighting, and so on.

   Investment in capital goods must be regarded as a recurring cost. Once installed, the technology becomes an essential tool, difficult to do without and often stimulating more uses and applications than originally anticipated. Organizations often underestimate this growth in demand and choose systems with insufficient enhancement capabilities.

(2) *Continuing modification, extension and replacement of systems*. The rapid rate of development of the technology means that the time between upgrading the system is likely to be quite short. The evaluation of systems should therefore be seen as a continuing process, with regular analyses being

made to compare benefits and costs of new developments with those for carrying on with existing, possibly outdated, hardware and software.

(3) *Operating costs*. There are continuing costs for running systems, such as telecommunications charges, the provision of accessories like printer ribbons and special stationery, and many other items that may be overlooked when evaluating costs, but which can prove to be substantial.

(4) *Support for people directly or indirectly involved with office systems*. Although accounted for in a different way than capital investment, support costs can be substantial as they include the following:

  (a) Costs for managers, computing specialists and others to conduct a detailed feasibility study into where and how systems should be applied, including the search for, and evaluation of, different technical and design options.
  (b) Transition and conversion to the new system requiring important expenditures on, for example, the education and training of all managers and staff affected by the new system, provision of extra staff to carry out the normal workload while people are learning the new system, and employment of skilled staff to perform technical conversions when moving software and data between old and new computer-based system.
  (c) Availability of skilled staff who can provide assistance when technical problems occur or when the system needs to be repaired or modified, or a new system needs to be developed. These specialists may already be in the organization, but new staff may need to be recruited and/or external consultants or vendors may need to be employed. Such skilled staff usually demand high salaries and fees.
  (d) Regular and well controlled monitoring of the quality of information input to the system to avoid allowing the old computing adage to come true: *Garbage In, Garbage Out* (GIGO). This can be demanding in terms of manpower, but is worth the investment because systems soon lose their credibility if data is found to be ou of date or incorrect. The system itself should also perform some validation of input, for example, checking that values are within a specified range or that inappropriate characters do not appear in a particular field, such as numbers where only alphabetic letters are expected.

As hardware prices continue to fall, a higher proportion of the total cost will derive from software and the human element in office systems. Some organizations have already established budgets for staff training equal to those for their capital expenditure on information systems.

Hidden costs

Many of the costs incurred by developing and introducing new office systems are not obvious. These need to be investigated and brought to the surface to ensure that evaluations reflect the true balance between costs and benefits. Six main areas of hidden costs are of particular importance:

(1) *Time, skills and energies consumed by individuals at all levels in the organization*. Some of the investment in human resources may be explicitly accounted for as part of the project management process but the vast majority remains hidden in the daily activities of a large number of people. It includes the time users spend familiarizing themselves with the new system, exploring and playing with its facilities, solving difficulties and problems as they arise, informally assisting others, and introducing minor modifications to suit particular needs. In the longer term, office workers can use the technology to reach a new understanding of their own situation, leading to radical changes in work procedures. The overall investment of time by managers, specialists and staff can be considerable.

(2) *Standardization policy*. One of the central issues for many organizations who are planning and implementing new office systems is the extent to which different elements of hardware and software are to be standardized. There can be many incompatibilities between software, data, storage media, telecommunications and other capabilities. Attempts to keep everyone to the same standards can be so complex that it leads to long delays before particular units can get their own systems, resulting in extra costs through the loss of benefits that could have been achieved by the units who have to wait. To allow complete autonomy, however, can lead to duplication of effort and an ultimate inability to support and link incompatible systems. In one organization, the operations research department developed its own microcomputer-based system. After the operations research department had been disbanded, it became necessary to modify and extend

the system's software. The information systems department, however, had nobody skilled in the appropriate programming language so, eventually, a completely new system had to be developed.

Many organizations have sensibly pursued a middle course. In the shorter term, they have decided that they neither want nor are able to co-ordinate all systems development. In order to retain a measure of compatibility, however, all those who implement new systems are required to select from a range of specified hardware and software. This means that an appropriate level of systems support can be provided and the option is kept open to link up independent systems at a later date. Even this approach could lead to extra cost; an organization may commit itself to a vendor whose later equipment proves to be incompatible with earlier models.

(3) *Integration of information*. One of the benefits of a computer-based system is its ability to integrate information and activities of different people and groups across the enterprise. This can greatly assist in management decision making, co-ordination and control, but the experience of many organizations suggest, however, that there may be hidden costs as well as benefits.

If total integration is attempted, all users of the system must agree on a common basis for describing and categorizing items, be they products in an inventory control system, drawings in computer aided design tasks, or personal information in a personnel records system. While this may create no difficulties in many situations, the more varied the background of the users and the more different their working contexts, the greater is the potential for problems to occur in trying to standardize data. People may not understand distinctions between different categories of data, thereby creating many errors. They may feel that the distinctions do not suit their particular needs, so fail to use the output from the system effectively.

Integration can also lead to an increase in the complexity of management control because it increases the interdependence between hitherto relatively separate departments and divisions. The system is likely to be modified frequently because many parts of the organization are involved, each with differing and developing needs. This causes technical problems in co-ordinating the system's evolution and managerial challenges in agreeing and implementing the necessary changes.

(4) *Vulnerability*. As organizations become more dependent on computer-based systems, they can also become more vulnerable to any failure of the system through errors, accidents, crime or sabotage. This vulnerability is greater if the system is more centralized and integrated, but the use of more decentralized and independent systems can involve increased capital expenditure. The vulnerability risk should therefore be carefully weighed and necessary costs to assist the security of the system should be considered (*see* Chapter 9).

(5) *The costs of failure*. A computer-based system can have far reaching consequences for an organization, which could lead to extra costs if there are major failures. This occurred when a system was introduced by a hospital to improve financial management[1]. By providing a more systematic method for collecting information, particularly on the treatment given to each patient, the system could be used by the hospital to improve all aspects of financial management, from patient billing to forward planning. In practice, it generated a great deal of interdepartmental conflict and nearly brought many hospital activities to a standstill, illustrating the problems that can arise when trying to integrate and streamline information systems, as discussed above. The designers had failed to recognize that procedures to facilitate one department's working may inconvenience other groups. Doctors, for instance, gave little priority to recording every patient-related activity in the full detail required by the accounting system. Yet, without complete and timely input, the whole system ground to a halt. Few of those required to contribute to the system received anything of practical value in return and had little appreciation of the needs of those who did benefit because the participants were so far removed from each other.

(6) *The risk factor*. Any significant venture into new office technology has an element of risk: it may succeed or fail to varying degrees. Managers should therefore ask two key questions. Firstly, what else could be achieved if the human and financial resources involved were invested differently? Secondly, what may be lost by not making this investment in new systems? Although it is not possible to answer these questions with certainty, they focus attention on the need to consider the relative merits of different choices.

There is another hidden aspect, concerned more with shifts in costs between groups rather than necessarily increasing overall costs. For example, one of the effects of having an integrated information system is that the costs of gathering data may be moved between departments and groups. This is indicated by the hospital system described earlier, in which operational units had to take on extra work in providing detailed information to the computer. Such a shift can please some units, for example, the accounts department which is relieved of some of its information gathering responsibility, but can be a cause of unhappiness in others.

Balancing the costs and benefits

I have deliberately described the benefits and costs of new office systems in general terms. The importance attached to individual attributes, indeed whether or not a factor such as integration is seen as a cost or benefit, depends on the work environment in which the technology is to operate. For example, the opportunity to communicate across geographical distances is likely to be valued differently in a large multinational than in a small, single location company. Those organizations and departments whose primary contact is directly with customers and clients will place a higher premium on the production of high quality documents than those who communicate exclusively within the enterprise. Balancing costs and benefits therefore requires careful consideration of the overall organizational context[2].

In considering the management and control of any enterprise, computer-based systems are just one of several elements which need to be mutually supportive. New technology has important implications for the style and culture of the organization and makes substantial demands on its people and structure. The size of the organization is also an important consideration in assessing the value of the technology.

Comparing large and small organizations

Much marketing information on office technology emphasizes the savings to be achieved through increased efficiency in administrative activities. In smaller organizations, however, there is generally less administration overheads, so the potential savings in this aspect may not be as significant as for larger organizations. Of more importance to the small organization is the assistance the technology can give to increase its business and handle more work without the commensurate expansion of office staff.

The small organization can have several advantages when implementing new office systems. It is generally easier for a senior manager, sometimes the owner, to make a commitment and convey enthusiasm for the technology. There is mounting evidence to show that such personal commitment from top management is of great importance in achieving success with the technology[3]. Employees in smaller organizations often adapt and change their working arrangements more easily because there is greater informality and less specialization than in bigger enterprises. On the other hand, this flexibility can be a potential problem if new office technology seems to increase formalization in office work. The standards and control procedures imposed by the system may seem disproportionately time consuming and costly, without having a clear, acceptable pay off. Having to update database files regularly according to strict standards, for example, can seem to be a tedious, unnecessary chore. If expected procedures are not followed, however, the database becomes unreliable and the whole information system can fall into disrepute.

In absolute terms, the size of an office information system for a small organization may not be very great, but can be significant relative to the total operations of the enterprise. The smaller organization may be particularly vulnerable to any problems or failures of the system, particularly as it has fewer resources to buy its way out of trouble.

In the larger organization, the potential savings and benefits of information technology may be more apparent but, at the same time, more difficult to achieve. The scope for integration is greater, but also more problematical because it can give rise to intra-organizational rivalries and managerial power battles, as well as having to bring together a wide variety of specialized activities. Even the decision to go ahead with a project can be more difficult because it has to be approved by so many different people and functions. Although the idea of change may be welcome, latent inertia in large groups tends to mean it takes longer to achieve such change than in smaller enterprises. Perhaps the biggest danger for large organizations is that computerization can encourage managers to think in terms of a single large system rather than viewing their operation as a collection of semi-autonomous units working towards a common goal. This big-systems thinking can lead to increased organizational complexity resulting in a failure to deliver the expected benefits.

Aims and objectives of new office technology

In my discussions with people in a wide range of organizations, I have found, in addition to replacing obsolescent equipment, three main reasons for introducing new office systems:

(1) *To solve a particular problem.* This type of application is motivated by the need to remove or alleviate what is perceived, by at least some people in the organization, as a problem. It is usually based on the detailed analysis of a current set of activities, with a clear specification of how performance should be improved. Typical tasks tackled are the introduction of word processors to increase productivity and cut down overheads, the use of computer aided design systems to improve the efficiency of product development, and database systems to meet growing customer demands for better and more timely information. American organizational specialist James March suggests that such *problem-oriented* approaches normally occur in more tightly constrained organizations and are usually applied in a relatively localized and intense manner. They promise a high return on investment, but are unlikely to lead to new ventures or ways of working that are of deep significance to the enterprise's future development[4].

(2) *To seek new opportunities.* In these circumstances, the technology is regarded more as an experimental aid: a solution in search of a problem. Innovation may be driven by a general belief that the organization must move with the times, the 'me too' syndrome, or by a recognition that new technology is a vital element in giving the organization an edge over competitors, the 'automate or die' fear. March[4] has discovered that this type of development is more likely to occur in times of an excess of resources and in decentralized organizations. In such situations, as in many smaller organizations, key individuals may be more willing to experiment, take a risk, and go ahead without a guaranteed return on the investment. For example, the managing director of a small firm making scientific products for medical applications obtained a microcomputer system for his company, initially to assist with clerical operations but with an undefined longer

term hope that it would become a resource to assist future, unpredictable business development. The computer has now helped in the expansion of the company in a variety of ways, such as by exploring new markets through a careful analysis of customer records and selected mailing of personalized marketing material.

(3) *As an element in broader organizational change*. Developments such as the reorganization of departments, setting up of new ventures, and redistribution of managerial responsibilities generally encourage a re-examination of information and communications systems. For example, the creation of a new division and the move to a new building stimulated a multinational company to make a detailed study of a range of office technology applications to assist its new organizational unit.

Many different applications in an organization may be motivated by each of these aims, while there may be more than one objective within one application. For example, a decision to invest in a microcomputer system may initially be made as a broad solution in search of new opportunities, although the implementation of particular tasks may appear closer to problem-driven concerns. More significantly, different groups of managers may see the chance to pursue diverse priorities and objectives within the same application. Some managers tend to emphasize the longer term strategic aspects of systems while others, often those in more junior line management positions, are more concerned with shorter term control objectives. It is crucially important to recognize that this variety of approaches and expectations can have a significant influence on what objectives are set and the characteristics subsequently looked for when evaluating the costs and benefits of the technology.

There are two contrasting approaches to the task of project analysis and evaluation, *planning with goals* and *directional planning*[5].

Assessment with goals

The classical approach to decision making recommended in many management textbooks specifies a series of clear-cut stages requiring a lucid, precise and generally quantitative statement of goals and objectives. Thereafter, the process involves the identification of alternative ways of achieving objectives and selecting the option that comes closest to satisfying the required criteria. To be complete, the effects of implementation should then be carefully monitored and, if necessary, adjustments made to bring performance in line with expectations.

This method is exemplified in office systems developments by *cost benefit analysis*. As its name implies, this attempts to identify the full costs and benefits and to express these in a common unit of measurement – money. Choice then involves selection of that option for which the benefits most exceed those of other alternatives or for which the benefits most exceed their costs.

A word processing case study

A cost benefit analysis was carried out by a large international company when deciding to implement word processing at its headquarters in London. The company set out to reduce costs by tackling two of the most important problems experienced with typing staff: individual typist productivity and labour turnover. The following were the main elements in the analysis:

(1) A detailed calculation of the full costs of employing typists, including such overhead items as the costs of office space in central London. This enabled the organization to investigate the relative benefits of increased productivity assessed against a higher level of employment.

(2) A detailed calculation of the costs of labour turnover, including advertising, recruitment and training of new staff. This helped to work out the savings to be gained by increasing the average length of employment of typists.

(3) A work study of the typical typists's day, classifying the proportion of time spent typing new words; correcting errors; retyping material; handling paper; and idle time. As a result of this study an objective was established to increase productivity by reducing error rates and the amount of retyping and paper handling needed. This would release typists to spend time on new work.

(4) A survey to find out what typists liked and disliked about their work and its environment.

(5) An assessment of the costs of making those changes to the office environment found desirable in the survey of typists' likes and dislikes.

(6) A survey of word processing systems. Emphasis was placed on finding a system that would be extremely easy to use

because this would not only make it more acceptable to present employees, but also would reduce the amount of time required to train new staff. In addition, comparisons were made between the costs of alternative systems, including the costs of installing hardware in the building, charges for maintenance contracts, and so on.

The service finally selected established several typing pools, each with a set of workstations linked to a central computer and with printing separated from typing activities. An evaluation of the system after it had been operational for some time indicated that productivity had increased by more than 200 per cent, largely because of a reduction in the amount of time spent retyping text and correcting errors. The rate of staff turnover had been reduced, partly because working conditions had improved. Overall, the financial breakeven point was achieved earlier than anticipated.

There were, however, several sources of dissatisfaction that were difficult to resolve. For example, some problems arose from the separation of printing tasks from typing operation. The move to centralized typing pools was also not universally popular. It was difficult to compare the benefits of a higher quality of completed work against the costs to certain groups of a reduced level of typing support because of their physical separation from typists in the central pool.

Key issues in cost benefit analyses

A cost benefit analysis can stimulate the collection of much useful data to aid decision making, but the experience of many organizations suggests that a large number of other issues also need to be addressed by managers. These relate to technicalities of the analysis and to some fundamental questions about the basic assumptions underlying its philosophy, including the following key aspects:

(1) *Basic elements in cost benefit calculation are neither absolute nor completely objective.* Each financial appraisal incorporates significant subjective judgements, by those in charge, about what should be included in the assessments. Far from being an absolute or objective assessment, the quantification process reflects the assumptions, standards and objectives thought to be appropriate in a specific context at a particular point in time. For example, there are alternative ways of evaluating the indirect costs mentioned above. In fact,

whether they are assessed or allocated at all is a matter of judgement. In identifying the cost of a new application, say, only extra costs directly attributable to that task may be included or it may be decided to incorporate a proportion of the overhead of having corporate computing systems and specialist staff. Various methods of calculation may be valid, though they may have completely different implications for decision making.

(2) *Costs and benefits do not all occur in the same place within the organization.* For example, the benefits to the customer accounts department of an integrated information system may be experienced as a cost to the other departments who may have to modify the way they provide their information, as in the example of the hospital financial management system. Centralized typing pools have been shown to increase throughput and save on the costs of providing equipment, but they may provide a less useful service to certain users and reduce the job satisfaction of those who work in them[3]. In considering the implications of any evaluation of the technology, managers should examine whose perspectives have been adopted in defining the nature of the costs and benefits and whose may have been ignored.

(3) *Analyses concentrate entirely on those factors which can be measured.* This can produce an undue emphasis on quantity at the expense of quality in setting objectives and assessing performance, such as specifying number of words typed, pages of paper printed or documents produced, in an analogous way to output targets in product manufacturing. It is difficult, perhaps impossible in some cases, to attach a precise value to important qualitative improvements, such as having more effective communication in the organization or a more personalized, responsive service to customers or clients. The quantifiable performance of a system may, indeed, not be translated directly into the desired organizational performance precisely because it ignores the crucial influence of qualitative factors. For example, a word processing system in one organization produced a sixfold increase in total output per typist. The useful output, however, only doubled because managers were so poorly trained in exploiting the new system that they asked the typists to make many unnecessary changes and amendments to text[3]. Concentration on the volume of information processed and produced may also lead managers to concen-

trate on the total *quantity* of data generated and to overlook the fact that it is the *content* of information and how it is used which is of prime importance.

(4) *Decisions are treated primarily if not exclusively, on the basis of economic considerations.* This arises partly because all aspects need to be compared in similar terms. While the financial implications of behaviour are important, there are many equally significant social and political dimensions to be considered in making choices about office technology. For example, the value of a communications system cannot be fully judged purely in terms of the speed, volume and cost of transmitting messages. Communication is a fundamental means by which people learn about each other and the world about them. It is part of the social glue of the organization, the way in which individuals in the enterprise come to a shared understanding of their mission and to forge and sustain personal and institutional linkages. To increase the efficiency of message transmission, with reduced interpersonal contact, may bring short term savings, but also longer term costs. As well as being a place where specific work tasks are undertaken, an office is where people meet to establish the trust and understanding necessary to make the organization function. Cost benefit assessments, however, rarely include an evaluation of how the technology may disrupt this social process and what mechanisms exist to facilitate the development of suitable alternatives.

(5) *Focusing primarily on the technology assumes that nothing else changes when new systems are introduced.* The conditions for a soundly based cost benefit evaluation of office systems are rarely to be found because they require that the outcome of innovation can be attributed totally, or mainly, to the impact of the technology. As shown throughout this book, however, the implementation of new office technology is almost always associated with other organizational changes, including the redesign of existing jobs, the creation of new ones and modifications to the responsibilities of departments.

Why an alternative approach is needed

Quantified goal-oriented assessments provide a rational, analytical model of how systems should work. There is an overwhelming amount of evidence to show, however, that many decisions do not, and cannot, fit that model[4]. The net effect of such cost benefit analyses is to produce conservatism in the implementation of change. The logic of the approach applies only to well understood, routine problems in an environment with stable conditions so that predictions about the future can be made with a high level of confidence. Attention is therefore mainly concentrated in those activities that are tangible enough to suit these methods of measurement.

This is an important reason why the initial thrust of new office technology was directed towards the more defined and easily measured work of secretaries and clerks, rather than managers and professionals. Within secretarial work, it has also caused too much emphasis on typing activities, primarily because it is easier to demonstrate performance improvements in such highly structured tasks, although most studies agree that typing consumes less than 20 per cent of the total time of secretaries. Overall, secretarial and typing personnel constitute typically less than 10 per cent of total employee costs, while managers and professional staff can account for over 60 per cent. The goal-oriented assessment method therefore led to the targeting of new technology on activities that were far less important than the evaluations suggested. In the London-based company installing word processors, discussed earlier, management recognized that the method used for cost justifying the system had led to insufficient attention being given to managerial jobs and non-typing secretarial activities, particularly administration and filing, which provide greater scope for significant, although less tangible, savings and benefits. A similar view has been reached in many other organizations.

The goal-oriented method of evaluating costs and benefits can lead to less creative innovations, emphasizing short-term benefits and paying less attention to long-term effectiveness. It is a technique that can be successfully applied to limited and tightly defined problems and is most suitable for applications stimulated by the need to solve specific problems, although even here it may produce an unduly narrow definition of the problem. The objectives of cost benefit analyses may be difficult to set clearly, there may be little agreement amongst different users about priorities to be allocated to different factors, and outcomes cannot always be predicted with a high degree of accuracy. In a dynamic environment, the organization may need to evolve in an organic way rather than having new mechanistic ways of working imposed on it. An alternative method should therefore be considered.

Directional assessment of office innovations

Goal-driven planning pushes the organization towards the achievement of specified and measurable objectives. Directional planning, in contrast, is based on a broader definition of aims and tasks, as in the process described in Chapter 7, which involves producing a statement of an organization's information system strategy that offers a wide and flexible blueprint for development. In this approach, the decision makers state the general area in which the organization wants to work and the direction in which it wants to move. For example, a project may be initiated to gain familiarity with office technology, to assess its potential by stimulating its implementation in different parts of the organization, and to encourage innovation through applications instigated and steered by users.

Directional assessment allows for the fact that new goals are often discovered as a result of behaviour rather than being specified in advance. For instance, an English local government authority has been experimenting with office technology to find ways of easing communications between geographically separate offices. In doing so, it has discovered for itself the advantages of having connections to other locations, thereby opening the way for having more office work performed at home. The authority can now see that the technology can assist a new policy objective: employing a larger percentage of physically handicapped people who can work more easily from home than in an office.

The directional approach is most appropriate when it is too early to set clear goals, when the environment is unstable and the future uncertain, and where there is insufficient agreement on common objectives. It may be especially valuable in the early, experimental stages of a project and is more suitable for solution-driven applications and for some complex organizational changes. In all cases, it emphasizes the need to establish processes that enable individuals and groups to reflect on what they have discovered and to communicate this in the interests of organizational learning.

The experience of organizations using directional planning has demonstrated that this technique places considerable extra demands on management, and the organization as a whole, compared to goal-oriented techniques. It requires a greater need to process novel information relating to the consequences of change over a considerable period of time, because planning and acting are seen as clearly identifiable stages. It also runs a greater risk of producing an inefficient use of energy as there is a higher probability of following false leads and duplicating effort. Directional planning does, however, offer the prospect of discovering how the technology can make a more significant contribution to overall organizational effectiveness than less adventurous cost benefit analyses.

Which evaluation approach to adopt?

The characterization of goal-oriented and directional methods as distinct modes of planning reflects divergent assumptions about the degree to which all aspects of a problem can be precisely analysed, defined and quantified. The approaches also vary with respect to the range of factors taken into account in the evaluation. Typically, directional planning includes social as well as economic values whereas cost benefit analyses usually concentrate exclusively on financial factors. Directional planning is more likely to recognize and take into account that both formal and informal information processes and networks are important in understanding how an organization operates and they need to be represented in any assessment process (*see* Chapters 6 and 10).

Perhaps most significantly of all, the two methods are based on contrasting assumptions about the way organizations operate and the extent of the change likely to follow from the introduction of new technology. Goal-directed assessments assume that the majority of the real costs and benefits, and certainly the most significant ones, can be identified and attached to a specific set of people, activities and groups. It views the role of planning as being primarily concerned with control. The directional method emphasizes planning as a learning process and expects many of the real costs and benefits to emerge over time, often in tasks and areas far removed from those which were the focus of attention when changes were initially discussed. It aims to identify and handle these changes as they occur by establishing appropriate mechanisms to deal with them rather than by treating them in an *ad hoc* way because they could not be anticipated in formal cost benefit studies.

The decision about which approach to adopt will depend on the basic style of management in the organization and the nature of the applications being evaluated. While they represent markedly different perspectives, they can coexist. As has already been stated, the directional approach is most effective at earlier planning phases. Cost benefit analysis, however, can be effective at a more detailed, tactical level, once a specific aspect has been identified within a broader context. The information gathering aspect of cost benefit analysis is particularly useful, provided limitations of this method are borne in mind, such as its inability to be as precise about qualitative implications as it can be for measurable aspects.

Whatever method is adopted, managers should be aware that there is no single, objective way of accurately pinpointing all likely costs and benefits. Their own beliefs, prejudices and expectations can influence the results of evaluations, so a balanced view should be obtained from those who will be affected by innovations in office work.

The role of assessments in decision making

An American management specialist, Henry Mintzberg, has suggested that there are three fundamental ways in which a manager makes a choice from a selection of options: by analysis, by judgement and by bargaining. In planning and assessing new office technology, all three methods can be employed. The assessment process itself can also be of symbolic importance in the organization.

Analytical assessments

Analytical approaches to decision making involve the systematic evaluation of options in terms of their consequences for stated organizational goals. They can appropriately determine a decision only to the extent that all aspects of the problem can be defined and quantified, which is not possible when considering behaviour in organizations. The less tangible, but more important, broader impacts can be incorporated in assessments only through the processes of judgement and bargaining.

Making appropriate judgements

The subjective judgements of individuals play a vital part in weighing and augmenting the findings of any formal analysis because so many crucial aspects cannot be reduced to quantitative assessments. Since the experience and perspectives of different interests in the organization may vary, there are strong arguments for including a wide spectrum of people in the processes that identify the likely costs and benefits of new technology. Many of the potential users of the system may be physically remote from the technology, but are directly affected by procedures built around it and by the information it produces, so their views should also be taken into account.

Bringing together people from different parts of the organization may stimulate the discovery of new priorities and understandings. The ensuing process of discussion, assessment and review may be more important than the actual product of the evaluation in contributing to an overall understanding of how the organization operates.

Bargaining and negotiations in assessments

Negotiations and bargaining between different, interested parties are a necessary precursor to many important organizational choices (*see* Chapter 10). The subject is highlighted here because it recognizes that not everyone in an enterprise shares the same objectives and priorities. Where there is a conflict of interests, assessments may serve a variety of purposes.

For example, the evaluation process may be used to justify a particular viewpoint by providing propaganda that brings exaggerated good news about the potential benefits of a particular development. Alternatively, assessments can be used to delay unwanted changes, with those who oppose change providing calculations to show that the return on investment is insufficient. Assessments may become games to test the commitment of those involved or they may be advertisements intended to persuade key people and groups that a chosen course is the right one. Whatever the particular form the negotiations take, the existence of conflicting interests ensures that, whatever else assessments achieve, they provide ammunition in the game of organizational power and influence.

The symbolic influence of evaluations

Assessments are important not only for their impact on the eventual outcome chosen but also for what they represent. For example, managers may use them as a symbolic expression of their belief in sound management in which action is taken only on the basis of reasoned analysis. The decision style of the enterprise may be such that it requires a detailed, economic justification of capital investments and organizational change, even when many of those involved recognize its limitations. In such circumstances, it may be politic to present a decision as if it had been adopted primarily as the result of a conventional cost benefit analysis, although it is accepted in private that this is not the primary justification for the development. Similarly, an assessment may be used to signal to important outside groups that appropriate processes have been followed even if, in reality, they have not determined the actual action taken.

Organizations and managers often gain and retain their legitimacy by following the procedures and practices widely recognized as being desirable at the time. The importance attached in some quarters to rational, analytical processes is so great that organizations must, at least occasionally, be seen to be adopting them as a basis for decision making. Evaluations can also signify that something apparently systematic has been done in circumstances that may be characterized by a large number of unknown factors, such as with most computer-based office innovations.

Conclusions

Developments in new office technology provide significant new opportunities to improve performance, to enhance the working environment and to generate new services and products, but the potential of the technology has not always been realized in practice. Not only do many systems fail to meet their stated formal objectives, but they may become an additional source of problems to the enterprise. This disappointment is most likely to occur when those implementing systems take an unduly narrow perspective on information and its role within the organization. The real benefits of computer-based information systems, many still to be discovered, are more likely to be obtained through greater experimentation and a realistic assessment of the organizational setting in which office systems are embedded.

Recommendations

(1) Consider carefully what are the primary and secondary objectives for introducing new office technology. Where does the balance lie between problem-oriented, solution-oriented and change-related applications? If the main purpose is to reduce costs or solve a particular problem, study

the proposed actions to ensure that they do not lead to a narrow approach to the technology and its organizational context.

(2) Examine the organizational setting in which the technology will operate. In particular, carefully consider the following factors:

(a) The needs, expectations and skills of individuals and groups at all levels in the organization, giving thorough consideration to the apparently simple question 'Who will use the system?'. All those who will be affected by the system should be taken into account.

(b) The structure and style of the enterprise and the various groupings within it, remembering that there may be more variations between different interests than is initially recognized.

(c) The enterprise's complex network of suppliers, customers, clients and external regulatory bodies and legislation.

Thought should be given before going ahead with a system that conflicts with the basic way the enterprise operates; if it is necessary, extra managerial time and attention should be made available to oversee its implementation.

(3) Examine which of the factors in (2) are likely to alter in the future and discuss what this implies for the need to have a system that is sufficiently flexible and adaptable to cope with the developments.

(4) Identify what it is reasonable to expect from the assessment process. This should include the following:

(a) What is the decision making style of the enterprise? How does it expect decisions of this sort to be taken and justified? To whom must they be justified? The nature of the assessment may need to reflect this style, although other objectives could be considered informally.

(b) Having analysed and listed the more visible costs and benefits, investigate the main hidden ones. Identify how you will take account of the factors that are not amenable to quantitative measurement and analysis.

(c) If there are several different, perhaps conflicting, aims and expectations for the system, determine how these divergent views will be represented in any evaluation of the proposed changes. Examine whether evaluations are geared to support all, or only some, objectives.

   (d) Decide what role the assessment will play in choosing and implementing a system.
   (e) Recognize that assessments rarely anticipate all the major costs and benefits of planned changes.

(5) Set up a mechanism to find out what people have learned through implementing the technology, recognizing that there are likely to be successes and failures.

(6) Regard assessment as a continuing process that provides valuable understanding and information when the time comes to consider further developments (*see* Chapter 9).

References

1. Malvey, M., *Simple Systems, Complex Environments: Hospital Financial Information Systems*, Sage Publications, Beverley Hills, Ca (1981)
2. Hopwood, A.G., Evaluating the real benefits, in Otway, H.J. and Peltu, M., *New Office Technology: Human and Organizational Aspects*, Frances Pinter, London; Ablex, Norwood, N.J. (1983)
3. Buchanan, D.A. and Boddy, D., *Organizations in the Computer Age: Technological Imperatives and Strategic Choice*, Gower Press, Aldershot (1983)
4. March, J.G., Decisions in organizations and theories of choice, in Van de Ven, A.H. and Joyce, W.F. (eds), *Perspectives on Organization Design and Behaviour*, John Wiley and Sons, New York (1981)
5. McCaskey, M.B., A contingency approach to planning: planning with goals and planning without goals, *Academy of Management Journal*, **17** (2), 281–291 (1974)

Bibliography

The following publications are also relevant to topics discussed in this chapter.

Argyris, C., Organizational learning and management information systems, *Accounting, Organizations and Society*, **2** (2), 113–123 (1977)

Axelrod, C.W., *Computer Productivity: A Planning Guide for Cost Effective Management*, John Wiley and Sons, New York (1982)

Burchell, S., Clubb, C., Hopwood, A. G., Hughes, J. and Nahapiet, J., The role of accounting in organizations and society, *Accounting, Organizations and Society*, **5** (2), 5–27 (1980)

Feldman, S. and March J.G., Information in organization as signal and symbol, *Administrative Science Quarterly*, **26**, 171–186 (1981)

Galbraith, J. R. *Designing Complex Organizations*, Addison Wesley, Reading, Mass (1973)

Mintzberg, H., Planning on the left side and managing on the right, in Kolb, D. A., Rubin, I. M. and McIntyre, J. M. (eds), *Organizational Psychology: A Book of Readings*, Prentice Hall Inc, Englewood Cliffs, N.J. (1979, 3rd edition)

9

Managing the Introduction of New Office Systems

Gerdie Nillesen
and Paula Goosens

Introduction

Technology enthusiasts often suggest that the implementation of computer-based systems involves an effortless attainment of perfection in new forms of office work. The task of introducing new systems can be made to appear as simple as unpacking and assembling hi-fi audio equipment, requiring just a few elementary skills to set up and operate. This image is far from the truth. The introduction of new office technology is neither a short nor a simple activity.

This chapter examines the manager's role in ensuring that the operational systems meet appropriate objectives and continue to provide an efficient and effective service over a long period. It provides guidelines to assist managers in dealing with the challenges that arise from redesigning office jobs and applying new technological tools. It discusses the importance of adequate education and training, the part that should be played by technical experts and how to handle labour relations aspects. The aim is to provide a general framework and methodology that can be applied to the specific problems and circumstances faced by managers.

Turning objectives into real systems

The office of the future is often portrayed as a technological fix to all problems. An eminent computer scientist, Nicholas Negroponti, encapsulated this view at an international symposium in Japan in 1981 when he said 'The office of twenty years from now will weigh about two pounds, be battery powerered . . . . will have access to all the information in the world, will be able to see, hear and talk, will probably be flexible so I can take it to bed with me and waterproof so I can use it in the bathtub'. This book shows, however, that there is more to an office than a collection of technological wizardry.

There is a slogan: 'Organizations get the systems they deserve'. This is meant as a sceptical comment on how computer-based technology has often been implemented in the past. Many investments in computer-based systems have been made with great hopes for improving efficiency, competition and the working environment. The introduction of a new system, however, has often led to lengthy periods of upheaval, stress and frustration, eventually giving way to the operation of a system that falls far short of the high hopes that inspired it.

Managers cannot sit back and allow the technology to take its own course, pulling the organization behind it. They must take an active role in ensuring that the organization 'deserves' the best system. This means not only establishing the strategic vision and appropriate assessment techniques (*see* Chapters 7 and 8), but also creating satisfactory mechanisms to co-ordinate the introduction and operation of systems.

Even when technology seems to answer many of the theoretical criteria set for it, problems can arise if insufficient thought is given to the manner in which it is put to use. For example, top managers in one company made a quick decision to purchase new equipment when administrative personnel refused to lick an additional 2000 envelopes a week. The envelope-sealing technology worked well, but was moved from the troublesome administration department to the mail room. Within two weeks, many problems arose which had little to do with the particular equipment. For example, 'Did the mail room personnel have to lick envelopes if the machine broke down?', 'Should the mail room take over bulk mailing tasks handled by other departments?', 'Which managers or departments could make the decision?'.

Managers had taken the view that their prime responsibility was to get the best technology installed as quickly as possible. With more consideration for the non-technical aspects, they could have avoided, or limited, the subsequent organizational upheavals that arose. If this can occur with the relatively simple technology of envelope sealing, imagine the possible ramifications of making similar short-sighted decisions with computer-based technology.

Office technology in smaller organizations

Many of the specific management procedures and structures discussed in this chapter are applicable mainly to medium or large organizations. The processes and objectives discussed, however, are of relevance to even the smallest organizations, although the responsibilities may be the concern of only one or two managers and any technical expertise will come mainly from outside consultants or vendors of systems. Smaller organizations obviously have fewer problems relating to intra-organizational changes and personnel policies. Nevertheless, careful consideration must be given to these aspects in terms of immediate needs and possible future growth.

Anticipating implementation requirements

Many experiences with computer-based systems have shown that their benefits can be frittered away and the potential left largely untapped if organizational and personal adaptations have not been carefully considered and managed *before* the system is introduced. In one English company, for example, so much effort and resources were invested in the technical workings of an advanced office system that little time or money was available to consider other aspects. As a result, three months after implementation, the financial director decided to stop the project and send the equipment back to the supplier because the system had caused so many problems amongst users and disruptions to how the organization operated.

Before a system is introduced, much needs to be done. People who will be affected by it need education and training, which should continue once the system is operational. Authority and communications channels need to be scrutinized. Personnel policies should be adapted to new job, career and rewards patterns. Jobs must be redesigned, preferably to maintain and enlarge the job satisfaction of all employees. Without clear, visible benefits being delivered to individual users, potential gains in organizational efficiency and effectiveness are unlikely to be fully realized.

Work enjoyment and efficiency are not independent or conflicting purposes. People tend to work better and deliver higher quality output if they are motivated to do a job well and feel a commitment to the organization. This is particularly important when a possibly threatening innovation is introduced to a reasonably smooth-running operation. Neither software nor hardware computing power is a source of the creativity and energy that ultimately distinguish success from failure. These are achieved only by people willing to use the technology as an effective aid to do their jobs.

Effective implementation leadership

The manager or group responsible for handling the detailed design and implementation of a new system should have the ability to understand and deal with a broad range of issues. In the past, however, the people responsible for these functions have often been selected on the basis of their technical competence and their ability, or apparent ability, to meet budgets and deadlines. This tended to favour computer specialists, who generally underestimate the *managerial* task involved in implementing new systems. Although many data processing projects were established and run within a narrow technical and quantifiable framework, computer systems have been notorious for overshooting budgets and deadlines. The extra costs come from unplanned direct costs, as well as a variety of hidden costs (*see* Chapter 8).

Latent weak points and deficiencies in the organization will not be rationalized away by new systems: automating an inefficient operation could make it more inefficient. Computing aids can boost the apparent quickness of reaction and busyness in an organization without improving the quality of work or decision taking. Giving managers new systems to remove mundane work and to allow them more time to think is pointless if the managers are ill-equipped to take advantage of the extra time. The leadership of an office technology project must therefore take an open approach to change, seeking out and managing all the underlying issues. It must be strong enough to stand up to the scrutiny its decisions will come under and should have the authority to examine all relevant information and work activities (*see* Chapter 7).

When planning is not in your own hands

Many managers and professionals are faced with a *fait accompli* when it comes to new office technology. They are presented with a system, often without any previous consultation or explanation of the rationale behind changes because senior executives have taken the view that technology should be introduced as quickly as possible and that the results will inevitably be a success. This type of approach can succeed superficially in the short term, in the sense that new technology is installed and operated. The problems that have been overlooked, however, may eventually erupt. The individual faced with the imposition of the system will probably feel resentment and antagonism. Lack of preparation is also likely to mean that users are not educated and trained to understand, operate and exploit the system.

If you are faced with such an imposition, you should try to make a systematic, carefully considered case to suggest how the existing system can be improved. You should find practical evidence to convince the decision makers that their systems would have been of greater benefit to them and the organization, as well as to yourself, if there had been broader participation in its design, evaluation and implementation.

Preparing people for the system

To make best use of technology, users need to be prepared in two main ways:

(1) *Educated in new attitudes* to job tasks, interpersonal relations, work habits, and organizational procedures and responsibilities.
(2) *Trained in new techniques* to apply the technology effectively and to operate specific systems.

Education should mobilize people for change. It should start before systems are installed and be concerned with strategic issues in a continuing process, providing a forum to discuss and develop new approaches and new systems. Training should mainly be propaganda for the particular route chosen and cover aspects of the system's impact beyond its specific technical and operational characteristics.

Management education

Education should teach people to invest time in order to save time. It aims to take people from their current awareness and set of working routines to an understanding of new techniques and a new working lifestyle. New habits take a long time to sink in, so education should start as soon as possible and should continue for as long as necessary. With new office technology, an education programme should consist of the following:

(1) *Analysing existing work*: its faults, strengths and the influences that could help or hinder future developments.
(2) *Finding better ways* of reaching corporate goals.
(3) *Implementing* the new strategy for improved performance.
(4) *Creating new attitudes and behaviour* as an integral part of daily life.

Management education should focus on:

(1) *The process of decision making and planning*. Managers make decisions on the basis of intuitive skills developed from experience (*see* Chapter 10). New office technology offers a variety of aids to decision making, such as tools to analyse data, receive information and model future behaviour (*see* Chapter 4). The advantages and limitations of alternative aids should be fully discussed and individuals given the opportunity to become familiar with several approaches. This is an area that can be threatening to managers so requires intensive guidance and an appreciation of the continuing need for traditional management expertise.
(2) *Control and co-ordination*. Computers will make what people do or what they *don't* do more visible (*see* Chapter 5). Education is needed on the appropriate use of new capabilities for increased surveillance and monitoring, how people in lower echelons can cope, and how everyone can ultimately gain something.
(3) *Division of work between manager and secretary*. Habits in the relationship between management and secretarial and clerical staff are deeply rooted in traditional behaviour and personal status and motivation. Education programmes should explore new ways of organizing this relationship (*see* Chapter 5).
(4) *New management responsibilities*. The educational process should help the search for more effective and productive ways of organizing management and departmental responsibilities.

Management training

After giving users an initial familiarity with a new system, serious training should start one or two weeks after the system is installed, when users have had some chance to try the system and can begin to ask sensible questions. It is better not to teach too much at once. If an individual feels that insufficient initial training has been provided, it is better to give follow up assistance at a later stage than to extend the initial period, so that some hands-on experience can be gained to clarify the issues about which the user is uncertain. Attention should be given to changes in work practices other than those related directly to operating the system. Training should therefore not be conducted by computing specialists alone. If training is given too early, before key decisions have been taken about its implementation, too much emphasis will be given to technical operational aspects.

Training programmes should ensure the following:

(1) Specification of systems with good human–computer communication and built-in software training aids, like Computer Aided Learning and Help facilities, to enable systems to be used and understood without having to learn too many new computing concepts.
(2) A thorough discussion of basic equipment, new applications and task adjustments.
(3) Use of understandable language by the trainers and in documentation.
(4) A clear explanation of what the system *cannot* do as well as what it can.
(5) Familiarization of users with basic operations, such as using a keyboard or mouse, giving a feel of how the system works in live operation. Later, possibly in follow up training, specific developments, enhancements and intricacies can be explored.
(6) Provision of a basic understanding of how the system structures and processes information. This helps the user feel more comfortable in adjusting and extending the system in the future.
(7) Production of easy to reference, slim training manuals and documentation to back up formal courses.
(8) Instruction on how to adjust the system to local needs.
(9) Advice on suitable work tempo when using new office technology, particularly if the user is likely to spend long periods at a workstation.
(10) Some indication at the end of training to assist self confidence and morale, such as a certificate or a change in job title. This is more important for lower management levels and secretarial and clerical staff.

For managers, the following are particularly important aspects of training.

(1) *Support for beginners*. Training in advanced skills for managers or professionals already familiar with technology should be separated from training for newcomers. Fears about what will happen to their own jobs can make beginners extremely anxious. A sense of confidence and command should therefore be built up gradually. Time should be given to the individual to 'give it a go' on their own, without always being forced into group work where managers may be frightened of exposing their lack of knowledge in front of colleagues or subordinates.

(2) *Consideration for older managers*. Young people tend to be more open to learn about computer-based systems, particularly because they are more likely to have gained an awareness of the technology either at school, at home or playing arcade games. Training for older employees should take account of the greater strains on them both to learn new skills and to face up to the changes in their jobs and career prospects.

(3) *Resistance to training*. Many managers dislike spending time in training, either because they are frightened of failing or feel it is a waste of time. Top management must therefore take positive steps to ensure managers attend training. Senior executives should be seen to be trained themselves and the training programme should include the provision of practical skills that can be quickly applied.

(4) *Follow up*. Active support and assistance should be provided on a continuing basis. Encouragement should be given to forming groups, networks and workshops so that users help each other by exchanging experiences. The way systems are being actually operated should be checked soon after initial training, then six to nine months later (and periodically after that) to sort out any misunderstandings and problems. The amount of time and resources needed for follow up, and the importance of providing it, should not be underestimated.

(5) *Training in writing programs*. The availability of end user languages (*see* Chapter 2) and other software aids means that managers should rarely need to program their own software. Training courses should be provided, however, for those with a special need or interest in programming. These should take at least a week and be oriented towards creating dummy programs that can be thrown away later rather than trying to

develop software of crucial importance to live working.

The role of computing specialists

Computing specialists have many skills relevant to the implementation of new office systems. They are also often hardworking and dedicated to the task they are carrying out. A method should be developed that makes use of computing specialists within a framework that enables managers with a broad perspective to steer developments in the appropriate corporate direction.

Data processing professionals have often suffered from two drawbacks in relation to new office technology. Firstly, their technical orientation has been towards centralized mainframe systems. Many of them failed to take an interest in word processors because they regarded them as uninteresting in terms of computer systems design. The emergence of the microcomputer was also dismissed by some DP staff as of interest only to computing hobbyists and home enthusiasts.

Secondly, they have often lacked an understanding of, or interest in, human and organizational consequences of the changes they initiate. They have tended to regard the person who is meant to benefit from the system as somewhat remote from their own, mainly technical, considerations: hence the term *end user* to depict the manager, secretary or clerk whose job depends on using the new system. Computing specialists' experiences with relatively highly structured work in traditional data processing tasks have made them view office work in a similar vein, emphasizing those aspects that increase formalization, structuring, preprogramming and monitoring of work.

Information centres to support users

The views of computing specialists, however biased, are likely to be highly influential because of their technical knowhow. Management should therefore create a new structure and process that enables managers, users and computing specialists to work together towards a common aim. The *information centre* or *user support centre* provides such a solution for many organizations; the establishment of user and related teams, discussed later in this chapter, should also be considered.

Information centres are decentralized focal points where users can gain practical experience of new systems and obtain advice on how to apply computer-based techniques in their own jobs. This could involve having a *walk-in service*, so managers and others can come to seek *ad hoc* assistance. A variety of hardware and software in the information centre can be made available for hands-on demonstrations and experiments. *Flying squads* of specialists and trainers can be provided to respond to calls from users for specific assistance at their own workplaces.

In some organizations, information centres have remained under the control of central DP departments although they are located close to the offices where systems are actually being used. While it is important that the centre contain people skilled in relevant computing techniques, the management responsibilities and goals for an information centre should aim to achieve corporate goals. Computing specialists must adjust to the fact that knowledge about computer-based information systems no longer gives them an exclusive hold on the technology as an influential powerbase. Their role must emphasize *service* and *consultancy* rather than the control of designing and producing systems that determine how other people work.

Managers and users should neither stand in awe of the technical specialists nor should they reject their advice out of hand because they have often failed to provide the required systems in the past. The notion of service from an information centre is crucial. Staff working in it should not feel bound to support any particular method but should aim to assist users in finding the best solutions to their particular needs. The technology is changing so quickly that nobody should feel incompetent if she or he cannot answer a problem without first having to do some research. Managing an information centre will be difficult because it is trying to blend different skills, expertise and objectives, but it is necessary to pursue a course such as this if office technology is to be introduced in a humane and productive manner.

Traditional ways of co-ordinating implementation

The management structures and methods used to co-ordinate and control the implementation process are of great importance. In the past, two techniques have been particularly popular.

Steering committees

Steering committees have been widely used with data processing systems, bringing together a group of weighty figures in the organization who monitor the work of specific task forces. Such a technique may be useful if the new system is of vital strategic significance to the organization's survival and needs the constant attention of many senior managers. Steering groups, however, do not always steer. They often lose any sense of mission after the first few meetings leaving it to a few active individuals, typically technical specialists, to dominate the committee. Managers and computing experts in the group can play a cat and mouse game, batting the question of who is ultimately responsible between each other so that, in the end, nobody really takes decisive action to steer the development of the system. Many key human and organizational issues involve talking about individuals, which is difficult to do in a committee. Important issues may therefore be fudged or dodged. Particular user problems are often ignored or overruled and those who participate as user representatives may effectively become hostages who lend some credibility to a process over which they had little real influence.

Project management

A project management approach brings together individuals from many activities in the organization. This can be a useful way of combining different experiences and skills if it is effectively organized, with due and explicit prominence given to social and organizational objectives. In practice, however, many problems arise.

In organizations with rigid, hierarchical boundaries, the final decisions may be left to a senior manager who is remote from the detailed discussions and who may be unwilling to make important changes if they offend particular line managers. Project management can be suitable for relatively self-contained tasks but is generally unsatisfactory when policies that last longer than the lifetime of the project need to be developed and implemented. If the project carries on for too long, it can become institutionalized, fighting its own battles rather than acting to co-ordinate the needs of others.

A new approach to office technology implementation

A strong theme developed in this book is the importance of managers taking personal responsibility for the design, introduction and use of systems within their local workplace. Having evaluated many experiences of the implementation of computer-based systems, we believe this can best be achieved by integrating new office technology developments within normal organizational functions. This requires that a senior manager, possibly an information manager, has overall authority for the establishment and co-ordination of corporate policies and standards, within which local control over implementation is handled by *user teams* and specialist *related teams*. The overall strategy lays down standards for activities like establishing the telecommunications infrastructure and selection of the vendors of key systems. Corporate co-ordination is carried out through a *sounding board*, the equivalent in stature to a steering committee, but more open in listening to and reflecting the differing requirements of local management. The sounding board should be involved primarily in creating the commitment to the strategic vision and policy while the user and related teams control the shaping of policy (*see Figure 7.4* in Chapter 7).

The user team

The user team should consist of the relevant line manager plus representatives from all levels of staff, supplemented by specialists in computing and personnel management skills. It undertakes the main work of implementation, decides between possible alternatives and has an important say in monitoring and controlling schedules. The manager leads the team as part of his or her normal role. One manager should have sole responsibility for all aspects of installation so that disputes do not arise about who is in charge of specific aspects, such as hardware, software, cabling, new furniture, and so on.

The computing specialist acts as a consultant, advising on the technical feasibility of proposals, suggesting alternative courses, and liaising with the related main computing team. The involvement of an expert in personnel management helps to ensure that the changes to an individual's job, labour relations and organizational design are considered from an early stage. Both experts need to take steps to show why and how they can contribute practically to the implementation but, at other times, they should step back and learn from the rest of the team how their own specialization is affected.

The manager should lead the team by formulating possible ways ahead and focusing attention on key issues. Time should be given for members of the team to undertake their own fact finding without having any predetermined solutions. Feedback on the team's performance and progress should be given continuously by the manager, who should also explain how the team's efforts fit into corporate plans. Members of the team should not be expected to answer specific questions until they have mastered the technical language and concepts.

The user teams needs to assist in the following phases:

(1) Preparing and carrying out necessary educational programmes.
(2) Problem definition and goal setting.
(3) Evaluation of technical systems.
(4) Assessment of local and corporate organizational aspects.
(5) Choosing between alternatives and reporting why.
(6) Gaining approval from the sounding board.
(7) Allocation of resources and purchasing/rental of systems.
(8) Undertaking any necessary work and structural reorganizations.
(9) Planning and providing necessary training.
(10) Experimentation and operational use of the system.
(11) Evaluation of actual use and reporting results to the sounding board.

An important early task is to describe the specific problems to be solved with new equipment in a report that will be used by senior management as the basis for allocating people and resources to the implementation process. This report should include the following main points:

(1) Answering the question 'Why are we changing?' in terms of a definition of the actual problem and the setting of realistic, achievable goals.
(2) A detailed description of the current state of affairs, to be used as the basis for assessing future performance.
(3) An analysis of costs and benefits (*see* Chapter 8).
(4) An estimation of the proposed changes in work procedures, job definitions and technical systems.
(5) A method for monitoring and evaluating the effectiveness and quality of implementation.
(6) An assessment of the implications for other departments

affected by the system.

(7) Plans and schedules for demonstrations, education, training, and research into suitable systems, including visits to other users.

Related specialist teams

The computing and personnel specialists within a user team must liaise with related teams of experts who co-ordinate corporate activity in their areas:

(1) *The Information Systems (IS) team* oversees all technical issues relating to computer-based information systems, defining how the technology can best meet user requirements and providing any necessary support services.

(2) *The personnel team* includes specialists who can help with:

(a) *Personnel planning*. Recruitment policies to take account of changes in skills and qualification requirements over a five to ten year period.

(b) *Education, training and retraining*. The kind of education and training needed and how it can best be provided (in-house, with the assistance of vendors, external courses, etc.).

(c) *Appraisal and compensation systems*. How work can be assessed and compensated for once new systems are introduced. Sometimes a one-off payment may be made to smooth transition to the new system.

(d) *Job descriptions and ratings*. Defining new working roles and grading them to ensure their rewards match the new responsibilities.

(e) *Job satisfaction*. How new job roles should overcome potential stress, alienation and other problems identified in Chapter 5.

(f) *Career development*. How new career paths can be plotted to exploit technology related skills; how career development for existing staff may be altered; and how to ensure that there is sufficient flexibility in personnel procedures to allow for the necessary mobility.

(g) *Job security, redundancy and redeployment*. The degree of job security that can be offered, such as no compulsory redundancies; how to compensate for any necessary reductions in staff levels, say through early retirement or voluntary redundancy; and plans to train staff who can be redeployed in new job roles.

(h) *Labour relations*. See discussion later in this chapter.
(i) *Conditions of employment*. Health and safety in the working environment (*see* Chapter 3); possible changes in work location, such as the use of home-based workstations; and revised, more flexible working hours.

The sounding board

The sounding board is a group of top managers with interests and expertise that can contribute to the development of new office information systems. It is the central forum for discussing organizational, financial, social and technical aspects of innovations, but does not aim to steer all parts of the organization in the same direction. It listens to, and discusses, progress reports from user and specialist teams and, if necessary, counsels them on what to do.

Meetings of the board should not be inquests or trials. They should stimulate and motivate, and provide practical support in assisting users to gain insight into their own requirements, say, by comparing experiences and results with other groups using similar systems. The last part of the meeting should be taken up with budget control, scheduling task assignments, and identification of key problems and actions. All parties should know who is expected to do what. Managers, staff and union representatives who wish to familiarize themselves with developments should be allowed to attend sounding board meetings.

Steps towards a full system

The pace of implementation is likely to speed up as individuals and the organization gain experience of a new system and understand its limits and potentials (known as the *learning curve*). Bearing this in mind, many organizations prefer to try out systems before going ahead with the full solution. This can be prudent to avoid the risk of making a major mistake through inexperience. Two methods have been widely used to make the early steps more of a learning experience than a direct attempt to achieve all working goals at once: *pilot projects* and *prototype software*.

Pilot projects

Pilot projects are self-contained systems applied in a real working environment, but whose main aim is to gain experience that can be applied to other live systems. The following are important factors to consider in managing pilot projects:

(1) *Objectives*. The pilot should be neither so limited that it is guaranteed to succeed nor so ambitious that it tries to prove the impossible. It should provide tangible benefits to the individuals and groups involved, who should not be treated as purely experimental guinea pigs.

(2) *Evaluation criteria*. Pilots tend to be more suitable for tasks that can be easily measured, such as costs and technical feasibility. As they are self-contained with limited time scales, it is difficult to obtain meaningful data from pilot projects on broader, qualitative social and organizational issues. Care should therefore be taken to understand the limitations of any conclusions that can be drawn.

(3) *Leadership*. Ideally, the pilot project should be led by a manager who understands people and technology and can act as a facilitator to resolve the variety of issues involved. Such individuals are difficult to find but top managers should give visible personal backing to the person who has to manage this role.

(4) *Size*. Management systems consultant Alexia Martin, from the Stanford Research Institute (SRI), recommends an optimum size of between ten and twenty people with common tasks, but a variety of roles, for projects involving personal communication and information retrieval aids. Pilots covering managerial and professional text processing systems, she recommends, should have at least fifty principals. If a project is too small, its results will have little general value. If it is too large, it becomes too complex and difficult to manage.

(5) *Location and visibility*. Some specialists, like Alexia Martin, recommend that the pilot project should be highly visible throughout the organization so its results will be accepted by other parts of the organization. High visibility, however, means a high risk factor if something goes wrong in what is an experimental project.

(6) *Transfer of results*. Experience gained in pilots should be used to assist other projects, but it would be dangerous if the results of one project dictated the procedures of all later implementations.

Software prototypes

In the past, software has either been developed from scratch to a detailed specification or ready-built packages have been bought from software vendors. Prototype software is developed gradually through close interaction between the software experts and the user.

The basic concept behind prototyping is that users can respond more realistically to a tangible system than to a theoretical design. The software developers therefore produce an initial system very quickly, knowing that it will be raw and unrefined. This rough outline could be drawn up in a few days and the first prototype could be ready in ten to twenty days after that. The users try out the system and adjustments are made as necessary. A sequence of prototypes evolves towards the required system, resulting in software that should be tailored to real user needs. Users involved in the process should be given sufficient technical education and training to allow them to contribute to a dialogue with software specialists. Rigorous testing is vital before any prototype moves into an environment other than that for which it was originally developed[1].

Labour relations

The changes in office work caused by new technology mean that labour relations implications must be considered from an early stage. Trade unions have often requested that the introduction of new systems be preceded by negotiations for *new technology agreements* covering aspects such as: the provision of full and timely information; consultation and participation in decision making; job security; redeployment and redundancy payments; training; health and safety regulations; job enrichment; work monitoring; data privacy; and access to outside experts by unions. Many countries have legislation and guidelines in some of these areas, particularly health and safety aspects and some form of co-determination in decision making[2].

The reaction of unions or other staff representatives to new office technology will depend largely on the prevailing labour relations climate in the organization and, to some extent, in the country as a whole. That is why it is important to involve personnel specialists from an early stage, as discussed above.

Job security and consultations with unions

The two issues that most affect labour relations are employment levels and participation in decision making. Ideally, unions would like the same number of jobs to be maintained after the technology has been implemented. This contradicts the frequent management aim of using technology to reduce staff costs. In many cases, however, a compromise has been reached by management agreeing to have no compulsory redundancies and to achieve any necessary staff reductions by *natural wastage* (not replacing staff who leave voluntarily), staff redeployment, early retirement and voluntary redundancy with adequate compensation.

In the past, unions tended to respond to technological change after systems had been chosen, so their main role was in negotiating rewards for operating the new systems and making relatively minor adjustments to the system. The tendency more recently has been to try to influence systems *before* they are designed and chosen. Managers and computing specialists often regard this as an unwelcome interference with their own powers, although they accept that more user participation generally produces more effective systems.

In some countries, such as the Federal Republic of Germany, *works councils* have been established with legislative backing to provide a mechanism for staff participation in decision making. These councils have rights to receive timely information on key changes affecting work practices. In practice, members of works councils generally have too little knowledge to become involved in the details of computer systems design. In Scandinavia, unions have made a more concerted effort to receive adequate computing training, particularly for *data stewards* or *technology representatives* who sit on technical design teams. Research into such methods of co-determination indicates that, while trade unions 'sit at the table' and voice their opinions, they generally have little real influence on major aspects of systems development. There has also been a tendency for trade unionists who receive special training to become so involved in the technology that they lose sight of the user perspective they are meant to represent.

Managers should avoid viewing all union or staff requests in a confrontational context. There are many aspects of new technology agreements, such as ergonomics, increased user participation, adequate training and an element of job security, that can be of great benefit to office innovation, if handled in an appropriate manner.

The implementation process

Implementation of new office technology is a social and human process, as well as a technical change. This must be borne in mind when progressing through the following main stages in introducing new office systems.

How to start

Before proceeding with implementation, have a carefully prepared, phased plan. It is usually preferable to start by taking a small step in the direction you want to go with the full system. It is less costly and risky to start small and then expand facilities when users have gained more experience, either by an extension of the initial system and/or by introducing the same system elsewhere in the organization. This is why important evaluation criteria for new systems should be their ability to grow in an evolutionary manner and to be compatible with other key systems used in the organization.

What to avoid

Do not be too futuristic or raise hopes too high. For example, an accounting department in a manufacturing company was told how a new system could help them in one of their most time consuming tasks, filling information in on forms that were sent daily to the production plants. Later, management decided that this would be too expensive. Expectations had been raised only to be shattered. So keep the benefits and limitation of technology within a realistic context and avoid giving too much credence to the over optimistic views of vendors and technology enthusiasts.

How to proceed

Implementation should proceed in a gradual manner, with well defined milestones and stages. An opportunity should be given to evaluate progress regularly, learn from experience and adapt objectives, schedules and systems accordingly.

Lessons to be borne in mind

The experiences of those who have been involved in developing complex computer-based systems should be given weight. Many of these have been summarized with insight and humour by John Gall[3] such as in the following axioms:

(1) In setting up a new system, tread softly: you may be disturbing another system that is actually working.
(2) Systems develop goals of their own the instant they come into being.
(3) A system that performs in a certain way will continue to operate in that way, regardless of the need or changed conditions.
(4) New systems generate new problems.
(5) Great advances are not produced by systems designed to produce great advances.

What the system should achieve

The system should fullfil the following main requirements:

(1) The new system must be at least as good as the previous, possibly manual, system.
(2) The system should contribute additional value and quality.
(3) Targets that can be quantified in a meaningful way should be set and met.
(4) The new system should provide immediate, practical benefits to users, as well as any long term advantages.
(5) Human–computer communication should be of a high standard (*see* Chapter 3).
(6) The needs of *all* users should be met.
(7) The system should be flexible and capable of local adjustments.
(8) Individuals' job satisfaction should be enhanced.
(9) The system should support people working as a group and individually.

Integrating all management objectives

All technical, financial, human and organizational aspects should be evaluated systematically (*see Table 9.1*) so that those involved in development and implementation will appreciate the broad range of impacts caused by the new system. It is better to consider all aspects within a consistent framework, rather than to deal with

Table 9.1 Chart to assist integration of all aspects of office innovation

Alternative solutions	*Technical merit*	*Financial benefits*	*Human aspects*	*Organizational impact*
(1)	+	0	++	+
(2)	--	++	-	0
(3)	0	-	0	-
(4)	++	+	+++	++
.	.	.	.	.
.	.	.	.	.
.	.	.	.	.

Note: 0 is neutral; number of '+' marks indicates positive value; '-' marks show the degree of negative assessment.

each aspect separately, and then try to create the appropriate blend afterwards.

Keeping systems close to actual working needs

Consultation from the earliest stages with users is an important way of ensuring that the final system bears a close relationship to what is actually wanted. Many managers fear that such consultation will inevitably be a time consuming activity that is likely to stimulate resistance from some quarters. Failure to involve users, however, has been one of the major causes of the poor working performance of many computer-based systems. Managers should keep users informed and allow them to participate in shaping the final system in a manner that suits the prevailing corporate management style; this helps to facilitate, rather than hinder, the development and implementation of effective systems.

Possible stumbling blocks and problems

Managing the implementation of new office technology is unlikely to be completely smooth and trouble free. The following are some difficulties that may be encountered:

(1) *Technical problems*. Computer-based systems are complex entities. It has been common for software, in particular, to

have many errors (*bugs*) that crop up after implementation and which can be difficult to identify and eradicate (*debug*).

(2) *Conversion problems*. Moving from a manual system to a computer one, or from one computer-based system to another, can be time consuming, costly and fraught with difficulties. Transferring data from manual files to computer storage can be a major task. Incompatibilities between software, computer storage and the telecommunications capabilities of equipment can also be a significant obstacle.

(3) *Vendor and supplier difficulties*. Vendors may not live up to their pre-sales promises and insufficient maintenance and support may be provided. In some cases, the vendor may go out of business completely, a problem that occurs most frequently with very small software suppliers.

(4) *Management style*. The way the office technology project is managed can cause problems if it is at odds with corporate style, for example, if an attempt is made to have an open, participatory approach to office technology within a culture that emphasizes closed decision making by top managers. In such circumstances, an attempt should be made to achieve the desired approach, but with techniques adapted to the prevailing management climate.

(5) *Reactions to changes in status*. Tension and friction can be generated because the power and status relationships between individuals and groups may be changed by the advent of the new system. Small scale reorganizations could be used to assess likely changes and trainers can assist managers and staff to prepare for their new roles and relationships.

(6) *Work performance changes*. Computer-based systems can generate exaggerated expectations, causing frustration and anxiety even though the new system is operating more efficiently than the previous method. For example, a manager may have been content to wait half an hour to have a document retrieved in the past. Now, if the computer does not respond in a few seconds, the manager may become angry. The time taken for a system to respond to a user (the *response* time) is therefore an important evaluation criterion.

(7) *Misunderstanding the system's capabilities*. This is caused by poor training and provision of insufficient product information. A frequent problem with word processing, for example, is that managers can expect secretaries and typists to handle too much work, too quickly, and force documents to go through too many drafting phases. The result has been

friction between managers and secretaries and inefficient use of resources, including, for example, an increase in the amount of paper generated by the unnecessary number of drafts. One secretary even started using a manual typewriter for some executives to prevent them continually changing text.

Preparing the environment

Changes may have to be made to the physical environment, such as providing new ducts for cables, more ergonomic lighting, more points where workstations can be plugged to networks, and special environmental controls[4]. Costs for such changes can equal or exceed those for the hardware and software. The later such changes are made in the life cycle of new systems, the greater is the cost because operation of the system will have to be interrupted.

Security and privacy

If the computer-based information system is damaged through a breakdown, accident or deliberate sabotage, the organization could lose a great deal of money and even be forced to close. Much of the information held on the system is important because it represents private details about individuals or because it indicates monetary values, as in a banking system. Managers therefore need to take measures to protect systems, particularly in the following aspects:

(1) *Physical security*. Access to locations that contain computers, workstations and information, such as libraries with magnetic disks and tapes, should be carefully controlled.
(2) *Systems back-up*. Precautions need to be taken to ensure that facilities are available to recover from a breakdown or that there is sufficient *back-up* resource, such as a duplicate processor, that can be switched into action when some parts of the system are faulty. Copies of key data should be stored in secure sites remote from the main office, so that files can be recreated if something happens to the live system. Arrangements should be made with users of similar systems, or the vendor, to allow some programs to be run on their machines in emergencies.
(3) *Choosing reliable and resilient systems*. Important evaluation criteria should be the *reliability* of a system (how frequently it breaks down) and its *resilience* (the quickness and ease with

which it can recover from a breakdown). Systems should be able to operate at reduced performance if some elements fail (*graceful degradation*).

(4) *Privacy and data protection*. Many countries have *data protection* and privacy laws governing an individual's or a group's control over private information. These include the right to be able to check the accuracy of information held on you and to prevent information collected for one purpose, say medical records, being used for another, say by an employer when assessing an individual for a job. Systems should have built-in software checks, for example, the need to give a password before access is allowed to particular classes of information. Managers should become familiar with data protection legislation in all countries where they operate, or to which they may send information, because these laws can have significant practical implications, such as obtaining a licence to operate a database and incorporating data protection checks into the system.

Negotiating the contract

Vendors usually have standard contracts that are biased in their own favour. If something goes wrong, it can be difficult for the user to get recompense through contractual liabilities. Managers should therefore ensure that the contract explicitly contains clauses covering points of potential dispute, with clear guidelines of what performance is expected. Where a number of suppliers are involved, the responsibilities of each should be spelt out. Expert legal advice should be obtained before signing major contracts.

Insuring the system

It is relatively easy to obtain insurance covering the physical hardware value of systems but more difficult to determine the value of the consequential loss to an organization if information or software is lost or stolen. Insurance companies are more likely to consider reasonable requests if there is evidence that detailed consideration has been given to security aspects.

Delivery of the system

An example of the need for managers to be involved in all details of a system is the question of the delivery of equipment. Some vendors deliver only to the door, or the street sidewalk outside the door, as part of the standard contract. Either extra money has to be paid to the vendor to install the system or the user organization must make its own arrangements.

Handling the final transition

Once a system has been installed and is working, it is often desirable to have a period of *parallel running*, during which both the old and new systems are operational. This obviously requires extra money and staff, but is usually worthwhile during the initial period of any major computer-based systems, when technical problems are most likely to occur. Management must ensure that the old system is discontinued immediately the new one is working satisfactorily.

Monitoring and evaluating the system

It cannot be overemphasized that the introduction of a computer-based system is not a once and for all exercise. The system, like the organization in which it operates, is likely to be in a continuous state of evolution as the business, economic, technical and legislative environments change. Management must ensure that the way the system is working is frequently monitored and systematically evaluated by a broad range of people. Basic points to be considered in the evaluation include the following:

(1) How have the original promises for increased cost effectiveness and productivity been realized? Such analyses should go beyond superficial examination of measurable criteria.
(2) What are the strengths and weaknesses in the redesigned office?
(3) Is the system being operated according to intentions implicit in the design? If not, why not? What spin-offs and side effects have there been?
(4) How has the behaviour of users and others affected by the system changed? What changes have there been in influence and dependency between individuals and groups?
(5) How have staff levels changed? How have the contents of jobs changed? Are staff more or less motivated and committed to their work than before?
(6) Are there functions that have been underused? If so, why? Are the underused facilities unimportant or should more use of them be encouraged?
(7) What new facilities are most needed? Can they be provided

by extending the existing system or should a major new office technology project be initiated?

(8) Are there sufficient workstations or too many? Should schedules for access to workstations be revised?

(9) Is the administration and maintenance of the system satisfactory?

The manager's role: balancing and optimizing

Managing the introduction of new office technology is often a question of balancing many pros and cons, resolving conflicting aims and making choices that optimize the final performance of the system. It requires an ability to handle small details and also to have strategic vision and the expertise to implement significant changes that affect many people. Senior executives have often underestimated the impact of new office technology. Small changes were allowed to happen in an unplanned way, eventually building up into major organizational and job alterations.

Managers should play an active and positive role in all stages of the introduction of new systems, including the following activities:

(1) Assessing the system and maintaining an overview of the variety of people and interests that need to be considered.

(2) Ensuring that all important topics are addressed and that particular groups, such as technical specialists, do not have undue influence on the course taken.

(3) Conceptualizing future possibilities and incorporating any missing dimensions in current proposals.

(4) Anticipating potential conflicts and problems and bringing them into the open.

(5) Maintaining open communication channels with relevant interests to discuss and resolve possible difficulties before they can sour the system.

(6) Helping to formulate problems clearly, with a broad understanding of the rationale behind the establishment of clear, tangible goals.

(7) Providing the necessary education, training and retraining.

(8) Ensuring adequate financial and skilled human resources are available.

(9) Liaising with other managers, say through a sounding board, to establish the necessary co-ordination and awareness.

Recommendations

(1) Regard the implementation of new office technology as a continuing process with broad ramifications throughout the organization.
(2) Ensure that the management structure handling office innovation includes representatives from all interested parties and from all those with relevant special skills, such as personnel management and computing experts.
(3) Integrate the introduction of new systems into the normal management of the organization.
(4) Top management should establish corporate policies and guidelines for all information management and computer-based systems in the organization. Detailed implementation, however, should be left to local managers and users.
(5) Expect the provision of computing expertise to be a service and advisory function, whether it is provided by external consultants or an in-house information systems or data processing department.
(6) Have a phased, step by step introduction schedule, starting with smallish developments.
(7) Establish necessary education and training programmes backed by suitable resources.
(8) Make explicit all organizational, human, financial and technical objectives. Set up mechanisms to ensure they are integrated systematically into procedures for the design, implementation and evaluation of systems.
(9) Monitor and evaluate systems on a continuing basis. Initiate a new project when major change is identified.

References

1. Gremillion, L.L. and Pyburn P., Breaking the system development bottleneck, *Harvard Business Review*, **61** (2), 130–137 (1983)
2. Evans, J., Negotiating technological change, in Otway, H. J. and Peltu, M. (eds), *New Office Technology: Human and Organizational Aspects*, Frances Pinter, London; Ablex, Norwood, N.J. (1983)
3. Gall, J. *Systemantics*, Kangaroo Books, New York (1978)
4. Duffy, F., *The Orbit Study: Information Technology and Office Design*, DEGW, London and EOSYS Ltd, Slough (1983)

Bibliography

The following publications are also relevant to topics discussed in this chapter.

Makower, J., *Office Hazards*, Working Women Education Fund, Cleveland, Ohio (1983)

Marshall, D. and Gregory, J. (eds), *Office Automation: Jekyll or Hyde?* Working Women Education Fund, Cleveland, Ohio (1983)

Peltu, M., *Successful Management of Office Automation*, National Computing Centre, Manchester (1984)

Schlefer, J., Office automation and bureaucracy, *MIT Technology Review*, **86**(5), 32–40 (1983)

Vonnegut Jr., K., *Player Piano*, Dell Publishing Co, New York (1952, 1980)

Warren McFarlan, E. and McKenney, J.L., The information archipelago – plotting a course, *Harvard Business Review*, **61**(4), 145–156 (1983)

10

Management Autonomy in Bargaining and Negotiation

Brian Wynne

Introduction

The key to successful management is to nourish the interpersonal skills needed to bargain, motivate and negotiate effectively and to encourage sufficient autonomy and discretion to allow these skills to produce changes suitable to particular needs. Technically oriented computer systems designs, however, often fail to recognize this (*see* Chapter 6). They assume that organizations run on the basis of unambiguous, unified definitions of job roles, authority structures and information channels, whereas they really operate as complex, dynamically changing coalitions that represent disparate goals and interests.

This chapter focuses on the bargaining and negotiation requirements for managers as receivers and implementors of new office technology because of the central importance to managers and organizations of these processes. It draws together some of the themes discussed in the rest of the book in examining the kinds of management and organization styles most appropriate for handling computer-based systems. The types of management skills and negotiation approaches that are most likely to succeed are analysed, with stress laid on the importance of understanding the historical and cultural context in which managers operate.

Living with new office technology

The planning and introduction of new office technology should be the subject of much negotiation at all levels within an organization (*see* Chapter 7). In addition, the technology offers new instruments to be used in bargaining over what organizational goals should be. A distinction has therefore often been drawn between the role of managers in implementing such technologies and their subsequent responsibilities in living with the new systems once they are installed. Experience has shown, however, that this is a false dichotomy.

Implementation cannot be regarded as a once and for all event. There must be regular iterations between designers and users: making changes to the design on the basis of trial and error, repeatedly scanning the market to look at available systems, developing or buying special systems to fill gaps in the original development, and so on. 'Implementation' as such may never end, particularly given the rapid innovation rate of the technology. The second phase, living with the system, is also intimately bound up with the way implementation is carried out. Implementation and live operation therefore form a continuous, evolutionary process, rather than clearly demarcated activities.

Nevertheless, some useful observations can be drawn by considering the different strands in this interlaced process. The same manager can, indeed, play different roles in relation to the technology, even when implementation and operation run concurrently. This can lead to new stresses and conflicts. For example, a manager may have the implementation of a new system imposed on her or him from above while still being responsible for its advent and acceptability in the eyes of subordinates, who clearly see flaws in the system. Managers who have the authority to initiate their own office technology development may become ensnared by important new constraints on their job when learning to live with their system.

Management roles and organizational structures vary so much that it is not possible to provide a general prescription for the ideal way in which managers can handle their new roles. Three key principles can be identified, however, as the basis for finding particular solutions:

(1) *Access to the main decision process*. Managers must be able to influence decisions which shape the way new systems are introduced and developed in their real, social context. Decision making must be seen as a continuous process, not as isolated events.
(2) *Degree of formalization*. Managers should have a say on how far and in what areas management activities can, and should, be subjected to the formalization which computer software requires.
(3) *Management style*. The effective implementation of new office technology usually requires that even more attention

than usual be paid to human negotiation processes and accommodations[1]. This is true even though the technology is often sold with the implicit promise that it will avoid the less 'tidy', less 'rational' business of human interactions.

Implications of distributed computing

The management issues raised by new office systems can be illustrated by examining a move typical in many organizations, that from centralized to decentralized information systems. Developments in microelectronics and telecommunications have made it possible to link traditional data processing capabilities to the more personal facilities of the office. Equipment on office desk tops can now represent powerful and functionally rich computing systems. Managers may therefore want to take more detailed direct control over office equipment, such as telephones and keyboards, rather than leaving it largely to their secretaries. There will, at least, be some redefinition of the relative scope of the manager's and secretary's freedom and responsibilities over what have now become the real symbols and tools of power.

The availability of relatively low cost computing capabilities can also lead to changes in the relationship between the centre of the organization and individual managers. A local manager now has the capability to own and control databases and software tools tailored to personal or departmental needs. This reduces and blurs his or her dependence on, and responsibility to, central departments and provides the technical freedom to create localized financial management, scheduling, work styles, and priorities which differ from corporate standards.

Distributed computing creates a momentum towards a diversification of management approaches, although corporate requirements tend towards expecting uniformity throughout the organization and predictable behaviour from all managers. On the other hand, the availability of flexible new office technology offers new opportunities for improving overall efficiency. The resultant tensions need to be handled by renegotiating centre–individual relationships in parallel with other aspects of technical and organizational change. This can be accomplished in an acceptable way through private accommodations and the generation of trust between affected parties, as illustrated in the successful case study in Chapter 6. If, and only if, *ad hoc* negotiations fail, then external 'legislation' from above may be the only way of resolving the conflicts.

Preparing tomorrow's successful managers

The design and implementation of computer-based office systems involve more and richer forms of human interaction and negotiation than many managers have been accustomed to. Managers therefore need to draw on a wide range of analyses and experience of negotiation to assist them to enact the new systems properly. The richest seam of knowledge and expertise about the arts of negotiation lies with competent managers themselves, not with overly academic studies of the subject. The fund of tacit knowledge gained by managers in the past will be of continuing importance in the face of new technological innovations and their attendant experts.

The most critical question in bringing office automation constructively to management roles is proper discrimination between those aspects which are repetitive, mechanical and automatable, and those which are not. This varies within a given management role as well as between roles. It is possible to view management activities within specific categorizations, such as the stratification described in Chapter 4, or within the more conventional groupings of *supervisory*, *advisory* and *top* management. In practice, each role has a mixture from a very broad spectrum of managerial tasks. Apparently unstructured work involving a great deal of human interaction may actually consist primarily of mechanical supervision that follows clear corporate guidelines. On the other hand, a technical director whose responsibilities involve reasonably structured methodologies may be faced with unstructured design or innovation problems to solve. Many managers have part of their work structured by external 'objective' needs but with room for local manoeuvring. Generally, the mix moves towards more unstructured work for higher management levels.

Office technology can replace the more structured tasks in a mechanistic way while enhancing the more unstructured work through, say, decision support aids. The extent to which such changes have a positive or negative impact depends on whether the organizational context encourages or inhibits either mobility between roles or internal development within a role. For example, the replacement of a mechanical task may be good for a manager if the organization allows him or her to develop more rewarding activities, but not if it makes the manager into a machine operator or, even worse, completely redundant. It follows that managerial roles with mixed tasks are likely to be the ones that can be successfully adapted to new office technology.

Building on experience

Managers do not start from scratch or suddenly change radically overnight when establishing the new accommodations and co-ordinations necessary to make new office systems effective. They depend crucially on existing mutual expectations between parties that have evolved from a seamless web of historical experiences. Constructive negotiation is more likely, for example, where managers have been expected to maintain a supportive rather than a controlling relationship with subordinate departments or individuals. The formalities of acting as a controller can be a cause of executive alienation and chronic interdepartmental problems[2]. Factors such as these need to be carefully considered in understanding how management tasks and relationships are defined.

The most sophisticated and important parts of management activity are often beyond formal specification. They are based in 'craft skills' and tacit knowlege built up from practical experience, which cannot be abstracted into universal skills to be taught through routine training. These skills include an ability to recognize the real problems and to select the most appropriate means of solving them by drawing on knowledge gained from the results achieved in the past in similar situations. The recognition of management as, to some extent, a craft has two main implications:

(1) There are intrinsic limits to the extent to which management roles can be preprogrammed, even those which appear to be largely based on formally specificable routines.
(2) Personal judgement and responsibility should be given high priority.

Decisions or advocated actions often emanate seemingly *ex-cathedra* from an analytical process which, for all its technical sophistication, may only be a repackaging of personal values or prejudices in 'objective' form. Personal characteristics and the specific situation in which managers operate are often the main determining factors. Managers should therefore be expected to bear the responsibility of identification with decisions rather than hiding behind a formal process. The personal reaction of a manager, say to the taking of risks, can be a more relevant indicator of that manager's real authority than any technical ability to manipulate analytical managerial procedures.

The five ages of managers

Managers acquire their skills and tacit knowledge in a gradual way as their careers progress. Stuart E. Dreyfus has defined five main stages which provide a useful framework for considering managerial developments[3]:

(1) *The Novice*. When a manager has little or no previous experience to go by, the structures of tasks need to be clearly understandable without reference to other situations. Clear rules of response need to be provided which assist in deciding what to do in various circumstances.

(2) *The Advanced Beginner*. As managers gain experience, they will begin to identify recurrent meaningful *aspects* or components of their roles, as well as the predefined formal attributes. They also begin to use experience-related *guidelines* to assist them to make appropriate responses. Dreyfus explains that 'This human ability to recognize something on the basis of experienced concrete examples, without consciously doing so by applying strict rules to objectively identifiable components of the scene, simultaneously accounts for the improvement of human performance with real-world experience and the impossibility . . . . of constructing formal models representing what has been learnt.'

(3) *Competence*. This stage is typified by the relatively inexperienced middle manager who begins to perceive longer range goals and values which help to select and focus attention on *salient* attributes and aspects of a problem and its context. The manager is also able to start determining appropriate elements which can be built into a planned response.

(4) *Proficiency*. This level is typical of the more experienced middle manager who has seen and been involved in sufficient different situations to have a sense of the likely consequences of various actions. The proficient manager has built up a network of perspectives evolved from experience which 'present themselves' to him or her in any new problems setting. Decisions tend to be derived from *maxims* which are distilled from those elements which the manager can identify and knowingly abstract from all stimulae, conscious and unconscious. Such managers can evaluate whole situations intuitively but their schooling, their habits acquired at lower experience levels, and their need for self-justification in the organization, motivate them towards taking decisions on the basis of 'objective' comparisons between salient elements of alternatives.

(5) *Expertise*. The highest level comes when the manager's repertoire of experience is so great that he or she no longer needs any explicit analytical principle to relate his or her grasp of the general situation to specific action. This ability to use intuition successfully is not refined from some mysterious inner power but through the accumulation of concrete experience, skills and tacit knowledge.

Authority, autonomy and ritual

One of the skills gained at the more advanced levels described by Dreyfus is the ability to know how far formal rules can be reshaped to maintain local viability. Experienced managers often take the attitude that, within bounds, deviations can be made to official procedures 'provided nothing is put in writing' and 'the results are successful'. Less skilled or less confident managers may not be so flexible and want to stick to the rules at all costs because they are less able to compromise on formal procedures. This has important implications for managing new office technology.

Chapters 6 and 7 explain the importance of developing systems which can be adapted to changing needs and having top management establish policy and then remain in charge of its implementation. The social interactions and experience necessary to maintain a degree of necessary local autonomy and authority are part of the tacit knowledge gained by the skilled manager. If implementation is left to relatively junior managers and technical experts, the outcome could be an over rigid system that destroys important informal accommodations needed to keep the system tuned to real needs. In practice, however, implementation is often wrongly regarded as a relatively trivial task and, therefore, is thought to be appropriate for lower level managers. The importance of considering management roles as a mix of ever developing skills is also vital when considering how much of a manager's job to automate. It has been frequently argued by proponents of the technology that computer-based systems can 'release' managers from their routine, programmable 'drudgery'. Such routine work may sometimes be needed by managers, however, as a way of refreshing themselves and relaxing from the more exciting, but stressful, unstructured, and non-formalizable tasks. Taking the routine work away could be counter productive.

At first, managers may welcome computers which perform elaborate analyses. Skilful managers can even use them to reduce the heat of negotiations by giving their personal preferences the mantle of objective, quantified facts disgorged by a complex technical system. Later, the use of computers may come to be perceived as an obligatory ritual in management negotiations. Computers may take over the 'programmable' aspects of management decision making but, unless they are carefully designed, they may be inappropriate to the task being analysed (*see* Chapter 4). In addition, computer-based systems may remove managers from the conceptual tools and manipulative routines needed for creative thought, which previously they would have gained through the experience of actually doing the routine work. This has important implications for future generations of managers.

Computer-based management aids should avoid imposing external constraints which stop managers learning and exercising vital skills. They should, instead, provide a framework to be used as a common arena, focus and language within which to negotiate and resolve important issues. Managers responsible for introducing office innovation must be sensitive to the fact that there may be groups or individuals who will have their influence enhanced or reduced and that some may be excluded. Previous clear and secure boundaries between roles may be dissolved when new systems are introduced. The creation of workable new balances and role boundaries will be subject to intense and continual negotiation.

Toughening effective management skills

An understanding of the central influence of craft skills on management effectiveness is of practical importance because it calls for a fresh approach to the types of personal characteristics to be selected and cultivated in training tomorrow's successful managers. It also has implications for how to approach the design and implementation of new office systems. Craft skills require that there should be a building up and toughening of existing informal processes to encourage the evolutionary development of expertise based on practical experiences. An overemphasis on formal skills and computer systems that try to control and automate management tasks will bypass vital experiences and negotiation procedures which provide the imagination and ability to cope with the unexpected.

While most management theories recognize the importance of concrete experiences rather than abstract analyses, there has been a tendency to regard all proper skills as ultimately measurable against explicable principles, rules and standards. The approach highlighted by Dreyfus suggests that there are some key informal skills and processes for which it may never be possible to find formal explanations and descriptions. Computer systems should therefore be designed to accommodate and support implicit knowledge and craft skills wherever possible.

Underlying this discussion is a further question about whether behaviour and beliefs are chosen by individuals, rather than being ingrained as a result of social experience and cultural reinforcement. The *voluntarist* approach, which gives primacy to individual choice, takes it for granted that each person (and by aggregation, an organization) has multiple, fixed and clear interests and values. This offers a relatively simple account of what is being negotiated when people interact and is therefore more amenable to computerization and simulation.

The *interpretative* view is more complex, but gives more insight into what usually occurs. It stresses that an individual's (and organization's) values are often vague, uncrystallized, open to tacit negotiations and, to a significant degree, adjustable according to each particular context. It does not reject the likelihood that some aspects of work can be formalized and programmed. It does, however, argue strongly that formalization should not destroy the freedom to adapt, which keeps individuals and organizations alive and resilient.

Styles of negotiation and organization cultures

The common model of organizations as functional hierarchies encourages the false idea that those functions can be defined in detail for the subsequent automation of some roles. As has been already emphasized, organizations usually work as coalitions between different subcultures and groups in a continual state of negotiation. In some cases, the style of negotiation is explicitly accepted as bargaining by compromise. On the other hand, opposing parties may take dogmatically asserted stances, based on statements or edicts of 'objective necessity', which quietly yield to each other's counter arguments.

Even policies or arguments which are expressed as if beyond negotiation can be a tacit first step in negotiation processes. In many areas of life, a policy is initially put forward couched in rhetoric which stresses that it is an inevitable decree of nature, money, deities or history. Many technologies have been advanced as the unavoidable result of 'objective' *technological determinism*, the supposedly ever unfolding and unalterable laws of science and technology. If faced with such rhetoric regarding new office technology in their sphere of influence, managers should identify and challenge aspects with which they disagree. The impression that there is no room for negotiation may come from an unconscious infatuation with the technology or from an attempt to avoid negotiation over many design and organizational aspects of the technology. No technology of the complexity and scope of computer-based systems can be successfully exploited without extensive and continuing interaction and bargaining amongst the interested parties.

The culture and management style of an organization have a strong influence over negotiations. Organizations having a firm hierarchial structure will define roles rigidly with inflexibly stratified authority structures and constrained information flows. More egalitarian organizations may have stronger external boundaries but little internal structure, with a seething ferment of debate and negotiation going on about all aspects of collective life.

For example, in one scientific organization, decisions were handed down from a remote management structure. These were accepted and then adapted to local realities with little concern about the group's boundaries with other organizations. In a rival organization, decisions tended to be negotiated openly at agonizing length. Once made, these decisions enjoyed more intense loyalty and enthusiastic support, but there was a sense of jealousy and competition with other groups and organizations.

The past shapes the future

A great deal of modern management science theory has been built on the concept of negotiations as one-off events that can be reduced to models which rationalize gambling risk decisions. Parties involved in negotiations, however, have a continuing relationship to maintain and hence *recurrent* negotiations are the norm. The parties come to any new negotiation with previous experience of the relationships as well as future expectations, which deeply influence negotiation behaviour, for example, how far one party is prepared to trust another partner to follow a responsible course of action if given more autonomy or responsibility. Any attempt to understand the process of negotiation which does not take account of past interactions and the negotiators' expectations and reputations will fail to explain what is going on and could hamper the effective introduction of new technology.

Past behaviour and perceptions can determine whether those

involved in discussing new office information systems regard each other as collaborators or competitors in the system's design and implementation. Previous experiences and relationships should, therefore, be very carefully charted to avoid an innovation being immediately labelled as yet another example of some past exploitation or insensitive treatment. Many early experiences with new office technology implementations have run up against historically induced suspicions that any external intrusion into working practices is an attempt to test performance rather than to help it develop under some local control. Participants in office technology innovations, as in other negotiations, often spend an enormous amount of time and energy trying to reconcile apparently irrelevant past incidents before tackling the present and future issues.

The process of change is usually multilayered, with many undercurrents. The main task for senior management at the start of an office technology venture may be to induce an atmosphere of co-operation between the implementing agent (such as the Data Processing Department) and the users, to replace a mood of mistrust and competition that has been built up in the past. This may require immediate, visible action, like offering some guarantees of job security and/or full participation in the implementation and review, followed by patient, longer term work to gradually establish a more positive atmosphere. This requires that all those involved feel they are part of the same culture or community, with a similar identity and fate, rather than feeling they are bound together in a purely contractual relationship with the organization.

For strategic reasons, however, top management may deliberately encourage an unremittingly aggressive organizational style which discourages co-operation. Loyalty to an organization is often regarded as an important attribute, but it can lead individuals and groups to identify with particular structures. When it becomes necessary to have some form of reorganization to accommodate new computer-based systems, the preservation of the *status quo* may become an issue of moral principle rather than merely a question of trading *interests* in the common good. Continuity and identification with the organization can provide a stable and constructive context for negotiations, but it can also lead to fundamentalist, recalcitrant attitudes that inhibit change. Sensitive preparation and negotiation of the design and implementation of office systems is therefore needed to maintain the right balance between these countervailing forces.

Settling disputes

If locally negotiated solutions fail, then other levels may be introduced, such as:

(1) Formal negotiations between organized labour and management representatives.
(2) Mediation by a third party, such as a consultant, professional arbitrator or 'elder statesman'.
(3) Formal adjudication, say by higher management remote from the heat of the local battle.

The relevance and potential of these different kinds of practical procedure depend on the kind of organization and the local characteristics involved. An aggressive business firm in a very competitive environment, for example, may not be prepared to adopt a longer-term perspective on mediation and patient bargaining.

Negotiated decisions are generally preferable to imposed, legislated or adjudicated ones because they create norms through *joint* discussion and thus engage the loyalty of the parties in the negotiations. An adjudicated decision applies general norms to a particular situation and may ultimately carry less authority. Negotiations are therefore worth pursuing even if mediators are needed to smooth out misunderstandings and if the process seems inefficient and time wasting. If people feel they have been responsible for their own solution, they will be more committed to it and a precedent for co-operation will have been established which can have increasingly positive effects in the future.

The organizational context in which bargaining takes place has a decisive influence on how a dispute may be resolved. Some local negotiations may involve an implicit threat to higher authorities, say if a particular division is discussing a system of consultation based on representative work groups with powerful decision or advisory rights. This can pose a threat elsewhere in the organization and on other issues, so any adjudication from corporate management would inevitably rule against such an outcome. A skilful manager will find room in which to conduct satisfactory local negotiations even if they are not formally recognized.

The shape of negotiations

Philip H. Gulliver has investigated disputes and negotiations in organizations with a variety of cultural styles[4]. In all of them he found a universal tendency to call upon the broader cultural context and historical norms and precedents in attacking the central current issues. This proved to be particularly useful where deadlocks had been reached. Attention was shifted from the point of immediate dispute and agreement was reached on some general principle of, say, systems design or career development, thereby creating a suitable climate in which the specific problems could be handled with more success.

Gulliver identifies eight phases, which provide a useful framework for considering the shape taken by most negotiations:

(1) Search for an arena of confrontation.
(2) Compile an agenda and define the issues.
(3) Emphasize differences and explore the limits of the dispute.
(4) Narrow differences and reduce issues, revealing the really obdurate aspects.
(5) Carry out preliminaries to bargaining on key issues, such as gathering information.
(6) Conduct final bargaining to an outcome.
(7) Provide a symbolic affirmation of the outcome.
(8) Execute the terms of the agreement.

The initial seeking of an arena of confrontation is of particular significance in relation to new office technology. The advent of a new system may not in itself be the main point at issue. Tensions caused by other factors often condense around technological changes, or the new system may open up a large range of important issues. A patient exploration is required at the outset to find out what really creates fears and opposition, and what alternative visions and ideas exist. This can be a traumatic phase, requiring expert management that is able to see computer technology for what it is: sophisticated and powerful machines which raise many human and organizational implications, rather than intelligent agents by their own right, to be revered and followed at all costs.

An important characteristic of the eight-phase negotiation process is the counterpoint nature of successive phases, the way the themes and shape of the negotiation change and intertwine. The context of the dispute is broadened in order to narrow down issues; sharpened in order to reduce its scope; diffused in order to focus again at another level. Managers must be able to handle this negotiating flow as well as engendering personal trust and confidence. For example, holding joint discussions on relatively trivial side issues or information gathering exercises can assist in working towards successful negotiations on bigger matters.

Changing basic beliefs

The progression to phase 6 in the negotiation process involves a move from reducing conflict over basic principles to issues where compromise and trades can be reached without loss of face. It is often felt that basic values are not negotiable, so when conflict remains on such beliefs external adjudication or legislation is thought to be required.

In practice, these beliefs *can* be adapted through negotiation even if it requires delicate rituals to ease and conceal the painful transformation. At times, a risk needs to be taken if particular groups or individuals in a multi-party negotiation remain recalcitrant by threatening to 'go public' prematurely. The obstinate group may then back down and accept the decision because it feels isolated in holding on to principles that may not stand up to general exposure. On the other hand, it can lead to the reactivation and exacerbation of confusion and opposition over basic principles. However it is achieved, negotiations must be about persuading participants not only to accept alterations to their optimal outcomes but also to change their views and expectations of each other and themselves.

Multi-party decisions

Negotiations almost always involve more than two parties. Even when there are two main protagonists, there can be dissension within parties. During intense negotiations a gap may open between the negotiator and the 'constituency' she or he represents. This can lead to agreements between negotiators which cannot be implemented because of opposition at the grassroots. Where there are more than two main parties, the increased complexity makes internal cohesion more difficult to achieve.

There are two lessons which can be followed to help overcome these problems:

(1) *Negotiations must allow for plenty of consultation within the different parties*. Managers must be alert to the need to keep internal co-ordination and must avoid looking only in one direction, at the other negotiators. A change as all embracing as that involved with new office technology has so many points for negotiation and potential disagreement that it is impractical to refer every item back to the negotiator's

constituency. Accepting a total systems 'package' is also no answer, unless it has been carefully examined for all implications which might unfold. The negotiator's constituency must be well informed about the rationale of proposals and counterproposals so that necessary changes can be made during implementation without destroying credibility in the whole agreement. Obviously, managers on good terms with colleagues are likely to have a sound intuitive feeling of how far they can go in yielding concessions or agreeing to design or organizational issue.

(2) *Where necessary, negotiations should be divided into subnegotiations in a co-ordinated structure.* Even in small organizations that propose to implement new office technology there will be diverse interests, not merely polar opposites between those who stand to gain from the innovation and those who may lose, or fear that they may do so. Negotiations between subgroups can be an effective means of building a solid foundation on which a small number of more monolithic interest groups can bargain over bigger questions. The balance between what are deemed local and large issues must be handled so that all participants feel they have a genuine say in the big decisions without requiring every significant design issue to be referred back to a subgroup before a decision can be made.

New patterns of management

New office technology can cut deeply into all aspects of managerial life. There can be major shifts in power relationships, which is why viewing the innovation process as a negotiated change involving some sharing of authority can assist in moving towards constructive modes of decision making in rapidly changing organizational environments. Job roles can change, for better or worse (*see* Chapter 5). If pursued strictly as office *automation* or the simple mechanization of isolated tasks, rather than as a way of offering new management aids, computer-based technology can remove personal responsibility over the origination of information and decisions and can create stress, tension and feelings of alienation amongst managers.

In the past, managers have understood the meaning of information and the reasons for decisions through networks of formal and informal human interactions. If this is replaced by an automated system which depersonalizes these transactions, momentum may be given towards increased fragmentation with individuals and groups withdrawing into identification with their own immediate groups. This can give rise to countervailing pressures for increased corporate identity campaigns. If the imposition of corporate norms radically alters the control and discretion that can be exercised when managers move beyond their local enclave, vital informal interactions will be jeopardized. Compensating mechanisms and new arrangements will therefore need to be established to rebuild trust.

New office technology therefore confronts managers with fundamental and complex challenges affecting their individual roles, relationships with colleagues and subordinates in their own groups, and interactions with the rest of the organization and the outside world. This intricate pattern of change can be successfully and effectively handled only by understanding the importance played by negotiation and bargaining in all aspects of organizational life. The organization should encourage the development of the necessary managerial skills and establish a corporate environment in which trust and openness predominates, rather than fear, suspicion and rule by paternal edict and corporate propaganda.

Recommendations

(1) Recognize that decisions result from historical processes rather than discrete events.

(2) Whatever specific organizational structure or office system is eventually chosen, senior managers must patiently build an image of the future from the earliest opportunity; a common framework of understanding must be provided for the whole organization within which negotiations over specific elements can take place.

(3) Ensure that the authority for implementation of new office technology is given to an experienced manager with sufficient confidence to recognize and respond to informal organizational realities as well as formal ones.

(4) Do not expect a computer-based office system to replace the need for *ad hoc* human discretion and negotiation; on the contrary, successful implementation increases the demand for such human interactions.

(5) Toughen and support practical and intuitive management 'craft skills' and informal processes because they are needed

to complement more formal skills and procedures.

(6) Allow parties to agreements over the design and implementation of new office systems to have some freedom to make adjustments in the future. Be prepared to accept that some agreements are best left without being made totally explicit.

(7) Pay serious and systematic attention to the phasing, scope and sequencing of negotiations.

(8) Avoid allowing computer-based systems to reduce individuals' responsibilities over the decision-making process.

References

1. Wynne, B., The changing roles of managers, in Otway, H.J. and Peltu, M. (eds), *New Office Technology: Human and Organizational Aspects*, Frances Pinter, London; Ablex, Norwood, N.J. (1983)
2. Hofstede, G., Alienation at the top, *Organizational Dynamics*, **4**, 44–60 (1976)
3. Dreyfus, S.E., Formal models vs human situational expertise, *Office: Technology and People*, Vol 2 (1), 133–165 (1982)
4. Gulliver, P.H., *Dispute and Negotiations: A Cross-Cultural Comparison*, Academic Press, New York (1979)

Bibliography

The following publications are also relevant to topics discussed in this chapter.

Dalton, M., Cooperative evasions to support labour–management contracts, in Rose, A. (ed), *Human Behaviour and Social Process*, Routledge and Kegan Paul, London (1962)

Daly, R., The specters of technicism, *Psychiatry*, **33** (4), 417–431 (1971)

Deal T.E. and Kennedy A.A., *Corporate Cultures*, Addison Wesley, (1982)

Douglas, M., *Social Factors in the Perception of Risks*, Russell Sage Foundation, New York (1983)

Eaton J. Smithers J., *This is IT: A Manager's Guide to Information Technology*, Phillip Allan, Oxford (1982)

Salaman, G. and Thompson, K., *Control and Ideology in Organizations*, Open University Press, Milton Keynes (1980)

Wynne B. and Otway, H., Information technology, power and managers, in Bjørn-Andersen, N., Earl M., Holst, O. and Mumford, E. (eds), *Information Society: For Richer or For Poorer*, North Holland, Amsterdam (1982)

Index